Perspectives on the Sociology of Education

Routledge Education Books

Advisory editor: John Eggleston
Professor of Education
University of Keele

Perspectives on the Sociology of Education

An Introduction

Philip Robinson

University of Keele

Routledge & Kegan Paul

London, Boston and Henley

First published in 1981
by Routledge & Kegan Paul Ltd
39 Store Street, London WC1E 7DD,
Broadway House, Newtown Road,
Henley-on-Thames, Oxon RG9 1EN and
9 Park Street, Boston, Mass. 02108, USA
Set in IBM 10/11 pt Press Roman
by Academic Typesetting, Gerrards Cross, Bucks
and printed in Great Britain by
Billing & Sons Limited,
Guildford, London, Oxford and Worcester

British Library Cataloguing in Publication Data

Robinson, Philip

Perspectives on the sociology of education. —
(Routledge education books)
1. Educational sociology
I. Title
370.19   LC191
ISBN 0-7100-0787-6 Pbk

For Nicky and Becca

Contents

Chapter 1

Changing sociologies

The world is not completely arbitrary. If it were, neither you nor I could manage our everyday affairs let alone try to reach a considered understanding of them. There are regularities; you know what is expected of you in most of the situations you face, and in turn, expect others to behave within a certain framework. Our expectations are not always accurate and at times we misinterpret the world. This unease may be because of our own uncertainty about appropriate behaviour, it may be because the world has changed in ways which we never anticipated. An example of the latter relates to students who entered colleges of education in England in September 1973. A sensible judgment at the time was that teaching was a secure job with plenty of opportunities for employment; but as these same students qualified in June 1976 they faced a world of teacher unemployment. In retrospect it is possible to put forward reasons for the dramatic change, though probably few student teachers in 1973 anticipated how very different the world was to look just three years later.

The possible relationships between man and society are unlimited, therefore any sociology can only be a partial account of the world. Some, like Parsons in this century and Marx in the nineteenth century, have tried to encapsulate the social world into an all-embracing theory. They built complex models which may strengthen our perception of the world but which cannot accommodate the many idiosyncrasies of the individual.

There is not one but many perspectives within sociology, and therefore there are many sociologies of education. This assertion may be more acceptable if one remembers that we are looking at individuals and society; the possible inter-relationships are infinite and the very terms 'individual' and 'society' are open to many interpretations. The complexity is compounded by the fact that neither is static, a frozen unit awaiting the sociologist's dissection, but is continually

1

changing. The present moment is made up of the past and an anticipated future; for each of us, the future passes through the present and into the past which is thereby changed with the addition of each 'present'.

There is an inter-relationship between you and society by which you are the product of society and yet at the same time help to make that society. In sum, you are a unique individual as a result of the family into which you were born and the street where you lived, and in turn the street and the family are different because of your presence. This is not to say that this is all you are, or that the total influence on the street is the people living within it. You are also quick-tempered, lazy, garrulous; your street may also be considered the 'best' in town, or may have the highest rate of unemployment. It is meaningless to debate how much you are the product of individual as against environmental factors; or how much the street is the product of historical and economic circumstances as against the interaction of its inhabitants. We are all products of genes, history, economics, politics and traditions; the characteristic shared by each sociological perspective is a recognition of the inter-relationship (sometimes called a dialectical relationship) between you and your society.

The word 'sociology' was first used by a French philosopher, Auguste Comte, in 1843. As a discipline, sociology originated as part of an intellectual tradition located within Western European and American thought. Its founders did not train as sociologists, but as lawyers, economists and philosophers, and before turning to the sociology of education as such, we must explore a little further this background from which the present perspectives have emerged. In this book I am not attempting to explain why sociology of education has taken the various forms it has, but am concerned rather with showing how the different perspectives describe and interpret the processes of schooling. In so doing, we start with those who laid the foundations of our present understanding, the founding fathers of sociology of education.

Émile Durkheim

Durkheim was born in Épinal, a small town in eastern France, on 15 April 1858. His father was a rabbi whose early hopes were that Émile would continue the family tradition of service to the Jewish faith. However Émile decided on a secular career as a teacher, first at the University of Bordeaux, where he taught from 1887, and then at the University of Paris, where he worked from 1902 until his death on 15 November 1917. His own death was about a year after his son, André, was killed fighting in the First World War, a holocaust which was also responsible for the death of many of Durkheim's students.

2

Throughout his working life, Durkheim lectured regularly on educational topics. His lectures are readily available, published under the titles *Education and Society* (1956), *Moral Education* (1961), and *Evolution of Educational Thought* (1977). In looking at his educational ideas it is important to remember that they stem from Durkheim's ideas as a sociologist. Writing in his *The Rules of Sociological Method* he gives his view of what sociology is: 'As a matter of fact, our principal objective is to extend scientific rationalism to human behavior. It can be shown that behavior of the past, when analyzed, can be reduced to relationships of cause and effect' (p. xxxix). Durkheim was convinced that we could understand the social world in much the same way as the natural scientist understands the material world, that through reason, rational thought, and the pursuit of logic, the complexities of the social world would be grasped by man.

Durkheim argued that we live in a world of *social facts* that are external to us (in that they exist apart from our conception of them) and which constrain our behaviour. The birth rate is an example of a social fact. In England and Wales the birth rate was 15.0 per thousand of the population in 1955 when 674,000 babies were born; by 1964 the rate had increased to 18.6 per thousand and a total of 876,000 babies were born, but by 1977 the rate had dropped to 11.6 and only 569,000 babies were born. We assume that the decision to have a baby is a personal one, yet collectively, and for every region of England and Wales, these individual and private decisions had resulted in 300,000 fewer babies in 1977 than in 1964. The birth rate is a social fact, a trend which is open for explanation and which cannot be reduced to the psychological disposition of the individual decision-takers. There is an analogy between social facts and the actuarial principles used by insurance companies in calculating risk. One cannot predict who is going to have a car accident, though the chance of a student having an accident is greater than that of someone in their mid-forties. Insurance companies work on the assumption of such social facts.

Throughout his career Durkheim was preoccupied with the nature of *social solidarity*; what keeps society together rather than falling apart. He argued that in modern societies the form of solidarity has changed from mechanical to organic. Under *mechanical solidarity* the individual is strongly determined in his behaviour by the *collective conscience*; that is, the traditions and beliefs of his society. He is born, has his existence as a child and adult, marries and dies in the manner of his ancestors. Throughout life he knows his obligations and the rights which he has; religion is strong and the law repressive, for to break the law is to challenge the very existence of society. As the population of society grows in size so the division of labour becomes more complex and the nature of social solidarity changes to *organic*.

3

Organic solidarity is sustained by the dependence we each have on each other. We need the services of hundreds of others to sustain our daily life; people to provide our energy, food, attend to our health, leisure and education; in turn we also contribute to the sustenance of others. This inter-dependence is built on neither you nor I as specific individuals, but on the roles which we occupy as student, mother, teacher or son. Each role is part of the *collective representations* of society; that knowledge we have of what is expected of us in our behaviour – though to say we know how we *ought* to behave, does not mean that this is in fact how we *do* behave. The collective representations are the beliefs and common-sense knowledge of our society, but not the determinants of our action. In Durkheim's words, 'It is indeed true that the world only exists for us in as far as it is represented or is capable of being represented to our minds; in as far as it cannot affect our intelligence it is as if it did not exist' (1977, p. 50).

As we shall see below, the dominant philosophical tradition in America at the turn of the century was that of pragmatism. This was a movement which Durkheim found interesting, though fearing that, 'In our time we are witnessing an attack on reason; actually it is an all-out assault' (1964, p. 386). As a 'rationalist', Durkheim held that it was possible to know the truth about the social world. He saw pragmatism as an attempt to soften the truth, 'to make it less rigid . . . to free it, in short from the discipline of logical thought' (1964, p. 428). For Durkheim, on the contrary, the existence of truth resides in the universals within society; the form of the family, religious practice, morality or political organization may be culturally and historically relative but we can still identify social interaction which we label 'family' or 'religion' or 'politics'. 'Truth is not the working of experience but men have always recognised in truth something that in certain respects imposes itself on us, something that is independent of the facts of sensitivity and individual impulse' (1964, p. 430).

At both Bordeaux and Paris, Durkheim taught courses in pedagogy. Fauconnet (1923, p. 537) explains Durkheim's interpretation of pedagogy as,

> neither the educative activity itself, not the speculative science of education. It is the systematic reaction of the second upon the first, the work of thought, seeking in the results of psychology and sociology principles for the direction and for the reform of education.

This inter-relationship is clearly seen in *The Evolution* in which Durkheim relates the actual practice of education in France to the changing intellectual traditions of the country. He anticipates the work of a contemporary French sociologist, Pierre Bourdieu, in noting that,

'Educational transformations are always the result and the symptom of the social transformations in terms of which they are to be explained' (1977, p. 166). He explains, for example, the moral and intellectual revolution of the Renaissance as being partially caused by the increase in public wealth: 'A people which grows rich discovers new needs. The luxury which develops renders character more delicate, more gentle and less brutally aggressive' (1977, p. 198). The old curriculum, which was rooted in Scholasticism (exercises in logic, reasoning and debate) was irrelevant to a new age attracted by quality of taste and aesthetics.

As the curriculum changed, so, Durkheim argued, did the accessibility of knowledge change (1977, p. 206):

> Neither Erasmus nor Vives had any awareness that beyond this small world [the aristocracy] which for all its brilliance was very limited, there were vast masses who should not have been neglected, and for whom education should have raised their intellectual and moral standards and improved their material conditions.

Here Durkheim as an optimist sees education as the right of all and also as a channel through which the poor might rise to become leaders of society. The new curriculum of the Renaissance celebrated an exclusive elite culture denied to the majority of the population. Though the old curriculum was formal and pedantic, it was also universal, based on what was thought to be essential principles of logic.

Durkheim's sociology of education is rich in its conceptual development. It touches on issues which were largely neglected for half a century after Durkheim's death, like the sociology of the school curriculum and of classrooms, as well as the problems of selection and allocation in education. Durkheim is the most important theorist in the sociology of education and throughout this book we will be returning to the contribution which he made to the subject.

Karl Marx

Less directly concerned with education than Durkheim, Marx's influence has been less on the substantive development of sociology of education than on the way of thinking about education and society. He was born into a prosperous, middle-class family of lawyers in Trier, in the Moselle district of what is now western Germany, on 5 May 1818. He spent over half his life in London, coming to England as a political refugee in August 1849 with the expectation that his stay would be short. It lasted until his death on 13 March 1883. He had been a student at the University of Bonn, where he read law, though after a year he continued his studies at the University of Berlin which he entered in

5

October 1836. Georg Hegel, one of the most influential Western philosophers, had been Professor of Philosophy at Berlin from 1818 until his death in 1831. His influence was still strong at the university when Marx arrived; former colleagues and friends of Hegel formed a circle to promote his teaching. One of these 'Young Hegelians', Edward Gans, taught Marx; others, like Bruno Bauer and Ludwig Feuerbach, became close friends and fellow members of the Berlin Doctors' Club, 'formed as a discussion group for radical Hegelians' (McLellan, 1969, p. 14). By 1844, however, from whence Marx's close and lasting friendship with Friedrich Engels develops, Marx had rejected the philosophy of Hegel and was beginning to develop his own.

Hegel had developed what some felt to be the ultimate philosophy. Gans wrote, for example, 'philosophy has now come full circle; its progress is only to be considered as the thoughtful working over of its material in the manner which [Hegel] has so clearly and precisely indicated' (quoted in McLellan, 1969, p. 1), Hegel's philosophy is labelled idealist: our knowledge of the world stems from the ideas we have about the world; these ideas are changed and developed, but ultimately it is we who create the world.

Marx is often said to have inverted Hegel, to have approached Hegel and, finding him on his head, to have turned him around to stand on his feet. Rather than starting from the ideas we have about the world, Marx and Engels 'set out from real, active men, and on the basis of their real life-process we demonstrate the development of the ideological reflexes and echoes of this life process' (Marx and Engels, 1970, p. 47). Or, in another well known quotation, 'It is not the consciousness of men that determines their being, but, on the contrary, their social being that determines their consciousness' (*Selected Works*, Vol. 1 p. 363).

Marx's *materialism*, his view of how we come to know about the world, is *dialectical* in that he sees us in constant interaction with the material world. We change that world, but in turn are changed by it; truth is revealed by *praxis*, or political action, where our ideas are put to the test in the world. One of the attractions of Marx's philosophy is that it leaves the scholar's cell and engages with the experience of everyday life: 'Philosophers have only interpreted the world in various ways, the point is to change it.'

The driving force for Marx's system stems from the relationship which we have with the *means of production*; in other words, the control we have over our labour, its inputs, outputs and the necessary technologies to complete the tasks. Marx argues that under capitalism man's real condition is one of *alienation*, a term which McLellan (1973) shows that Marx uses in three senses. Man is alienated from the product of his labour in that he is just an appendage to the production process, a machine-minder or bureaucratic paper-mover. Man is also alienated from his self in that his labour is forced, with the result that man is turned into an animal, 'for he only felt at ease when performing the animal functions of eating, drinking and procreating' (McLellan, 1973, p. 111). Finally, man is alienated from his fellow men: 'Thus in the situation of alienated labour each man measures his relationship to other men by the relationship in which he finds himself placed as a worker' (quoted in McLellan, 1973, p. 111). The relationships of the workplace permeate the whole of life so that man becomes what he is in labour.

The nature of man therefore depends upon the conditions determining his production. Even the system of beliefs which we hold, ideology, is a consequence of the division of labour. 'The ruling ideas are nothing more than the ideal expression of the dominant material relationships' (Marx and Engels, 1970, p. 64). The ruling group in a society controls not only the productive forces within society but also the ways of thought. They legitimate what is right and acceptable and provide the very framework within which thought is possible. The problem presented by Marxist analysis is that of transcending this framework, of removing the class bias in one's own thought.

This dilemma can only be resolved through the process of class struggle (Marx and Engels, 1960, p. 15):

> Our epoch, the epoch of the bourgeoise, possesses this distinctive feature; It has simplified the class antagonisms. Society as a whole is more and more splitting up into two great hostile camps, into two great classes directly facing each other – bourgeoise and proletariat.

The emancipation of the proletariat, the oppressed class, implies for Marx the creation of a new society in which the contradictions of capitalism will wither and die. Capitalism contains within itself the seeds of its own destruction. As the ownership of wealth becomes concentrated in fewer hands and the individual is further degraded by the minute divisions of labour, a point is reached where the existing structure cannot contain the estranged social relations and a new order is born in which the contradictions of the old will cease. The proletariat develop a consciousness of class and take action to resolve the contradictions of that position within capitalism. It is this action, praxis, which is action in truth and not in the context of the ruling class.

An appeal of Marx's view is the seeming inevitability of change; the poor, through struggle, will inherit the kingdom of earth and the rich will be overthrown. The new utopia, as viewed by Marx, is seen in the following quotation from *The German Ideology* (Marx and Engels, 1970, p. 53):

As soon as the distribution of labour comes into being, each man has a particular, exclusive sphere of activity, which is forced upon him and from which he cannot escape. He is a hunter, a fisherman, a shepherd, or a critical critic and must remain so if he does not want to lose his means of livelihood; while in communist society, where nobody has one exclusive sphere of activity but each can be accomplished in any branch he wishes, society regulates the general production and thus makes it possible for me to do one thing today and another tomorrow, to hunt in the morning, fish in the afternoon, rear cattle in the evening, criticise after dinner, just as I have a mind, without ever becoming hunter, fisherman, shepherd or critic.

There are many interpretations of what Marx intended in parts of his theory; much re-analysis of his work to demonstrate its relevance to the contemporary world. The subtleties and nuances within the perspective has led to much discussion between Marxists as different camps try to establish their direct descent from the original work. The value of a Marxist perspective to education lies in its illumination of conflict. There is a contradiction, for example, in many of the methods used to teach primary school and 'non-academic' children in the secondary school, and the nature of their eventual employment. The former may stress individual autonomy, creativity and the importance of a unique response to experience while the employment opportunities available require uniformity, regularity and conformity. A Marxist analysis ties down this contradiction to the economic relations of production within society and the concomitant domination of one group by another. The weakness, or romanticism, in Marxist analysis is in going beyond the statement of contradiction to a prescription for its removal. A feature of all societies is the regulation of contradiction not its elimination, as in the tension between freedom and equality. Educational policy must attempt to accommodate both, yet complete freedom of choice entails a lack of equality and the imposition of equality denies freedom. A Marxist analysis is a perspective on the nature of the inter-relationship between schooling and society, not a revelation of absolute truth.

George Herbert Mead

Mead was born on 27 February 1863, in South Hadley, Massachusetts (between New York and Boston) and died on 26 April 1931 in Chicago, having taught philosophy and social psychology at the university there since 1894. When Mead arrived in Chicago it was to accompany his colleague from the University of Michigan, John Dewey, who had been appointed Head of the Department of Philosophy at Chicago's new university. To say Mead taught philosophy and social psychology is to understate his interests; Miller (1973) quotes one student who took thirteen different courses taught by Mead amongst which were courses on Aristotle, Hume, French Philosophy, The Philosophy of Eminent Scientists, Problems in the Theory of Relativity as well as courses on social psychology. Mead published some forty papers during his life though did not produce any fully worked out statement of his position in a book. The editor of *Mind, Self and Society* published in 1934 as a collection of Mead's lectures, notes, 'That he (Mead) was not the writer of a system is due to the fact that he was always engaged in building one.'

Mead was a social behaviourist; this must not be confused with the behaviourism of psychologists, like Skinner, who ultimately reduce everything to neurological stimuli and response, but must be seen as indicating that the social world can only be known through the observation of behaviour. The stress is on the word 'social'; we become individuals only through the social. The self, your concept of who you are, is not the product of a basic personality structure which would have been much the same as it is had you been left on a desert island from birth. Rather the self is formed in interaction with others; self emerges and, importantly, continues to emerge and change. Mead views the individual actively participating in the social world rather than passively responding to events. In many ways his model has similarities to that developed by Piaget in the middle of the twentieth century. Thought is a process of adjustment to the world, but as in Piaget's model, the world is neither a fixed external object nor the creation of our will, but an interaction of the two. In adjusting to the world we change ourselves, but at the same time change the world. The world that exists is partly the product of our creation, the social structure accommodates and assimilates our will and is changed because of this process of adaptation. The influence most of us have is hardly felt outside the immediate world of our family, friends, neighbours and colleagues, though there are those whose influence transcends time, like Einstein, Mao Zedong, Nyerere and Christ. The self, then, is a process; mind is formed through social interaction and has the job of monitoring the adjustments that are continually on-going in our life.

The self emerges at the point where we can begin to view ourselves as an object. Mead illustrates what he means by contrasting *play* with *game* in the socialization of a child. At about the age of four, any child at play takes on the role of mother, father, baby, teacher, nurse and so on. As one listens to the constant conversation it is easy to pick out each role as the child switches from, 'I am mummy' to 'Now

I am daddy'. What is lacking is any developed concept of who the I is who is doing all these things. In the game the I is recognized; if one froze the action during any team game it would be possible to ask the players to plot on a diagram their own position, together with those of the other players. Part of the skill in team games is the ability to read the play, to know what is happening and where one's self should be for its most effective contribution. In this second example the individual has developed an understanding of the generalized other.

The *generalized other* is formed through the build-up of *significant symbols*, that is gestures and language. A gesture takes its meaning from the interpretation given by the other; by knowing that interpretation we come ourselves to know the meaning of our own gestures. Similarly language, or vocal gesture, becomes meaningful in use; through the process of communication we come to know what our words convey and because the meanings are shared they extend beyond our self to become objective. As the self emerges through interaction with others, through our being able to take on the role of the other, so within the self there is a constant interchange between the *I* and the *ME*. The ME, to take a geological metaphor, is the sedimented bit of self, the habitual, the known, that which has been formed over the years. The I is the innovative, that bit of the self responding to the changing world. Both the I and the ME exist simultaneously. In all of us there will be times when the I is relatively inactive, our routine is fixed, we travel to work, have lunch at the corner cafe, go home, watch television and go to the supermarket on Saturday mornings; little is questioned, life is taken for granted and more or less accepted. At other times, as the result of a particularly good film, the serious illness of a friend, or the affects of a petrol shortage, the I is dominant. We must consciously come to terms with the new situation in the context of the generalized other. We act towards our view of how the world is constructed and to an extent are constrained by that world of view. *Reflexiveness*, the turning back of the experience of the individual upon himself, is the essential condition within the social process for the development of mind.

The individual is both the active creator of the world and, at the same time, the product of that world. The social behaviourism of Mead has been developed into a school which is labelled *symbolic interactionist* (the term is Blumer's) and refers to a sociological perspective which holds three basic premises (Meltzer *et al.*, 1975, p. 54):

1. human beings act towards things on the basis of the meanings that the things have for them; 2. these meanings are a product of social interaction in human society; and, 3. these meanings

are modified and handled through an interpretive process that
is used by each person in dialogue with the things he/she
encounters.

Work within this perspective includes that of Becker on deviancy,
Goffman on total institutions and Hargreaves on schools. The focus
of the work is the individual actor who tends to be discussed without
reference to the historical and political context of behaviour. It is
this lack of context, the wider structural setting of action, which is *Note*
considered to be the major limitation of symbolic interaction. Although
this criticism holds for many empirical studies it is not a necessary
limitation of Mead's social theory which does recognize the possibility of the individual having a distorted view of the world, the exploitation of one sector of the society by another and the limitation
of individual freedom. The major challenge facing the theory is its
articulation in an empirical study that accounts for both the individual
actor making sense of the world, and also recognizes the structural
constraints which encompass that world.

Max Weber

A contemporary of Mead, though working within the different intellectual setting of Western Europe, Weber, also addressed the problem
of developing a social science which would be adequate both in explaining the individual actor making sense of the world and also recognizing
the structural constraints which encompass that world; in short, adequate
at both individual and structural levels. Weber was born in Erfurt, in
what is now East Germany, on 21 April 1864, and died in Munich on
14 June 1920. His initial training was as a lawyer and historian at a
time when discussion over the status of natural and social sciences was
almost an intellectual obsession. Heinrich Rickert, a colleague of Weber
at the University of Freiburg, argued that there were two approaches
to reality: that searching for general laws (nomothetic), characteristic
of the natural sciences, and that which focused on unique, particular
events (idiographic) or the social sciences. Although Rickert's ideas
had considerable influence on nineteenth-century thought, Weber
argued that the distinction between the two sciences was not helpful.
For Weber, reality is infinite and never completely knowable; the social
scientist can only make provisional statements about the 'truth' of
the world and in doing so must make use of whatever method seems
most appropriate.
  Weber defined sociology as 'a science concerning itself with the
interpretive understanding of social action and thereby with a causal

See | 34 bureaucracy.

explanation of its course and consequences.' Explanation within sociology must satisfy two criteria; it must be adequate at the level of meaning as well as being causally adequate. Weber was concerned both with the way in which we subjectively make sense of our world as well as with the fact that our world is in a particular socio-political time. Any explanation of behaviour must first of all make subjective sense – that is you and I can agree that the action is 'the sort of thing' that someone would do in a particular set of circumstances – or 'intuitive' sense. Although individual action is unique and part of the history of a specific individual, it is also shared action, part of a wider framework. As a teacher, I may act in a certain way because of my particular biography and specific location, and though my act may be different from yours in similar circumstances, nevertheless, it is still part of the wider discourse of teacher acts. It is possible to generalize from my action to make probabilistic statements about all teachers. This second aspect is what Weber means by causally adequate.

In gaining a purchase on reality, the social scientist develops what Weber calls ideal types of behaviour. An *ideal type* is a bench mark, a yard stick against which reality is measured. The ideal type is arrived at not by taking the average, or common aspect of a phenomenon, but by taking the logically extreme form. In developing an ideal type teacher, for example, one would not look for the qualities which all teachers have in common but for those which each has in extreme. The conceptual model thus developed becomes the mark against which actual teachers can be compared. In developing the ideal type the criteria of causal and meaning adequacy must be preserved so that the model makes intuitive sense as well as operating within a causal framework.

Weber classified social action into four ideal types; the first is where action is *goal-orientated*, that is behaviour is directed towards intended goals and is chosen from amongst a number of possible means, for example, 'She is staying in tonight in order to complete her essay'. Action may also be determined by belief or values alone, *value-orientated* action such as 'she is an ambitious student'. Both forms of social action are considered by Weber to be rational; the other two ideal types are classified as non-rational action. By this is meant that the actor is not making a conscious choice, his action being either *traditional*, the product of habit or convention, the way in which things have always been done; or *affectual*, the response to likes and dislikes such as, 'I know that I would hate eating frogs' legs even though I've never tried them'. The social action in which we are engaged every day contains bits of each of Weber's four ideal types; his purpose is to provide a conceptual tool which can be used as a reference point in the analysis of actual behaviour.

The hallmark of Weber's sociology is subjective meaning; our action is meaningful to us and can also be known by others. Our world is one of shared meanings in which we constantly read, and adjust to, our interpretations of others, modifying our own acts in response to our assessment of the consequences of our own behaviour. But in stressing the importance of meaningful behaviour, Weber does not ignore the constraints upon that behaviour. All individuals who are in the same position in the economy, or the market, are seen to be in the same *class group*. Class structures life-chances, it is the material basis of life, and like Marx, Weber saw the ownership of property as the crucial divide within society. Weber does not, however, see class as a determinate factor. Individuals may occupy the same class position in terms of their relation to the market but be unaware of their common ground. Linking class to individual subjectivity are *status groups*, those who share and are conscious of sharing the same prestige within a society and demonstrate this sharing in similar life-styles. There is no necessary connection between life-styles and life-chances; a minister of religion is the oft-quoted example of someone high in esteem but low in economic rewards, while a bookmaker may be given as an example of the opposite. The organization around either class or status forms a *party*, by which Weber means not only a political party in the conventional sense of the term, but also the formation of groups within normally accepted political parties; like, for example, the Manifesto Group in the English Labour Party, and the political groupings found within every formal organization including schools, colleges and universities.

Weber moves from the theory of subjective action, which has two levels of adequacy (interpretive and causal), through a discussion of the wider structural features of social life, to an analysis of class, status and party. Throughout his analysis is a concern for the legitimate order within which the individual act is located. For some, order is the consequence of power, which is defined as 'the probability that an actor will be able to realize his own objectives even against the opposition of others', in other words, my will prevails, with the power of the sword if necessary to ensure victory. In most organizations such naked power is replaced by domination, or authority, which is legitimated in one of three ways. The first is *traditional* authority, which is located in the long-established practices of the community and expressed through the imam, the village elders, or the chief. The second is *charismatic* authority depending upon the influence of a particular leader such as Gandhi or Hitler. The main problem faced by any charismatic authority is that of providing a basis once the leader has gone. This routinization of charisma was one of the major problems facing the Christian Church after the death of Christ, and is a problem faced in China by Hua Guofeng after the death of Mao Zedong. The final form of legitimation, *legal/rational*, is that of the modern bureaucracy. Those subject to authority are clear both as to their rights and obligations and there are checks on the use of power by those in authority. Obligations are not to a person, but to rules and procedures deliberately created, and with an army of lawyers ready to adjudicate as to a correct interpretation.

Our main debt to Weber is for his help in looking at schools as organizations, but we will also return to his work when considering examinations, the teaching profession and equality of opportunity in education. Contemporary work such as that of Collins (1975), Vaughan and Archer, (1971) and Bourdieu (1977), has drawn from Weber, as has the work of Schutz and through him the so called 'new' sociology of education.

Alfred Schutz

Born in Vienna in 1889 and educated at the university there, Schutz was particularly impressed by Weber's contribution to the social sciences. However he felt that Weber had not fully appreciated what was implied by 'interpretive understanding', and in developing a 'theory of meaning' (1972, p. 8),

> Weber makes no distinction between the *action*, considered as something in progress, and the completed *act*, between the meaning of the producer of a cultural object and the meaning of the object produced, between the meaning of my own action and the meaning of another's action.

In short, Schutz argues that Weber developed a sociology of meaning without discussing how meaning itself arises, is sustained and changed, a topic which in contemporary sociology is known as *hermeneutics* (see Bauman, 1977). In his analysis of Weber, Schutz draws heavily on the philosophy of Edmund Husserl (1859-1938) and Henri Bergson (1859-1941) and prepares the foundations of a *phenomenological* sociology as developed by Berger and Luckman (1967).

Like Weber, Schutz starts with a view of a reality that is infinite, thus all 'facts' about the world, either the social or natural, are interpreted facts, a selection from the world by our conscious being. There are endless inter-relationships and everything may appear to influence everything else, but at the moment you choose to attend to the amoeba, or to whether your lover is true, you freeze the on-going flow of consciousness. This act of selection is not arbitrary and random but taken against the common-sense knowledge which we all have about the world. 'From the outset all objects are objects within a horizon of familiarity and pre-acquaintanceship which is, as such, just taken for granted until further notice of the unquestioned (though at any time questionable) stock of knowledge at hand' (Schutz, 1953).

The true character of the world is not questioned in most day-to-day activity; we accept what is, we each have a series of *typifications* which confirms the non-problematic nature of the world. Our social world is inter-subjective, that is we accept that for all normal purposes the objects of the world mean the same for me as they do for you. In this, the world obtains its objectivity as its meaning is detached from, and is independent of, the definition of the situation and unique biographical circumstances of myself and the other participants. In engaging in everyday life we continually interpret the subjective meaning of other people; this process is on-going and is differentiated by Schutz into interpretations of *'in-order-to'* and *'because-of'* motives. The former refers to my future intended action and is subjective as only I have the possibility of knowing what my intent is by some future act. The 'because-of' motives are objective and represent the past as re-interpreted by the present. Such motives are not fixed and absolute, but change as the present changes and alters what is significant in the past.

For each of us, the members of our world consist of predecessors, those who provided our available meanings or the interpretations of the world that are accessible to us. There are also our successors for whom we provide their taken-for-granted knowledge, sometimes called *recipe knowledge* by Schutz. Finally there are our contemporaries, amongst whom are our consociates with whom we share a face-to-face relationship (Schutz, 1972, p. 46):

> Except in the pure We-relation of consociates, we can never grasp the individual uniqueness of our fellow man and his unique biographical situation. In the constructs of common-sense thinking the other appears at best as a partial self, and he enters even the pure We-relation merely with part of his personality.

Schutz joined the debate as to how a social science was possible. He argued that the social scientist has to replace the thought object of common sense, which relates to unique events and occurrences, by constructing a model of the social world within which only those typified events occur that are relevant to the particular problem which the social scientist is addressing. Like Weber, Schutz argues that the scientific problem should determine what is, and what is not, relevant to its solution, and thus relevant to the topic to be investigated. The social scientist constructs typical course of action patterns which correspond to observed events and grafts these onto a model of an

15

actor whom he imagines to be gifted with consciousness. In Schutz's terms, he constructs an *homunculus* (literally, 'little man'), invested with a system of relevances originating in the scientific problem of his constructor and not in the particular biographically determined situation of an actor within the world.

There are four ground rules which must be followed in constructing an homunculus; first the *postulate of relevance* – the model must be relevant to the interests of the sociologist as a sociologist; second the *postulate of adequacy* where the model must be understandable to the actor in the social situation under consideration. The next requirement is labelled the *postulate of logical consistency*, meaning that the rules of formal logic must be adhered to; finally there is the *postulate of compatibility* which states that the model must be compatible with the whole of scientific knowledge. Despite his intentions Schutz does not move much beyond Weber's notion of interpretive sociology, beyond the construction of ideal types which are adequate at the level of meaning and also causally adequate.

A recent extension of Schutz's ideas has been provided by Harold Garfinkel and labelled by him *'ethnomethodology'* to refer to the process through which we negotiate the routine of everyday life. Part of the process is managed through talk. An aspect of all talk is its *indexicality*; that is, the meaning conveyed is seldom fully articulated in the talk used. Instead, the speaker assumes a shared meaning with the listener such that the actual words spoken are interpreted in terms of the context that is implied, or 'indexed' by the speech. For example, the question 'How was teaching practice?' may mean many different things; your friend intends 'Did you manage to convince your tutor of your teaching ability?'; your tutor, 'Did you eventually manage the discipline problem with 4G?'; and your mother, 'Did you cope with the strain of getting up at six o'clock every morning?'

The talk used acts as an index to the meaning intended. As an index there must be procedures for moving from the talk to its intended meaning. These *interpretive procedures*, as they are called by Cicourel (1971) are the topic for ethnomethodological enquiry. They are the rules about rules that hold not only for talk but also for action, for example, there are rules about how close I can stand to you in conversation. If I come too close you begin to feel uncomfortable and question the nature of our relationship, too distant and you are convinced of your 'bad breath' and are again uneasy in the interaction. Ethnomethodology, then, is the exploration of the ground rules of everyday life as negotiated and practised by members.

This exploration of the ground rules of everyday life seems of immediate relevance to the sociology of education. This perspective holds the promise that the network of inter-relationships which characterize any school are open to investigation. In classrooms, children have to decide the indexicality within teacher talk if they are to understand messages; both teachers and pupils must negotiate the interpretive procedures which allow for order and enable teaching to be accomplished. Schools contain a series of typifications about what is a 'good' pupil, 'acceptable' behaviour or what counts as 'deviance'. The enthusiasm with which these ideas were incorporated into the sociology of education led, as we shall see in the next chapter, to the label 'new' sociology of education being applied to work within this perspective.

Talcott Parsons

A strong influence on the development of sociology of education, an influence which was increasingly contested in the 1970s, was the *structural functionalism* of Talcott Parsons. Parsons was born on 13 December 1902 in Colorado Springs, Colorado, and died in Munich on 8 May 1979 while on a lecture tour in Germany. His father was an academic and a minister of the Congregational Church, eventually becoming the head of a liberal arts college in Ohio, Marietta College. As an undergraduate, Parsons read biology at Amherst College in Massachusetts, changing to economics for his post-graduate studies. He spent two years in Europe, 1924-6, first at the London School of Economics and then at Heidelberg in West Germany where he began his doctoral thesis on the ideas of capitalism as contained in the work of Marx, Weber and Sombart. He returned to Amherst to finish this work and in 1927 moved eighty miles to the east to teach economics at Harvard. He remained at Harvard until he retired in 1973, moving into the sociology department in 1931 becoming Professor of Sociology in 1944.

Like Marx, Parsons was attracted by the grand scheme, an overall theoretical framework within which both man and society could be encompassed. Parsons saw reality as a social system in which the parts are related to the whole and which are explained in terms of their function for the whole. Thus classrooms are explained in terms of their function for the school, the school in terms of the educational system and the latter in terms of its function for society and so on. Parsons's 'grand theory' begins with an explanation of individual behaviour; he argues that all action is goal-oriented and that in pursuit of our goals we take into account the purposes of other people; this is not meant in any sense of having consideration for others in moral terms, but simply recognizing the social nature of our acts. In each of our acts we are confronted by five dilemmas, or *pattern variables*,

17

the first of which is the dilemma between *affectivity* and *affective neutrality*. This is the choice between viewing one's act as an end in itself or as part of some wider plan, a means towards the attainment of some further goal. The other dilemmas are *specificity* and *diffuseness*, or regarding the person with whom one is interacting in narrow specific terms such as 'shop assistant', or in wider terms such as 'close friend'; *universalism* and *particularism*, do you treat everyone in the same way or focus on some idiosyncracy; *self-orientation* and *collectivity-orientation*, the dilemma of viewing one's action as it benefits self or the wider group; and finally the pattern variable of *achievement* and *ascription*, the dilemma of treating someone in terms of what they have achieved instead of who they are, the daughter of the College Principal for example. As an illustration of the pattern variables, a father would tend to treat his child in ways which were affective, diffuse, particularistic, ascriptive and collectivity-orientated in the sense of acting for the benefit of the family as a whole; conversely an institute of higher education would tend to treat students in ways which were affectively neutral, specific, universalistic, achievement-orientated and also collectivity-orientated. These illustrations indicate a further dimension to the pattern variables, for as well as representing the dilemmas for individual action they also represent the dilemmas facing the social system itself as embodied within the family, church, school or trade union.

It is possible to analyse each social system by the response which it makes to four *functional prerequisites*. These are the requirements of *adaptation*, or how the social system manages the allocation of its resources, be they people, objects or symbols; *integration*, or preserving the commitment of members of the social system to the whole; *goal-attainment*, achieving a consensus about the goals which are to be worked towards; and finally, *pattern maintenance*, or the repair of any damage to system parts which arises from the workings of the whole. In all this, Parsons makes an assumption that all social systems ultimately share the same values, that beneath any surface differences there is a consensus as to the fundamental values which we all hold.

A development of functional theory which has also been influential within sociology of education is that of R. K. Merton (1957). Merton distinguishes between the *manifest function* of an act, that intended by the actors; and the *latent function*, that is the unintended or unrecognized consequences of action. Some would argue that although the manifest function of education is to stimulate curiosity and a sense of wonder at the world, its latent function is to kill any curiosity and make learning a drudge.

In using a systemic model, functionalism has the advantage of directing our attention to the boundaries of the model. In other words, in all analysis of a school focusing attention towards its boundaries with other systems and to the questions of who defines the boundaries, maintains them, is able to cross them, and how the boundaries are changed. In doing this, the model acts as a tool, an aid in the conceptualization of the school as an institution. The weaknesses of functionalism are, first, the assumption of value consensus. It may well be the case that in society there are incompatible values, such as those which support the individual's freedom as against those which stress the individual's responsibility to the collectivity. Second, to explain something in terms of its *function* is not to explain the *cause* of the phenomenon. The function of education may be, as Durkheim has it 'to arouse and develop in the child a certain number of physical, intellectual and moral states which are demanded of him both by the political society as a whole and the special milieu for which he is specifically destined'. But this begs the questions as to what these moral states are, why certain demands of the society are recognized in schools and not others, and why the child does develop in the way that she does?

Many perspectives or one?

The perspectives which have been introduced have been grouped by Dawe (1970) into 'two sociologies'. The first, represented in this chapter by the work of Durkheim and of Parsons, 'asserts the paramount necessity, for societal and individual well-being, of external constraint'; it takes the problem of *order* as the major topic for sociological investigation. The second group identified by Dawe, represented here by the work of Mead, Weber and Schutz, stresses 'autonomous man, able to realise his full potential and to create a truly human social order only when freed from external constraint' (1970, p. 214). In this group, the problem is the individual's assertion of *control* over the social world. This division has been criticized by Corrigan (1975) and Benton (1978) as being an unreal dichotomy, what Benton sees as two recognizably variant forms but within the same space; two sides to the same coin in other words.

Without doubt much of the debate between different perspectives is misplaced. The standard attack on the 'order' perspective from those who share a commitment to the 'control' perspective is that sociology has de-humanized the individual; that talk of bureaucracy, class and social structure denies the subjectivity of the person. The rejoinder comes that people are located within a specific political, economic and historical period; they exist through the social structure and to ignore this is to deny the reality of existence. Both views are correct and not necessarily incompatible, but rather raise the problem of the different levels of explanation within the social sciences. How near I stand to you in conversation may be culturally relative, but to make Durkheim's point again, in each culture there will be a point where my nearness will be uncomfortable. At the time of our conversation we may both be the victims of class oppression, both be prisoners of the 'relations of production', but to analyse our 'objective' class position is to move to a different level of explanation from an analysis of the 'indexicality' of my talk. Each level is a complement to the other and a full sociology of education needs both. This was recognized by Mills (1959) in outlining the promise of what he labelled 'the sociological imagination'. This requires the answer to three sorts of question: '1) What is the structure of this particular society as a whole? ... 2) Where does this society stand in human history? ... 3) What varieties of men and women now prevail in this society and in this period?' (p. 13). At best the sociology which has arisen from an examination of 'education' is an attempt to realize Mills's requirements of 'the sociological imagination'.

Chapter 2

Changing sociologies of education

What counts as the sociology of education is founded upon, and reflects, the changing theoretical bedrock of the parent discipline. At its best, sociology of education will reflect the three aspects of 'the sociological imagination' – historical, structural and biographical – which Mills identified as essential parts to an adequate social science. The emergence of sociology of education as a substantive area of inquiry is of fairly recent origin (despite Durkheim's work at the turn of the century and Karl Mannheim's contribution in the 1940s). When Halsey, Floud and Anderson published a collection of readings in the sociology of education in 1961, the subject was almost non-existent in the curriculum for intending teachers either at the then teachers' training colleges or at university departments of education. Well established degree courses in sociology, such as that at the University of London, allowed students to opt for demography, criminology, social policy and administration and comparative social institutions but not sociology of education. By 1977, when Karabel and Halsey produced *Power and Ideology in Education*, every university department, every college and polytechnic preparing teachers had courses in sociology of education. It is a regular option in undergraduate sociology courses, there are higher degrees in it, the British Sociological Association has a Sociology of Education section and there are Open University courses in the subject. In the sixteen years separating Halsey's two readers the growth of sociology of education as a teaching subject has been very rapid with frequent shifts of fashionable perspectives.

Reviewing the state of play in 1959, Floud and Halsey wrote, 'In England the scale of work remains restricted and socialist influence on the choice of problems remains strong.' They highlighted the tradition of *political arithmetic* which tended to be the sole movement within British sociology of education at the time. Political arithmetic was largely a British invention, a child of the 1830s, the product of a

21

rationalist faith which saw the collection of facts untroubled by opinion as the major task of the social sciences. By the turn of the century, this tradition had been seized by reformist groups like the Fabians under the influence of Sidney and Beatrice Webb, and institutionalized in the new London School of Economics. It inspired the early poverty studies and was the fold into which the early studies of educational mobility naturally fitted.

Political arithmetic was not the sole influence on sociology of education prior to 1960; Floud and Halsey point to the work of the anthropologist Margaret Mead, whose influential paper, 'Our Educational Emphasis in Primitive Perspective' was published in 1942, and to the work of Karl Mannheim. Mannheim had raised the possibility of developing a sociology of the school which would include how knowledge was organized as well as the way in which the assumptions held by teachers influence the nature of schooling and the experiences of children. Yet Floud and Halsey judged in 1959 (p. 168) that

> none of these writers seems to have faced the fundamental difficulty in the sociology of education; namely, that of presenting an orderly and coherent analysis of a set of institutions which by their nature confound social-psychological and sociological issues, straddling as they do the psychology and the organizational structure of society.

We are taken back by Floud and Halsey to the problems of levels of analysis with which we ended the last section. In the sociology of education there is a *macro level*, within which education is discussed as it relates to the economy and the opportunity structure, as well as to the attainment of political ideals, like equality of opportunity. There is at the same time a *micro level*, where the focus is on the child and the teacher, each shaping an educational identity in the context of a specific school. Some of the debates within sociology of education talk past each other as proponents defend either macro or micro interests as if the other were necessarily antagonistic to the view held. Others, like Bernstein in England and Bourdieu in France, accept the complementarity of levels and work at the interface between the two, accepting Floud and Halsey's injunction that (1959, p. 193),

> We cannot afford not to work at all levels simultaneously. We must have a general typology of educational systems in relation to social structure; we must apply it to the examination of the structure and functioning of schools, colleges and universities and we must look at the learning process in this institutional context.

Durkheim's work anticipated the challenge of Floud and Halsey to address the 'fundamental difficulty' in sociology of education. As mentioned in Chapter 1, he demonstrated that what was taught in schools was related to the political and moral climate of the time and also influenced the style of thinking of individuals. The resurgence of interest in historical research by sociologists may develop our understanding of how structural features of society relate to the everyday interaction and consciousness of individuals in schools.

Although some recognized the co-existence of identity and structure within sociological explanation, the empirical studies of the 1950s kept firmly within the tradition of political arithmetic. The work of Glass (1954), Floud, Halsey and Martin (1956) and the influence of Government Reports like *Early Leaving* (Central Advisory Council, 1954), Crowther (Central Advisory Council, 1959), Robbins (Committee on Higher Education, 1963), and Plowden (Central Advisory Council, 1967) kept alive a concern with access to education. In Bernstein's words, 'The basic concern was the *demonstration*, not explanation, of institutional sources of inequality in education' (1972, p. 101); a demonstration which was situated within a context of political optimism. It was believed that schools could change society; comprehensive, compensatory and community education were to be the vehicles at the front of the drive towards the eradication of inequalities within post-industrial society.

Political arithmetic was the dominant tradition within which sociology of education developed in the United Kingdom, a tradition reinforced by the growing theoretical model in the USA, that of *structural functionalism*, the roots of which may be traced back to Comte, Spencer and the early work of Durkheim in the nineteenth century as well as to the work of anthropologists like Malinowski and Radcliffe-Brown in the present century. Its contemporary development, however, lies, as we saw in the previous chapter, with the work of Parsons.

Before looking at the development of alternative perspectives it is important to explain the growth in the teaching of the subject which we have already mentioned. In doing this I am not arguing that growth determined the direction of theoretical development, though it did stimulate discussion of the strengths and limitations of both 'functionalism' and 'political arithmetic'.

Three factors may be isolated as contributing to the growth of sociology of education in the 1960s. The first was the changing nature of teacher education which started with the introduction of a three-year initial training course in the colleges in 1962. At the time of this extension, the upswing in the birth-rate of the mid-1950s was adding pressure to the existing trend of children staying voluntarily at school beyond the statutory leaving age to create a demand for many more teachers. Extension and expansion together produced a climate within which the nature of teacher education was to be examined; courses were criticized for their low academic level and for being little beyond

23

'tips for teachers'. In 1963 the Robbins Report on Higher Education contained a proposal that some students in the re-named colleges of education should take a further year's study to read for a Bachelor of Education degree. This second factor stimulated the development of what was thought to be an 'academic' study of education, and hence of the basic social sciences which underpin it, namely, sociology, psychology, philosophy and history. There was a demand for sociologists to teach on the new academic courses; a demand which stimulated university departments of education to mount diploma and higher degree courses to produce the manpower required.

The third factor is harder to specify but may be more important than either of the other two in explaining the subsequent development of sociology of education. This is the consequence of the change in mood in the latter half of the 1960s from 'optimism' to 'pessimism' in educational planning. The mid-1960s were boom years; students were plentiful, the economy was growing and reform was thought to be attainable through the existing political processes. In 1965, the British Labour Government accelerated the slow drift towards comprehensive education in an attempt to attack the existing inequalities of opportunity. In America the 'war on poverty' was well under way; Head Start had started as a programme of pre-school compensatory education and Coleman was engaged in his survey to chart the expected close relationship between educational achievement and educational provision. The concerns of the policy-makers complemented the interests of the sociologists, both exploring the patterns of inequality in society and the effects of social class on educational achievement.

When Coleman produced his report in 1966, and the Plowden Committee its report of 1967, the gap in educational provision was found to be much less than had been supposed. Doubt began to dawn as to the efficacy of reform programmes to implement and sustain change. Increasingly the sources of inequality were seen to lie outside the school; a realization which led to the role of schools as the front of the drive towards greater social justice being questioned. As the confidence in accepted policies was undermined so the sociology which had been coupled with those policies was found wanting. Functional theory seemed weak in predictive power and of little immediate relevance to the needs of the increasing number of student teachers preoccupied with the necessity of classroom survival. Signs of an emergent alternative perspective appeared in England in some of the papers presented to the British Sociological Association at its conference in Durham in April 1970. The signs were confirmed a year later, when M. F. D. Young published a collection of readings, *Knowledge and Control*, including two of the conference papers, those presented by Young and Bernstein.

To say the shift was from a 'macro' to a 'micro' perspective is an over-simplification; both Young and Bernstein continued to draw attention to the structural factors which impinged on the educational processes within the school. The originality of the emerging perspective lay in the recognition that educational institutions were 'knowledge processing'. That is, as well as processing people (children), the definitions of what counted as 'subjects', or as 'good' and 'poor' students, were also the product of social relationships rather than being predefined and absolute. The adaptation of the theoretical perspectives of Mead and Schutz, control theorists, raised the possibility that as knowledge was socially constructed, so it could be changed through human intent.

The expansion of teacher education stimulated a growth in sociology of education which initially was fed by the dominant theoretical perspective of functionalism. The apparent failure of reformist policies in the 1960s together with the increasing demand for sociology in teacher training resulted in a shift in perspective away from 'order' theorists towards the control theorists; a shift which Floud (1978) came to characterize as, 'Dehumanised, over-socialised, a-moral sociological man has given way to autonomous, creative, morally responsible sociological man' (p. 17).

The charge made by Young (1971), was that sociology of education had taken for granted the categories used in educational discourse. As a consequence sociological enquiry did not question the meaning of terms in general use like 'academic child', 'less-able' or 'the curriculum', but instead worked within a framework where the assumption behind these categories remained unquestioned. For Young, 'It . . . becomes the task of sociological enquiry to treat these categories not as absolutes but as constructed realities realized in particular institutional contexts.'

The terms which we use in discussing educational processes are not absolute, but the product of human action undertaken at a particular historical period and within a specific organizational setting. In this view, man creates the meanings through which he comes to reach his understanding of the world. 'Intelligence', 'deprivation' and 'creativity', for example, are each relative terms, indicating not an unequivocal and absolute property but a use specific to a particular context. The aphorism, 'IQ is what intelligence tests measure', reflects the point: IQ is the product of tests designed to elicit a concept of intelligence held by the test constructors. In Gorbutt's (1972) words, 'An interpretive sociology of education focuses attention on the social nature of educational categories and the social processes through which these are constructed and maintained.' Or in Bernstein's (1972) terms, the new sociology concentrates upon, 'the knowledge properties of schools . . .

25

as a result, curricula, pedagogy and forms of assessment are brought sharply into focus and their ideological assumptions and forms of legitimation are explored.'

'New directions' sociology of education?

In evaluating this shift in perspective it is appropriate to ask to what extent there was ever a 'new' sociology of education. Ten years later the substantive examples remain the work of Young, Esland and Keddie as represented in *Knowledge and Control* and in the Open University Course *School and Society*. Yet the criticisms are many, ranging from Shipman (1973) to Flew (1976), from Banks (1974) to Bernbaum (1977), and from Whitty (1974) to Demaine (1977). Though much anthropological, symbolic interactionist and phenomenological work was called to serve the new directions, there has been little growth towards a coherent position. Thus, almost at its birth, the seeds of replacement surrounded the new sociology of education. The major stumbling block in the 'new directions' perspective was seen to be its adoption of an extreme relativist stance, a radical solipsism.

The problem in seeing all categories as *just* the product of a particular time and place is that of deciding the grounds for choosing between categories. Young (1973) tries to solve this problem by arguing that a commitment to the idea of human liberation is the ultimate base for our action. But, as Bernbaum (1977) points out, this is no solution, as we are still left without the means of deciding between different commitments. The socialist and the conservative may agree that human liberation is the end for political action yet disagree as to the meaning of freedom. Though, for academic reasons, it might be interesting to view the world as if we as members were its active creators, we must also recognize that this is not a *sufficient* explanation. Inevitably, most of our time is spent operating within a world that is already ordered for us. As a teacher, we may wish to join our students in the pursuit of truth wherever this may lie, yet we also work with the structural constraint of a syllabus and examinations.

Young (1972) indicates a direction in which his own thought was to move in recognizing that what counts as knowledge within educational institutions is, in part, a political decision. Knowledge has different statuses, the 'pure' tending to be high- while the 'applied' is low-status knowledge. Such evaluations are not intrinsic to knowledge, Young argues, but the product of political processes. More explicitly, by 1977, Young and Whitty argue that the accepted definition of what counts as being educated is a reflection of the social relations of production. A capitalist society, like England, will produce an educational system which will reproduce the existing society. Schools are agents of social-ization into the existing order, breeding acceptance of the way things are and neutralizing the effects of alternative modes of living.

The basis for adoption of this Marxist informed perspective was present in the original formulation of the 'new' sociology of education where two separate strands to the theoretical discussion may be dis-cerned. The first views the teacher as the active creator, in partnership with his pupils, of the social world of the classroom. The failure of some children to succeed is because teachers impose definitions of the situation which do not fit the lived experience of the pupils. In this view, the task of the school is to enter into a joint understanding of the knowledge children have in the present; to develop and strengthen the child's own evolving picture of the world. As Jenks (1977) writes, 'Our writings attempt authenticity through making available the grounds of our understandings; as sociologists, as theorists, as members of a common humanity.' The call is to reach an understanding of the world through the exploration of our collective subjective interpretations. This is important; every day we try to reach the subjective understand-ing our friends, lovers, colleagues and acquaintances have to their world. To say the world is inter-subjective, however, is not to say that *this is all* that the world is. The second strand emerging from the 'new' sociology of education is to locate individual consciousness into the wider social structure. The morality of the 'new' directions, its con-cern with human consciousness, had an affinity with what might be loosely called 'Marxist' or 'Radical' writings, more specifically with the work of the French Philosophers Althusser and Bourdieu, and the Italian philosopher Antonio Gramsci.

Louis Althusser (1918-81)

Althusser sees the structure of society being determined, '*in the last instance*' by the economic base. Ultimately there is an economic determinism to the superstructure, segments such as education, politics and religion, but at any moment each segment is relatively autonomous of both others and the base. In this way, it is possible to view the history of education in nineteenth-century England in the context of domination by the religious sector. The relation between these seg-ments changes as society continually faces the problem of the repro-duction of the means of production. That is, part of the task of, say, any industrial firm is to obtain the materials and equipment needed to continue operating. One of the necessary requirements is that it con-tinues to have the manpower competent to undertake the many de-mands of the firm. Althusser argues that there is an increasing tendency

27

for these demands to be met through the formal education system rather than through apprenticeships and on-the-job training. The school in its role of cultural reproduction is not a neutral agency but part of what Althusser calls the *ideological state apparatus.*

Althusser (1971) argues that the state 'is a machine of repression, which enables the ruling classes ... to ensure their domination over the working class'. He asserts that this process operates both through the state's 'repressive apparatus' such as the police and the armed forces, and its 'ideological apparatus' such as education, the family and the mass media. Althusser sees the school taking 'children from every class at infant-school age, and then for years ... squeezed between the family State apparatus and the educational State apparatus, it drums into them ... a certain amount of "know-how" wrapped in the ruling ideology or simply the ruling ideology in its pure state' (1971). He recognizes that there are some teachers who, in dreadful conditions, 'attempt to turn the few weapons they can find in the history and learning they "teach" against the ideology, the system and the practices in which they are trapped'. The problem is a familiar one. If schools exert a crushing blow to individuality and indoctrinate pupils into the existing relations of production, by what means did Althusser himself come to recognize his 'true' position? Erben and Gleeson (1975) note that Althusser fails 'to explain how radicals emerge from, escape from and engage with the "crushing" influences of state apparatuses'. They argue that there are many similarities between Althusser's analysis of schools and the static functionalism of Parsons, both, in the last instance, working with a passive model of the individual who is more determined than determining. The importance of Gramsci's work is the recognition of human beings as the vehicle by and through which change can be developed.

Antonio Gramsci (1891–1937)

Gramsci saw 'intellectuals' playing a key role in the development of a climate for change, a movement which would be the result of a gradual and emergent change of individual consciousness, not the product of a single revolutionary act. In recognizing the importance of ideas and culture within a society Gramsci argued that the ruling class had established an *hegemony* (literally a leading influence) through which it was able to convince other classes to accept the values, morals, ideas of the dominant class as the most natural. As Williams (1973) has it, 'It is a whole body of practices and expectations; our assignments of energy, our ordinary understanding of the nature of man and of his world. It is a set of meanings and values which, as they are experienced as practices appear as reciprocally confirming.' Education has a critical role in legitimating the dominant hegemony, it teaches the young not only the facts about the world but an attitude towards those facts. Weber was saying something similar in his discussion of the examinations taken by the Literati of Imperial China; 'The examinations of China tested whether or not the candidate's mind was thoroughly steeped in literature and whether or not he possessed the *ways of thought* [emphasis in original] suitable to a cultured man and resulting from cultivation in literature.' In Gramsci's terms, 'Every relationship of "hegemony" is necessarily a pedagogic relationship.' Teaching helps to socialize the taught into the ways of thinking appropriate to the age.

The intellectuals play an important role in sustaining the existing order yet it is through the intellectuals that a counter-hegemonic culture will be born and through which the dominant culture may be challenged. The mechanism Gramsci advocates for the formation of the counter-hegemonic culture in some ways anticipates the work of Mao Zedong in China. The intellectual must remain in contact with 'the masses'; indeed the masses must become their own intellectuals, and work towards an understanding of practice as it is experienced rather than the elaboration of a theoretical model divorced from humanity. Mardle (1977) argues that, 'It follows . . . in Gramsci's analysis, that the real mechanism of change involved the development of the intellectual rigour which will enable man to recognise not only the contradictions of the real world, not only the contradictions of the intellectual orders through which the real world is made manifest', but, 'the ability to take control over both processes simultaneously.' Intellectual work is a struggle to reach an understanding of the historical background to contemporary culture. As Bates (1975) puts it, 'It is not enough for workers to gripe about the boss. They must make themselves better than the boss, not only in their moral conduct, but also in their technical know how.' The importance of Gramsci lies in moving beyond a simple determinism to a view of active man located in a social structure which is itself the product of man's historical acts.

Pierre Bourdieu (1930–   )

The idea of 'hegemony' is taken much further in the work of Bourdieu, the originality of whose thought may be seen in his being labelled a Marxist by some, (Kennett, 1973; Davies, 1976) a Weberian by others, (Swartz, 1977; Collins, 1977) and as developing from the work of Durkheim by others, (DiMaggio, 1979). The point being that Bourdieu draws from the work of many previous scholars to present a creative and unique theory of the maintenance of existing social orders.

The thesis which has been developed by Bourdieu is that capital may take many forms, economic, social and cultural, and if we are to understand the mechanics of its reproduction then we must look to the inter-relationship, or the *relative autonomy*, between the different forms. The established social order is not the result of physical coercion but the expression of *symbolic violence*. That is, the dominant class has the symbols (language, status, artefacts and customs) through which their ways of thought, the master patterns or 'habitus', becomes to be seen as the natural order of things. Bourdieu also uses the notion of habitus in the wider sense that each class, and factions within social classes, will develop its characteristic habitus or master pattern. In other words each will develop a perspective into which children will be socialized and through which they will make sense of their world and at the same time alter bits of their habitus.

The school, especially through the mechanism of awarding certificates and diplomas, is a crucial arena in which the maintenance of the established order is sustained (Bourdieu, 1966):

> It is in fact one of the most effective means of perpetuating the existing social pattern, as it both provides an apparent justification for social inequalities and gives recognition to the cultural heritage, that is, to a *social* gift treated as a *natural* one

The educational system maintains a stance of neutrality in that 'objective' examinations act as gatekeepers to the next stage allowing some of the dispossessed to succeed and failing some individuals within the dominant class. Bourdieu and Boltanski (1978) show that as the upper class become more aware of the importance of qualifications for the reproduction of their own capital – in other words instead of passing wealth direct to sons, the sons go to the university and take a qualification which admits them into the firm, the hidden nepotism of the modern firm – so at the same time those qualifications are devalued. Consequently the value of cultural intangibles like style, taste, background and connections remain the real criteria by which recruitment is managed.

The education system appears neutral and the proliferation of degrees, diplomas and certificates carries with it the idea that opportunity is increasing. But as 'everyone' gets a qualification actual selection is based on 'hidden qualities'. Bourdieu argues that, 'What the education system both hands on and demands is an aristocratic culture and, above all, an aristocratic relationship with it' (1966). Schools operate within the 'habitus' of the dominant group. The language, values, assumptions and implicit models of success and failure which are held by teachers within schools are those of the dominant group. In reflecting back *one* way of making sense of the world as the *natural way*, schools legitimate the cultural capital which is shared by the dominant class. As schools presently function, the oppressed classes need to learn how to relate to the school's culture before they can learn its message. In learning the message of the school, however, the oppressed classes are also learning an order of things which is not their order but that of the controlling groups.

As the individual from the lower groups moves up the educational ladder he becomes increasingly different from his peers as he accommodates the 'habitus' of the dominant class. As the few succeed, more in science and technology than in the arts, so their individual success reinforces the belief that the system must be just. Bourdieu's analysis illustrates some of the subtlety in the process of social reproduction (Bourdieu and Passeron, 1977):

> The educational system succeeds so perfectly in fulfilling its ideo-
> logical function of legitimating the established order only because
> of this masterpiece of social mechanics succeeds in hiding, as if by
> the interlocking of false-bottomed boxes, the relations which, in a
> class society, unite the function of inculcation, i.e., the work of
> intellectual and moral integration, with the function of conserving
> the structure of class relations characteristic of that society.

There are two problems in Bourdieu's analysis to which I wish to draw attention. As Johnson notes (1976), 'Schools . . . reproduce forms of resistance too, however limited or "corporate" or unself-conscious these may be.' The difficulty is probably one of the most profound, and possibly unsolvable, within social science. Any theory which suggests that we are in part determined by something, be this the economy or the cultural system, must also explain why it is still possible to see an alternative reality. Each political system, of 'right' or 'left', 'democratic' or 'communist', has its dissidents who occupy a 'habitus' which is not that of the dominant group. The fracture in social theory comes between individual and societal explanation, between an explanation of you and I as unique individuals and explanations of students and teachers as social groups. Bourdieu does not explain how a critical consciousness would emerge within society.

The second problem, as Davies (1976) points out, is the lack of a historical perspective, 'the historical dimension in his work which would enable us to see how it came to be like that'. As we have already seen in looking at Durkheim's work, the strength of *The Evolution* lies in its explanation of the change in consciousness; it is first and foremost a historical work which explains the present and as such is a dimension lacking in the work of Bourdieu.

31

Conclusion

Contemporary sociology of education has passed through a series of shifts in perspective. New positions have emerged only to be challenged and give way to alternatives, leaving at least Bernstein with the impression that 'the "news" of much contemporary sociology appears to be news about the conditions necessary for creating acceptable news'. It appears as if the empirical is dead and that the protagonists of each perspective defend their theoretical purity and lampoon the work produced within a different perspective, within a different 'problematic'. But this is an over-simplification; although there is a deep concern with theory within the sociology of education there is also, as we shall see, a strong tradition of empirical work which has grown out of that theory. Each perspective has tended to generate its own research style. Thus from political arithmetic has come the interest of the relative advantage of different social classes in access to education; from the 'new' sociology a concern with the curriculum and classroom interaction; and from the 'radical' an interest in the history of education, in attempts to account for and explain the consequences of the rise of mass schooling.

The designation of sociology of education into three perspectives – political arithmetic, new and radical – inevitably distorts the work of many. The labels are for convenience, for the purpose of helping our understanding of the many strands which inform contemporary sociology of education, and are not meant to be applied rigidly to any author or any work. Indeed, as we have seen with respect to Young's work, sociologists move across perspectives and draw from each. It may be, as Karabel and Halsey suggest, that a synthesis is required from the different perspectives to facilitate our understanding of the nature of educational processes. It could be that the complexity of the social world is such that any synthesis would only distort and that a tension between perspectives will better clarify our vision. As we turn to substantive areas of enquiry in the rest of this book something of a tension will be continually present as we view the emerging and changing patterns within the sociology of education.

Chapter 3

Socialization 1.
The child and the family

Having indicated that there are different perspectives within sociology and that these are reflected in the way sociology of education has developed, we turn now to an examination of aspects of that development. Starting with the child and her family, we take her into school where she will meet her peers in classrooms as well as meeting teachers, the curriculum and learning about her membership of a bureaucratic organization. In later chapters we consider the contribution that schooling makes to the attainment of political goals such as equality, as well as to the maintenance of existing hierarchies within society. In other words we travel from a micro to a macro perspective, shifting our attention from the formation of individual identities to a concern with the nature of social structure, and how this in turn influences and is influenced by those identities.

Any comprehensive sociological interpretation of real children, real men and women needs to be an amalgam made from each of the theoretical perspectives we have introduced so far. You and I are both determined by our world and yet determine that world; we are both products and producers, and the relationship between each aspect is constantly changing as we cope with the exigencies of our daily lives. Our consideration of how self develops begins with the process of socialization. This process continues throughout life, but conventionally social scientists label the initial period of socialization, that by which a child first acquires her identity as a person, as *primary socialization*; and the later socialization into membership of the wider society as 'school girl', 'student', 'clerk' or 'pensioner' as *secondary socialization*. In this and the subsequent chapter our emphasis is on the former and in later chapters the latter will be of central concern.

Passive theories of socialization

The dominant perspective from which the process of socialization has been viewed is that of functionalism, particularly the work of Talcott Parsons. Parsons (1951) comments that socialization, like learning, continues throughout life but that it is at its most dramatic when seen in relation to the child. He continues:

> There is reason to believe that, among the learned elements of personality in certain respects the stablest and most enduring are the major value-orientation patterns and there is much evidence that these are 'laid down' in childhood and are not on a large scale subject to drastic alteration during adult life. There is good reason to treat these patterns of value-orientation . . . as the core of what is sometimes called 'basic personality structure'.

Socialization is, for Parsons, explained in terms of his theory of functional prerequisites which we outlined in the first chapter. As the child grows and matures, she continually experiences frustration in her *goal attainment*; possibly because the demands upon her by parents increase and she feels in danger of losing their affection. The child thus *adopts* new coping strategies in order to meet her continuing goal of parental love. In so adapting her behaviour she also learns strategies which can be extended to cope with other, novel demands, that is *pattern maintenance*; finally she *integrates* the new behaviour into her emergent personality structure. The personality system becomes stable again in preparation for a new cycle of goal attainment, adaptation, pattern maintenance and integration as new demands are placed on the individual.

There are several problems with this essentially *passive model*. An assumption is made that the child is just responding to the stimuli of the parents and thus ignores the possibility that the child may well experience several conflicts within herself as to what the most appropriate behaviour is; the conflict, for example, between the guilt in hurting parents yet wanting to go against their wishes; or the conflict of knowing that one line of action, such as spending money on sweets, precludes another, such as buying a favourite game. Parsons's model also accepts that there is a 'basic personality structure' which once laid down in childhood is relatively static throughout life. Such an assertion needs to be demonstrated, with all the contingent problems this has of drawing causal links between you now and your judged personality when you were a child.

In an extension to Parsons's discussion, Kluckhohn (1958) has equated what Parsons labels 'value-orientations' to the culture of a society, suggesting that they emerge in response to five problems common to all human groups. The first is the orientation taken towards human nature; expressed in extreme forms this would be a belief that human beings are 'basically evil but perfectible' or alternatively 'good and corruptible'. The second is the orientation to Nature where a group might see the work of Nature as something over which we have no control as against a belief in people's ability to control Nature. The third is time orientation, or the relative emphasis placed on past, present or future, such as the belief in staying at school in order to obtain a good job. The next orientation asks what is the 'modality of human activity' or whether young people are seen in terms of what they are or by what they can accomplish. Finally Kluckhohn identifies as a problem our orientation towards other people, whether, for example, strong family ties should influence one's action.

From this analysis Klukhohn is able to conclude that the contemporary middle-class American family is the most suited to the rational, bureaucratic life-style of that country. Parents are concerned with the achievements of their children and train them for independence of action and initiative. Competition is applauded and the child is seen as the hope for the future by many families. The family does 'produce achievement-minded, independent and future oriented individuals who are largely free of ties that bind them in time and place.' There is, however, no necessary relationship between a participant type of nation state and the form of the family; Seymour (1974) for example, shows that many of the Iban in Sarawak hold achievement values and expectations of their children's futures which are similar to those which Klukhohn identifies as the symbol of WASP (White, Anglo-Saxon, Protestant) culture in the USA.

As part of a project under the joint direction of Parsons, Klukhohn and Stouffer, J.A. Kahl (1953) interviewed twenty-four boys, the sons of parents who viewed themselves as 'ordinary people', 'common man's boys', in his terms. His purpose was to try and explain why it was that though the boys had similar abilities and came from similar homes, half of them aspired to go to college (an aspiration which was later achieved) and half did not. Kahl argues that the difference between the two groups was 'parental pressure'; some parents wanted their children to strive for a better life and others were content with life as it was. Parents who were discontented tended to train their sons from the earliest years of grammar school to take school seriously and use education as the means to climb into the middle class. Sons who internalized such values were only the ones sufficiently motivated to overcome the obstacles which faced common man's boys in school; only they saw a reason for good school performance and college aspirations. The complexity of the causal link between parental pressure and educational attainment is clear from Kahl's data. Almost half of the

35

boys did not act in ways which support the overall thesis. It is not sufficient to identify something called 'achievement-minded' individuals and use this to account for the actual performance of children. This does not mean that high parental expectations are not important, but rather to stress that such expectations will be one of a number of factors which influence the child and whose influence may well be masked or neutralized by other factors. It is also important to note, as Colquhoun (1976) has stated, that 'It is reasonable to suppose that if people do want to "achieve", it is unlikely that they want to achieve in any and every area.'

The work on socialization which stems from Parsons's theoretical discussion is parallel to the social psychological theories of D. C. McClelland and his colleagues. McClelland (1963) argues that an important ingredient in the socialization process is the desire to do well, the attainment of a feeling of personal accomplishment. This he calls the 'need for achievement' and he reports that people who score high on tests designed to elicit this value 'tend to work harder at certain tasks; to learn faster; to do their best work when it counts for the record, and not when special incentives, like money prizes, are introduced; to choose experts over friends as working partners.' Rosen (1956) suggests that achievement orientation has two dimensions; the first is a personality characteristic towards achievement which provides an internal impetus to excel, the second is a cultural characteristic which upholds the value of achievement.

The arguments developed from McClelland's work have been used to explain why some nations are more advanced than others, and particularly to explain why lower working-class children do less well at school than their middle-class counterparts. Thus Hyman (1953), Winterbottom (1969), and Rosen and D'Andrade (1959) each conclude that a child who is encouraged to become independent from his parents will acquire the characteristics which result in his having a high need for achievement, a quality which is more often found in middle- rather than in working-class homes.

Each of the studies we have included within the functionalist perspective has adopted a similar method, that is, starting with the acknowledged variation in school achievement between social groups, the difference is explained in terms of some aspect of the child's primary socialization. Even if a relationship were to be established, this would not of itself explain the operation of the links between home background and school performance. Extending the work of Kahl and of McClelland, Swift (1966, 1968) attempts to move beyond a statement of association to explain *how* social class factors affect learning outcomes. Swift notes the danger of viewing the successful middle-class and the unsuccessful working-class child as part of a continuum where the latter comes from a family which exhibits characteristics which are opposite and inferior to those of the former. Having warned of the dangers, Swift's 'psycho-dynamic' approach tends to fall into the same trap. He identifies a type of academically successful family which is distinct from the middle-class stereotype and where the crucial variable is the high degree of 'mobility pessimism' in the father. This refers to the father's dissatisfaction with his own job opportunities, making him resolve that his children will do better through education and thus escape the monotony which he experiences. The inclusion of this category adds an extra point to the continuum but the process of socialization and the consequences for education remain hidden.

Role – active and passive models

The common factor in the models of socialization which we have discussed is that they each adopt a *passive* view of man. Socialization is something which happens to people, values are internalized, behaviour is changed as the child responds to the pressures upon him. The child is given no opportunity to create her own world, nor is the influence which the child has on the action of her parents or teachers a central feature of the passive view. The child takes her role within society. The meaning of role is ambiguous, some take it to refer to the *positions* within society such as teacher, student, mother and so on, and others to mean *performance* of people in the role. Despite this ambiguity sociologists have built a series of related concepts around 'role' including, *role set* or the set of expectations incumbent on any role performance; *role conflict*, or the at times difficulty in acting the role of, for example, boy-friend and son on the occasion of parents meeting a girl-friend.

As roles change so the individual must learn the requirements of new roles, a process of *anticipatory socialization* where you begin to learn what is required of you as, for example, a teacher, or when a couple expect a baby and begin to anticipate their future role as parents. Coulson (1972) has argued that we ought to abandon the concept of role altogether as it implies a consensual view of society. She argues that we might adopt instead the concept of 'structured network of expectation', a shift which would have the merit of alerting us to the conflict inherent in each of our social positions and stress how that conflict is related to the distribution of power within a society. The process of anticipatory socialization is not the gradual absorption of a new behaviour pattern. There is disagreement about how a teacher should perform her role and how a parent should perform his. You do not take on your role as you might your overcoat; each role has some built in *role distance*, Goffman's term to catch the detachment which we each have in our various roles. Individuals fight against being labelled a 'typical student' or 'typical teacher'. As well as *taking* on a role each individual also *makes* his role, a distinction made by Turner (1962) in arguing that the process of socialization into a new role is not one of passive acceptance but of active engagement with a world that exists, an engagement which changes that world and which also changes the individual.

Active theories of socialization

An alternative to the passive theories of socialization stems from the work of G. H. Mead, which we outlined in the first chapter. His *active* theory of socialization means, as Blumer (1965) has it, 'Action is built up in coping with the world instead of merely being released from a pre-existing psychological structure by factors playing on that structure.' People do not simply respond to their role, to the value-orientation or to the economic substructure, but actively create their roles in the material circumstances in which they live. The danger of the active theory is of implying that the individual has the freedom to do just as he pleases and of ignoring the power which some have to constrain the activities of others. There are limits to everyone's behaviour. As Davies (1976) argues, 'the social *is* control'. The point in Mead's discussion is that the self is a social being and can only be formed in interaction with others.

Mead's theory of socialization has been incorporated by Berger and Luckmann (1967) into their general social theory. They argue that we are each born into an objective social structure, a network of relationships existing before our birth, within which we meet the *significant others*, parents or those responsible for us, who will be in charge of our socialization. Thus the perception of the world by the significant others becomes the 'objective reality' for the infant. Through them is filtered a view of the world as natural or normal (Berger and Luckmann, 1967, p. 155):

> Primary socialization thus accomplishes what (in hindsight of course) may be seen as the most important confidence trick that society plays on the individual – to make appear as necessity what is in fact a bundle of contingencies, and thus to make meaningful the accident of birth.

The child learns, in Berger and Luckmann's words, 'that he *is* what he is called' and has little choice in the matter as he has no choice over who are to be his significant others.

As the child grows older so does his world of significant others expand; parents begin to share the position with teachers, a favourite relation, friends, idols and other esteemed people. In this changing emphasis that bit of the self labelled the 'I' by Mead is continually monitoring the formation of identity, reflecting on the 'ME' of everyday life (as we saw in the first chapter). In the process we are building a coherent view of ourself in which we may reject bits that have been internalized from our earliest significant others. At times this change is sufficient to prompt the comment of, 'I do not feel I know you anymore, as a father views his son, or as an individual revisits an old school friend', the discovery that their worlds are so far apart that there is little other than reminiscences to share. This process is not mechanistic; we are not determined by the labels and opinions of the wider significant others but evaluate their view of the world in terms of our emerging concept of ourself. The self is engaged in a dialectic, an interchange, both internally between the I and the ME, and externally with the shared experience of everyday life.

The process by which the self emerges has been further elaborated by Cicourel (1973). His analysis of self has similarities to that of Chomsky's analysis of speech. Chomsky has made the distinction between the surface structure of speech, our ordinary conversation, and the deep structure of grammar, or the implicit rules which we all invoke in constructing meaningful talk. Cicourel argues that the norms of behaviour are the surface forms and that the process of socialization is the acquisition of *interpretive procedures*, or the development of rules which guide our choice of appropriate behaviour within different situations. Interpretive procedures are 'rules about rules', a simple example is that in driving a car the expectations, indeed the law, in England is that one drives on the left-hand side of the road. There are occasions when it is possible to drive on the right; some are formally recognized, such as driving in a 'one way' street. Others are not so, such as in crossing open country on a twisting road where, if there is no other traffic, it is acceptable to use the full width of the road at each bend. Part of the knowledge required to drive a car is to know the 'rules about rules', to have the 'common sense' to modify one's driving in accordance with the prevailing conditions, keeping in mind the safety of oneself and other road users. We learn, then, the interpretive procedures which regulate our specific behaviour in particular circumstances.

Each perspective in socialization presents severe methodological problems. In our discussion of passive theories we raised the difficulty of showing that an association between two variables, such as 'need for achievement' and school performance, was a causal relationship. Even more with active theories is the difficulty of empirically demonstrating how interpretive procedures operate, what cognizance individuals actually make of significant others, or how people make their roles; as yet we must remain sceptical with all explanations of the processes of socialization.

Radical theories of socialization

Both the active and passive theories of socialization slide past what a third perspective, the *radical*, sees as its most important aspect; that socialization takes place within a stratified society. In most discussion social class tends to be seen as a descriptive, independent variable, the backcloth against which children become adults, instead of integral to the process. Clarke and his colleagues (Clarke and Jefferson, 1976; Clarke *et al.*, 1976) pick up Gramsci's concept of hegemony and argue that a critical feature of the social change in England during the 1950s and 1960s was the way in which the dominant groups in society were able to preserve their power through making their life-style appear to be part of the 'natural' order of things; Clarke *et al.* locate the 'confidence trick' to which Berger and Luckmann referred to the relations between social classes. The increased affluence of the period, which encouraged the ordinary family to strive for an automatic washing machine, colour television, newer car, a home of their own and a package holiday in Spain, neatly directed attention away from the real issues, the persistence of inequality between social classes. The fact that some working-class children went on to higher education and eventually obtained prestigious jobs perpetrated the myth of equality of opportunity by hiding the extent of the actual inequalities of opportunity. Building from a Marxist perspective and analysing the substantive topic of the formation and development of youth subcultures Clarke and his colleagues stress that socialization is class socialization: 'The young inherit a cultural orientation from their parents towards a "problematic" common to the class as a whole, which is likely to weight, shape and signify the meanings they then attach to different areas of their social life' (Clarke *et al.*, 1976, p. 29).

Although social class has been neglected in most discussion of the process of socialization its inclusion may suggest that one's class position determines behaviour. Clarke *et al.*, are well aware of the dangers of this position and try to overcome the problem by recognizing the many factors of culture, geographical area and economic opportunities which overlay and through which class factors are filtered. Nevertheless, such is the complexity of human behaviour that it is difficult to see in what meaningful sense one can refer to class factors, what dimension is critical to the formation of individual identity and consciousness. In their discussion of youth subcultures they recognize that 'the great majority of working class youth never enter a tight or coherent subculture at all' (Clarke *et al.*, 1976, p. 16). They note that at one period there were two clearly identifiable subcultures, Mods and Rockers, but it is not possible to explain within their perspective why some individuals became 'Mods' and others 'Rockers', nor why a particular historical period should see two distinctive subcultures, nor why both groups failed to attract the majority of teenagers; indeed it would be an interesting exercise to chart the boundaries of membership, what counted as being a 'Mod' or 'Rocker'.

In essence a social class analysis is an analysis of the distribution of power within society, where some have very little power over their own life-style and consequently over their sense of the possible, that sense of what human beings could achieve. As yet our understanding of the dynamics of class remains faulty and unsure, the process of socialization remains largely unexplained. There are a number of descriptive studies into patterns of socialization within the United Kingdom to which we will turn in a moment, but first we need to remember that the word 'child' is not as straightforward as one might at first assume.

The social structure of childhood

The categories by which we label the objects of socialization – child, adolescent, pupil and student, for example – do not have some inviolate, immutable existence. The contemporary use of each of these labels is different from that in previous historical periods; in fact we can assert that childhood and adolescence are both recent phenomena. As part of his study of the evolution of the modern family in France, Aries (1973) shows how the concept of childhood has changed over time. At the extreme the change is from the tenth century, where artists were unable to depict a child except as an adult on a small scale, to a position where childhood is almost a sacred concept and 'children are unique persons and their individuality is to be acknowledged and respected' (Brearley *et al.*, 1969, p. 159).

Aries identifies two *concepts of childhood*. The first, characterized by 'coddling', tended to see a sharp break between the world of the adult and that of the infant; the latter, as soon as he 'could live without the constant solicitude of his mother, his nanny or his cradle-rocker, . . . belonged to adult society'. During his dependency he would be 'coddled', touched, caressed and played with in a manner which led, Aries records, the sixteenth-century French writer Montaigne to declare that he could not accept this idea of loving children 'for our amusement, like monkeys'. The second concept, that of moral worth, saw children as 'fragile creatures of God who needed to be both safeguarded and reformed'. That is, the child must be protected from the evils of the wider society as must his own original sin be cleansed. To expedite the process a study of the psychology of the child was essential, hence the beginnings of the 'child expert' and the proliferation of manuals and guides as to the 'correct' way of socializing a child.

Schnell (1979) extends Aries's discussion and sees in the changing concept of childhood a justification for a common school: 'Seeing "childhood" as a dominant assumption of the middle class ideology provides us with a clearer understanding of the drive to institutionalise all children into a universal "childhood".' The growth of the common school is for Schnell 'society's most ornate shrine' to the concept of childhood, a concept which embraced the moral requirements of protection, segregation, dependence and delayed responsibilities. This protection of children within the walls of the common school is clearly evident in Platt's (1969) discussion of the child-saving movement in America, the precursor to contemporary programmes for 'delinquent' youths. Platt writes, 'the child-savers were prohibitionists, in a general sense, who believed that adolescents needed protection from even their own inclinations.' The model of human development which informed the child-saving movement was grounded in the conviction that children are bad as a result of their circumstances. Consequently what was required was access to green fields, hills and a sense of adventure; children had to be safeguarded against the evils of urban, industrial society.

As the concept of child changes with the different interests of social groups, so also does the meaning of adolescence. The *Oxford English Dictionary* gives the meaning of adolescent as the stage between childhood and maturity to be of late eighteenth-century origin; or as Musgrove (1964) has it, 'The adolescent was invented at the same time as the steam-engine.' Unlike the steam engine, however, it is not clear in what sense it is meaningful to talk about adolescence. There is a view which sees adolescence as a time of rebelliousness, a period when the developing person has a sense of his own independence without any of the responsibilities. Adolescents wear similar clothes, listen to similar popular music and enjoy the comparative freedom of association with members of the opposite sex. However, many 'adolescents' are not rebellious for much of the time, most not at all; many wear clothes which are identical to those worn by people a decade or two older. Many are not interested in popular music, or if interested neither more nor less than many non-adolescents, and finally relationships with members of the opposite sex continue to take many forms throughout adult life. The range of behaviour within adolescence is such that the category 'adolescent' has very little meaning, leading some to refer to 'the myth of adolescence' (cf. White, 1977, p. 117).

At the very least 'adolescence' would seem to refer to those half dozen or so years which begin at about puberty and last until the formal attainment of adult status, eighteen in England. The danger of the label is that it directs attention to the individual, to the adolescent, and sees the source of any problems stemming from the person to the neglect of the social structure. Thus many adolescents are rebellious at school not so much because rebelliousness is a characteristic of adolescence as that the organizational practices of some schools frustrate the needs of the individual. This recognition of the social context of behaviour does not exclude the fact that some individuals cause serious disturbances such that no conventional school could be expected to contain them. The point is more general, that is, as we shall see in chapter 8, some schools seem to allow the possibility for more disruptive behaviour than others and any complete explanation of adolescence must include the structural setting to individual action. The difficulty with such recognition is that discussion slips easily into passive terms, the circumstances 'cause' the behaviour, the boy was 'constrained' in some mechanistic sense by the social structure. Our discussion of socialization has shown some of the problems with the passive view and has also indicated some of the difficulties in developing an alternative active theory which could account for the behaviour of the adolescent at, for example, a football match. Ethnographic studies such as those of Patrick (1972), Parker (1974) and Willis (1977) are important beginnings for the generation of an adequate theory of youthful socialization.

Longitudinal studies of childhood

Another direction from which an adequate theory of socialization could emerge is from the series of longitudinal or cohort studies which are being conducted in the United Kingdom. Having surveyed the literature on social influences affecting educational attainment, Husen (1975) concludes that we are still far from the stage where we can begin to analyse causally how the relevant variables which determine educational achievement act and interact. Cohort studies may eventually enable us to identify these 'relevant' variables; at present they each give a careful description about the growth of the individual seen from the point of view of her parents and teachers and eventually, as the child reaches adolescence, from the individual herself.

The most widely known cohort study is that which has been directed by J. W. B. Douglas since 1946, the main educational findings of which are available in Douglas (1964) and Douglas, Ross and Simpson (1968). The study arose from the work of the Royal Commission on Population which had been appointed in 1944 'to examine the facts relating to the

43

present population trends in Great Britain.' As part of this investigation it was decided to look at the maternity services in the country and at the costs of having children, doing this by issuing a questionnaire to the mothers of all the babies born in the week 3–9 March 1946, some 15,000 in all. Having completed the maternity study, Douglas and his colleagues began to explore the opportunity of maintaining contact with the cohort, eventually being able to finance a study which included 'all children born during this week to the wives of non-manual workers and of farm labourers, and one-quarter of those born to the wives of other types of manual workers and self-employed persons' (1964), a total of 5,362 children.

For the purpose of analysis the parents of the 1946 cohort were grouped into four social class categories; upper and lower middle and upper and lower working class. The basis of the grouping was the occupation, background and education of the parents. Using tests of verbal and non-verbal intelligence and also tests of attainment the scores of the children were standardized to a mean of 50 with a standard deviation of 10. At age eleven, the upper middle-class children scored an average of 57; lower middle, 54; upper working, 50; and lower working class children, 48.

The value of Douglas's work comes from being able to follow the *same* children over time. In comparing the results obtained at eleven with those from the same children at eight, Douglas found, 'at eleven years the average test score made by children in the four social classes differs more widely than they did at eight' (1964, p. 76). One might expect that a consequence of school would be a reduction in the differences between the social class group, yet Douglas found the contrary so that, 'By the time he is eleven, the clever manual working class child has fallen behind the middle class child of similar ability at eight years', a difference which Douglas and his colleagues found to persist through the secondary school. In his introduction to *The Home and the School*, Douglas calculated that there would have to be 56 per cent more grammar school places in England and Wales to accommodate all the working-class children who at eight had the same ability as those middle-class children who eventually gained a place in a selective secondary school.

The critical factor put forward by Douglas in explaining the divergence between the social class groups is parental interest: 'High interest is closely linked to high attainment, good results in the "O" level examination and a long school life in the next generation, whereas low interest is associated with poor performance and early leaving' (Douglas, Ross and Simpson, 1968). This finding complements Kahl's assertions on the effects of parental pressure which we have referred to earlier in this chapter. Douglas measured parental interest by whether teachers assessed the parents to be taking a high level of interest in their children's work; if the father had visited the school to discuss the child's progress on more than two occasions; if either parent had sought further education after leaving school, and if the mother wanted her children to follow a full-time educational course on leaving school or to enter a profession. The great difficulty in measuring something like parental interest is in knowing what in fact is being measured; how the 'interest' as defined for inclusion within a questionnaire actually relates to the 'interest' shown by parents in their everyday care for their children. Even more elusive is the precise educational significance of the quality of care provided by the 'interested' parent as against that of the 'uninterested'. The attempt to gauge, in other words, how the quality of socialization affects school attainment, to move from descriptive categories to an understanding of the processes at work within the home.

A smaller yet complementary cohort study to that of Douglas goes some way to charting the dynamics of parental interest. This is the Nottingham Child Development Study directed by John and Elizabeth Newson from 1958. A cohort of children were followed at ages one, four, seven, eleven and sixteen. At each stage about 700 mothers were interviewed, losses being replaced by a newly drawn sample of mothers with children at the appropriate age. Using a modification of the Registrar General's designation of social class (see also chapter 9), the Newson study groups its sample into five; upper and lower professional, white collar (i.e. clerical) plus foremen, skilled manual, semi-skilled manual and unskilled manual. The sample was so drawn that there would be at least 100 cases in each of the smaller groups, like, for example, unskilled manual.

The first report from this project, which is explicitly about school (Newson, Newson and Barnes, 1977) gives two indicators of parental interest. The first is an index of General Cultural Interests which consists of items such as whether parents pay for extra lessons for the child, and if they take the child on visits to, among others, the cinema, theatre, museum, zoo and football match. The second indicator is the index of Home-School Concordance which is built from items such as whether the child takes things to school to show his teacher, whether the child asks about things she's heard about in class, and whether parents try to help with school work.

In summary, the two indices show a number of tendencies as one moves from the upper and lower professional group to unskilled manual. These are summarized by Newson *et al.*, (1977, p. 131) as follows:

1. The range of cultural interests experienced by children as members of their family group becomes more narrow and restricted.

2. Although children in all classes sometimes carry over school activities into the home, further down the scale they are less inquiring at home on school inspired topics.
3. Parents become less inclined to take up and expand children's questions, of whatever source, by whatever means.
4. Parents are, in particular, less likely to use books or newspapers to further the child's knowledge, and are more likely to attempt to conceal their own ignorance.
5. Children are less likely to receive help, direct or in the form of the encouragement of a 'hospitable environment' with school work other than reading.

The Newsons also report that the Concordance index scores are significantly higher for girls, suggesting that girls are more likely than boys to involve their parents at the interface between home and school. The most disadvantaged are the sons of unskilled manual workers, a disadvantage which is compounded should they also be members of a large family which has a low income.

This study begins to move beyond description to an analysis of the process of socialization by using a concept of *relevance*, the essence of which is that 'By taking him on visits to places of interest, making sure that he has access to the written media, answering his questions and seaching for answers elsewhere when her own knowledge is inadequate, the mother repeatedly characterizes cultural interest as relevant to herself, and by identification, to the child as well' (Newson and Newson, 1977, p. 85). There is a parallel here to Bernstein's discussion of family role systems. As part of his development of a theory of social reproduction, or how social control is maintained from one generation to another, Bernstein (1971) presents two ideal types of family, positional and personal oriented. The *positional family* is one where there is a clear separation of roles between members, such as mother, child or, at a certain age, grandparent. In such a family the child is socialized within a clearly marked framework, the 'children are expected to be seen and not heard' stereotype of the Victorian middle class. The *person-centred family* is one where the child is seen in terms of the unique characteristics which she has as a person. Her ascribed status, such as age and sex, is of much less importance than her personal and unique contribution to the life of the family. Consequently, Bernstein argues, 'person-oriented families, very early in the child's life, sensitize him towards and actively promote his language development in order that they can apply their favoured modes of control' (1971, p. 156).

The distinction between positional and personal-oriented families becomes, by 1977, the distinction between 'individualized and personalized forms of organic solidarity' (Bernstein, 1977, p. 125). The latter, the personalized form of organic solidarity, is dependent on a complex and elaborated form of speech which enables more of the child to be controlled. In the individualized, positional family, the child knows her place and in a sense her private world, her secret thoughts, remain her own property; there is no requirement to articulate what she feels about her life or what she thinks about her relationships to other members of the family. Within the personalized family, however, the child is encouraged to lay bare her thoughts and feelings, as do other members of the family, and as such she makes far more of herself available to the influence of the family, so much so that she feels intense pangs of guilt should she act against the perceived wishes of the family. The Newsons' concept of 'relevance' is an indication of the personalized family, the effective socialization of the child through the discussion of relevant cultural spheres.

The other major longitudinal study looking at the overall development of children is that of the National Child Development Bureau. (There are other, more specialized cohort studies like, for example, West's study of 411 boys in relation to patterns of delinquency; see West and Farrington, 1977.) As with Douglas's cohort, the National Child Development study began as an examination of the administration of British maternity services and the causes of still birth and deaths during the first week after birth (perinatal mortality). The sample taken was all births during the first week of March 1958. The children some 17,000, were followed up when they were seven years old (Davie *et al.*, 1972), again when they were eleven (Wedge and Prosser, 1973) and again at sixteen (Fogelman, 1976). Evidence from the latter report supports Douglas's finding that the gap between social classes increases during the period of formal schooling in scores achieved on reading and arithmetic tests. This is a finding of some concern given that the twelve-year gap separating the two studies was one during which there were vigorous attempts to promote more egalitarian educational policies.

Each of the cohort studies we have mentioned presents a picture of socialization and indicates the variation in the mode of socialization between different social groups. They are relatively atheoretical and essentially descriptive in nature, while Bernstein, on the other hand, uses a Durkheimian framework to explore how the form of transmission through language might influence the development of individual identities.

We have looked at different perspectives on socialization – 'passive', 'active', and 'radical' – and have shown how the concepts of the child and adolescent are not fixed, absolute categories but change over time. We turn now to look more closely at the family itself, for most people the setting for primary socialization.

Socialization 1. The child and the family

The family

The family has been variously seen by social scientists as beset by crisis, to be in inevitable decline, and to offer a richer source for individual fulfillment than ever. Briefly, in Great Britain in 1971 there were 6.4 million married couples with dependent children and 0.63 million single parents with dependent children; this last figure had increased to 0.75 million by 1976. During 1976 there were 406,000 marriages, an event which was a remarriage for either one or both partners in a third of the cases. Also in the mid-1970s the age at which people first married started to drift upwards having steadily declined throughout the earlier part of the century. In England and Wales in 1976, 146,000 petitions were filed for divorce as against 28,000 petitions filed twenty years earlier in 1956. From 1964 until 1977 the birth rate continued to fall, reaching its lowest level ever in 1977 when 569,000 babies were born, a crude birth rate of 11.6 births per thousand of the population. In 1978 the birth rate started to increase again and some 27,000 'extra' babies were born. Whether these changes are interpreted as a foretaste of disaster to come or an indication of the health of the modern family, all commentators agree that there have been important changes in the structure of the family during the past three decades.

There is little point in presenting a definition of 'the family', as Morgan (1975) says, 'I know who is "in" my family and the families of others appear to me to be recognizable entities.' There are families in this subjective sense where the adults are not married – they may even be of the same sex – and where the children are not the biological offspring of the adults. However, the most usual family is the one of Murdock's oft-quoted definition, 'The family is a social group characterized by common residence, economic co-operation, and reproduction. It includes adults of both sexes, at least two of whom maintain a socially approved sexual relationship, and one or more children, own or adopted, of the sexually co-habiting adults' (1947, p. 197).

Most of the discussion of the family has once again been conducted within the functionalist perspective. The functions of the family for the wider social system have been analysed, even though, as Morgan argues, 'there is little agreement as to what the "basic" functions of the family are, how many there are and to the extent and way in which they might or might not have changed' (1947, p. 56). Morgan continues that although many would agree that socialization is one of the key functions of the family it is unclear as to what is meant by this assertion; the family is not the sole agent of socialization, nor are its effects separable from those of other socialization agencies like the neighbourhood and the school. We are back to the dilemma we have already met in work within this area, where a common assumption is impossible to substantiate on any empirical grounds. Hence the assertion that the family is an agency of socialization, although correct, has little meaning.

The functionalist perspective, Morgan states, contains a conservative view of people such that biological features of the individual, like sex and age, are seen as determinants of behaviour rather than as limitations on individual action. Morgan argues for an examination of the family which takes as its central theme the 'project' of its members. The notion of 'project' shifts the emphasis away from the present or past action to that intended in the future. Morgan recognizes that we are each constrained in our future plans but the critical issue is whether or not we accept these constraints as part of the necessary framework of our action or something against which we struggle for change. In looking at the 'projects' of family members our analysis must also ask from whence the 'projects' originate. In this way we include background factors like family of origin, educational experience, the influence of the community and also the existence of other members. In including the latter, Morgan is recognizing that conflict may well be an integral and 'normal' feature of family living and not symptomatic of individual deviance.

There are similarities between Morgan's theoretical discussion of the family and the empirical exploration of the modern family conducted by Young and Willmott (1975). They make an analogy with a marching column which moves through three identifiable phases each of which exists at the present though the first two reflect past historical periods. The first stage is the *pre-industrial* where the whole family work together as a unit of production; this is the family of the eighteenth and early nineteenth century in Western Europe, the family whose internal structure was undermined by the process of industrialization. At this second stage, family members are seen as 'wage *earners*', as individual members of the new, factory-based economy and as such the family as a collectivity is under stress; this is the family described by Hoggart in 1958. Eventually, through growing material wealth, a new form of family is able to emerge where 'the unity of the family has been restored around its functions as the unit not of production but of consumption'. This is, in Young and Willmott's terms, the *symmetrical* family where the adult members are opposite but similar.

The symmetrical family has three characteristics. It is, first of all, centred on the home; it is what Goldthorpe and Lockwood have called the privatized family, 'manifested in a pattern of social life which is centred on, and indeed largely restricted to, the home and the conjugal family' (1969, p. 97). Second, the extended family of aunts, uncles, grandparents and cousins matter far less in everyday routines. Finally, inside the family, the roles between the sexes are less segregated so that the male may well feed the baby and change its nappy while the female mends a fuse and changes a plug.

Young and Wilmott speculate that a fourth phase may be emerging as a consequence of technological changes and the influence of 'feminism'. The former will tend to eliminate boring work but will also result in an expansion of shift-work as the expensive capital equipment is used around the clock, consequently some family members will be pulled away from the home at times when other members are enjoying leisure. The second influence is the recognition that 'Women should have as much right as men to seek, and to gain, fulfilment out of the home as in it'. They seek a move towards a time when both men and women have two jobs, one external to the home, the 'career', and the other the domestic role internal to the home. It is a process during which Young and Willmott see 'Strains will be inescapable. There will inevitably be more divorces because people will be seeking a more multi-faceted adjustment to each other . . . and because the task will be harder, there will be more failures' (1975, p. 278). In sum, the family is changing as its members come to terms with themselves in the context of changing technology, changing ideologies and changing values. It is a process which will result, Featherstone (1979) argues, not in the decline of the family but in its strength, 'changes in structure and function and individual roles are not to be confused with the collapse of the family'.

The ideological change of 'feminism' noted by Young and Willmott was stimulated by the work of radical feminists such as Mitchell (1971), Greer (1971) and Firestone (1972), contributing to a resurgence in the awareness of the oppression of women, an oppression which, in the view of many, was ultimately reducible to the relations of production under capitalism. There is no doubt that the contemporary United Kingdom is a sexist society where women are second-class citizens; indeed there is no country in the world where this is not the case. The moves in legislation to try and counteract discrimination towards women hardly touch the core of the problem, the formation and maintenance of negative sexual stereotypes towards women. To be a man in our society is to have one's sexual identity unquestioned, to be a woman is to have constant reference made to one's sexual identity; thus, Britain's first woman Prime Minister has received more public comment on her hair style and clothes than all her male predecessors together. The media does not report that a male Prime Minister was wearing a rather attractive shirt and matching tie or that a male trade union leader was wearing black shoes and fashionably cut trousers as he entered a factory. If a woman is appointed to an important position her sex is commented on whereas it would seem odd and superfluous to announce that 'Mr X has been appointed President of the Association; Mr X, father of two, is the 27th man to hold this position . . . ' .

Men and women are different. The problem is that biological difference is seen to be necessarily related to the social roles of male and female; that, in other words, *gender*, a cultural concept, is the direct result of *sexual* differences. There is greater variation of temperament, personality, ability and interests within either the female or male sex than there is between male and female. Yet so pervasive are the existing stereotypes that Sharpe (1976), Byrne (1978) and Deem (1978) each show how girls underestimate their abilities, have a narrow view of their occupational futures and see as 'natural' their future roles as wives and mothers. We have already made reference to Berger and Luckmann's view that primary socialization is 'the most important confidence trick that society plays on the individual'. The most successful aspect of that trick is to make half the population, the girls, view themselves as normally dependent on the boys as part of the natural order of things.

The recent interest in 'women's studies' is particularly significant for the sociology of education because discussion of the socialization of women highlights the relationship between biography and structure. Oakley (1972) demonstrates that the industrial revolution was instrumental in creating the division of labour whereby men service the factory and women the home. The expectation is that women ought to look after the children such that she feels guilty at neglecting *her* children should she decide to pursue an outside career. The topic of the socialization of women also illustrates the pervasiveness of existing hierarchies within society. Oakley writes, 'In the USSR, where the emancipation of women has been approaching the point where women . . . are liberated from their traditional gender roles, women still keep their two roles at work and at home' (1971, p. 192). The point is illustrated in the 'liberal' husband saying to his wife, 'I'll do the ironing for you'; one might ask, whose ironing is it? Here the husband has gone beyond the stage of regarding 'ironing' as women's work, but still preserves the division of sexual labour in making the assumption that somehow the ironing 'belongs' to his wife.

In English society during the first half of this century men were paid more than women for doing the same work. This was a structural advantage which underlined the apparent inferiority of women. However the removal of that structural constraint through equal pay legislation will not of itself bring about equality. Such structural change creates the conditions for the achievement of equality, but its accomplishment requires a change in assumptions made by both men and women. This in turn entails that during the socialization of children they be treated primarily as people and not as first of all boys or girls. This is not to deny *sexual* differences but rather to underline that it is up to those who wish to invoke these differences to show cause why it is relevant to discriminate on the basis of sexual identity.

Conclusion

In this chapter we have discussed three perspectives on socialization: passive, active and radical. The first draws from functionalist theories and sees the individual responding to the central value system of society rather like a puppet on a string. The second presents individuals who create their social world, negotiate shared meanings and define the situations in which they act. The third recognizes that all acts are part of a wider social structure and advocates a view of socialization which sees it as socialization into a particular world-view. We then discussed three specific dimensions to socialization; childhood and adolescence, the family and women. The latter, it was argued, was important in illustrating the link between biography and structure, in showing how 'social' divisions can become preserved as part of the natural order of things. In the following chapter, we stay with the theme of socialization, turning to a discussion of the processes by which socialization is effected.

Chapter 4

Socialization 2. Language, intelligence and ability

In the last chapter we discussed three different perspectives on socialization: passive, active and radical. We saw that each was limited and that our understanding of how the process of socialization works was still very incomplete. At several points in that chapter we identified a need for a detailed examination of the *process* of socialization, the careful observation and analysis of actual behaviour in much the same way Piaget developed in building his model of intellectual development. Such an examination would require an evaluation of the part played by language, intelligence and ability. The first, as Mead showed, is a major vehicle for socialization, and constitutes some of the most important significant symbols through which we come to exert our hold on the world. We talk about our problems, we discuss our relationships, we speak our apprehensions and hopes, if even just to ourselves. In so doing we are building an understanding both of the world and of ourselves. Referring to the process within marriage, Berger and Kellner (1971) write, 'In the marital conversation a world is not only built, but it is also kept in a state of repair and ongoingly refurnished', and they continue, 'Indeed, it may happen eventually that no experience is fully real unless and until it has been thus "talked through" ' (p. 27). Thus our first task is to clarify the part played by language in the process of socialization, a task which centres on the work of Bernstein.

It may be that the effectiveness of language in alerting us both to the world and to ourselves is dependent upon our ability; the 'more able' having a richer, more complete, and the 'less able' a poorer, more shallow, grasp of the intricacies of themselves and the world. We need, therefore, to look at what is meant by intelligence and at the way in which 'ability' is recognized and legitimated through examinations. These aspects of socialization are units of a process which is located within families and social classes and which ultimately contributes to a theory of social reproduction, the transmission of culture, inequality and power.

53

Socialization 2. Language, intelligence and ability

Bernstein's socio-linguistic theory

It is quite clear that people in different social groups talk in different ways; this would be particularly apparent were we to record the speech of the family of an unskilled worker and the speech of the family of a high executive. Having made this obvious point, what is implied by the differences? The topic of conversation may well be the same, each family being concerned about the price of food, the children's performance at school or the prospects of future employment, although the precise meaning of the conversation, that is its *semantic* level, may be equally obscure as we are unaware of the historical background to the particular speech recorded. The arrangement of words within the sentence – the *syntactical* level – and the actual vocabulary chosen – the *lexical* level – will, in all probability, not be the same. The same topic of conversation will be expressed in different syntactical and lexical forms. It is the essence of Bernstein's work on language, his socio-linguistic theory, that the difference in syntactical and lexical forms reflect different relationships between people and have consequences for the maintenance of social control within society. Bernstein argues that the form of the social relationship affects speech which in turn acts back on the social relationship: 'language is a set of rules to which all speech codes must comply, but which speech codes are realized is a function of the culture acting through social relationships in specific contexts' (1971, p. 173). For example, the speech which results from your foot being stood on in a rugby football scrum is different from the speech when your foot is stood on at the vicarage tea party; each social relationship realizes its own speech which reinforces the nature of social relationships.

The theoretical antecedents to Bernstein's work are mainly Durkheim, Marx and Mead. From Durkheim comes the idea that categories of thought are the product of society, as Durkheim puts it (Durkheim and Mauss, 1963, p. 82):

> The first logical categories were social categories; the first classes of things were classes of men into which these things were integrated.
> It was because men were grouped, and thought of themselves in the form of groups, that in their ideas they grouped other things.

This idea is at the base of the *Sapir-Whorf hypothesis* summarized by Trudgill (1974) as 'the speaker's native language sets up a series of categories which act as a kind of grid through which he perceives the world, and which constrain the way in which he categorizes and conceptualizes different phenomena' (pp. 24-25).

If there is a link, as Bernstein suggests, between speech and the form of social relationship, there is still the problem of understanding how this link operates. To resolve this, Bernstein turns to the work of Mead and particularly the latter's discussion of the formation of the self. Mead argues, as we outlined in the first chapter, that the essence of self is that it is reflexive – that is (1956, p. 203):

> The importance of what we term as 'communication' lies in the fact that it provides a form of behaviour in which the organism of the individual may become an object to himself . . . it is when one does respond to that which he addresses to another and when that response of his own becomes a part of his conduct, when he not only hears himself but responds to himself, talks and replies to himself as truly as the other person replies to him, that we have behaviour in which the individuals become objects to themselves.

Speech reflects back to the individual a view of the world formed in relation to others, yet still unique, as it reflects the idiosyncratic position of the speaker, the centre of that configuration of relationships which is his sole possession.

If we build our view of self and the world in interaction with others, and in interaction with ourself, if the symbols we have structure the world, filter the world, how is it possible to effect change? To solve this problem Bernstein turns to Marx and argues that the existence of cultural capital reflects the existing relations of production within society (1971, p. 172):

> It is not only capital, in the strict economic sense, which is subject to appropriation, manipulation and exploitation, but also *cultural* capital in the form of the symbolic systems through which man can extend and change the boundaries of his experience.

Consequently changes in the economic base will influence the nature of cultural capital, and with it the articulation of that culture in human relationships.

The distribution of cultural capital reflects the distribution of social classes in society. Part of Bernstein's concept of 'cultural capital' is 'the sense that the world is permeable' or the sense that change is possible. He suggests that cultural capital can be divided into two 'orders of meaning'; the first is *universalistic* where principles and operations are made linguistically explicit. By this is meant that nothing is taken for granted, the background to the conversation is given so that the hearer can quickly comprehend the speaker's intent. *Particularistic* meanings, on the other hand, are more context-bound; that is they are related to specific relationships, locked to a particular social structure. Most of the conversation you have within your family is particularistic, that is your talk is of family matters and presupposes that the listener shares the knowledge of the family which you have. Should you take a friend into the family you will probably spend some time 'filling-in' the background to the conversation, that is you will move towards universalistic meanings making few assumptions about the background knowledge that your friend has of your family.

Bernstein argues that the form of socialization points the child towards speech codes which control access to relatively universalistic or to relatively particularistic meanings, that of the working-class child tending to orient him through a *restricted* speech pattern to particularistic meanings, and that of the middle-class child through an *elaborated* speech pattern to universalistic meanings. The closer the identification of speakers with each other the more probable that the speech used will take a form which Bernstein labels restricted. In other words, speech between close friends will have a syntactical and lexical similarity which will be greater than the similarities in the speech used in, say, a seminar discussion.

As the form of the relationship is matched by a particular pattern of speech, so the speech acts back on the relationship and underlines, for the close friends, their inter-relationship. The seminar discussion highlights your individuality, how different the speaker is from the others, in fact much seminar discussion is an exercise in protecting the vulnerability of the self as you do not want to appear stupid, or want others to know that you do not understand the discussion. Bernstein argues that restricted speech variants realize particularistic meanings and give way to *communalized* roles; on the other hand, elaborated speech variants point to universalistic meanings and realise *individualized* roles. By communalized roles is meant a conception of self which emphasizes the links one has with others as against a view which stresses one's unique individuality.

From the publication of his first paper in 1958, the theme of cultural transmission has been a common thread to all Bernstein's work, more explicitly, 'It is reasonable to argue that the genes of social class may well be carried less through a genetic code but far more through a communication code that social class itself promotes' (1971, p. 143). As the child learns to speak so she learns the requirements of her social structure so that, 'children who learn different roles by virtue of their family's class position in a society, may adopt quite different social and intellectual orientations and procedures despite a common potential' (op. cit., p. 145). Bernstein identifies four critical contexts through which the child comes to acquire her cultural identity. The first is the *regulative* context, or the setting for the learning of authority relationships and morality; next is the *instructional* context where the child learns about the nature of objects and acquires skills; the *imaginative* context where the child is encouraged to re-create her world on her own terms; and finally the *interpersonal* context where the child develops her emotional, affective response to the world. The child's evolving models of the world, her taken-for-granted assumptions about the 'natural order of things', is learnt from the pattern of speech which articulates each of these four contexts.

A major difficulty with Bernstein's theory of cultural transmission is knowing what in fact is meant by the terms restricted and elaborated code. As they are not immediately apparent, but the underlying structure of communication, there is also the problem of demonstrating their influence empirically. Whatever they are, however, apparently all children have access to restricted codes because the social roles which the code presupposes are universal, 'But there may well be selective access to elaborated codes because there is selective access to the role system which evokes its use' (1971, p. 183). Thus as schools tend to operate within the framework of universalistic meanings, and therefore elaborated speech patterns, there may well be a tension between the school and the child whose socialization has been predominantly within the restricted variant (Bernstein, 1971, pp. 143-4):

> Where the child is sensitive to the communication system of the school and thus to its orders of learning and relation, then the experience of school for this child is one of symbolic and social development; where the child is not sensitive to the communication system at school then this child's experience at school becomes one of symbolic and social change.

It is this argument which has often been interpreted as meaning that working-class children fail at school as a consequence of their being socialized within the restricted variant. Such a conclusion ignores the continued qualifications made by Bernstein, the fact that he is always talking about tendencies rather than absolutes. It also ignores his reference to 'different social and intellectual orientations and procedures despite a *common potential*' (my emphasis), in other words, that he is not saying that working-class children cannot achieve in school, or that their speech variants are the cause of their relative failure, but that there may be a fracture between the child's articulation of the world and that presented by the school. It is the possibility of this fracture which led Bernstein to declare in an oft-quoted passage, 'If the culture of the teacher is to become part of the consciousness of the child, then the culture of the child must first be in the consciousness of the teacher' (op. cit., p. 199).

As already indicated, much of the criticism of Bernstein's work has centred on the concept of code, what is meant by 'code' and its use in our understanding of socio-linguistics. In an early evaluation, Coulthard (1969) argues that the theory 'offers an intuitively acceptable explanation of some of the socio-cultural causes of under-achievement by working-class children' but on examination of the thesis, Coulthard finds little support for the existence of restricted and elaborated sociolinguistic codes from the evidence produced by Bernstein. He continues with the charge that the validity of the theory is assumed and not demonstrated, in other words that Bernstein starts with the proposition that his theory is correct rather than showing why it is a necessary explanation of the effects of different speech styles. Jackson (1974) presents a similar criticism and argues that the codes refer to two different aspects of language. The first, the syntactic, is where by code Bernstein means different ways of expressing the same thing; here 'code' refers to the principles underpinning the syntactical arrangement of words in a sentence. The second use identified by Jackson, the semantic, refers to the principle regulating the amount of explicitness in a conversation. Jackson argues that there is no necessary connection between the two and sees a shift in Bernstein's work away from the first toward the second such that 'Bernstein has effectively abandoned the code theory, and adapted a (not wholly implausible) variety of role restriction theory instead'. Stubbs (1976) also identifies two uses of code in Bernstein's work and suggests that the only sense in which it is possible to talk about the existence of the socio-linguistic codes, 'is as *hypothetical constructs* intended to explain social class differences in language use and cognitive orientation' (his emphasis).

A different sort of critique has been presented by Rosen (1972) and by Byrne and Williamson (1972). Both papers show the concern of the authors at the way in which Bernstein's ideas have been taken up, as Byrne and Williamson write, 'crudely summarized as "working class children cannot speak properly" '. For Rosen the terms 'restricted' and 'elaborated' codes have become part of the vocabulary of legitimation whereby teachers are able to explain the failure of some children in terms of their language, 'after all, they have a restricted code'. For Rosen, Bernstein's theory has little relevance to the actual language of either working- or middle-class groups. Rosen agrees that there are speech patterns which in their economy, lucidity and resourcefulness 'give access to more powerful ways of thinking'; but points out that this is very different from arguing that these are located within a particular social class, or demonstrating that in practice a restricted speech style, whatever this is, results in a restricted thought style.

In a much reported paper, Labov (1972) presents evidence to show that what he labels 'nonstandard Negro English' (NNE), has a structure which enables the transmission of complex ideas to greater effect than is possible with the more verbose middle-class speech, an argument which, comments Edwards (1976), 'shows a triumph of good intentions over evidence, a willingness to match the gloomy guess work of deficit theory with optimistic guess work from the other side' (p. 133). Labov does show that what is often taken to be nonstandard and inferior English is in fact the product of the situation in which the speech was obtained. He illustrates how different contexts will result in different speech from the same child by giving extracts from an interview with an eight-year-old boy, Leon, and comparing these with extracts from a second interview where Leon is accompanied by his best friend, Gregory. In this instance, the interviewer had brought along a supply of potato-chips, sat on the floor and introduced taboo words and topics into the conversation. The result is one where the two boys have 'so much to say they keep interrupting each other, who seem to have no difficulty in using the English language to express themselves' (Labov, 1972, p. 191). Labov's purpose is to show how the prevailing social scientific view of the child as a deficit system, as lacking something rather than being different, has resulted in an inaccurate assessment of the Negro child as linguistically deprived.

Labov groups Bernstein with deficit theorists like Bereiter and Engelmann, a misunderstanding which appears to be a consequence of forming a view of Bernstein based on Jensen's (1968) account of one of Bernstein's earliest papers, 'Language and Social Class', published in 1960. At that stage Bernstein was still exploring 'linguistic differences, *other than dialect*' (my emphasis) which occur between middle- and lower-working-class groups; the concept 'code' had not been introduced, nor had the development of the thesis into a theory of cultural transmission been accomplished. Yet Labov is 'particularly concerned with the relation between concept formation on the one hand, and *dialect differences* on the other' (my emphasis), a project which is different to Bernstein's, more akin to linguistics and less to the sociological assessment of the consequences of different speech forms.

The whole of Bernstein's work may be seen as an exploration of social control. We saw in the last chapter that the 'personalized form of organic solidarity', for example, was dependent on a complex and elaborated form of speech which had the result of enabling more of the child's behaviour and values to be controlled. In this chapter, we have argued that the significance of Bernstein's work lies in exploring how the form of cultural transmission makes different demands on the child, so that those who experience elaborated speech variants also learn the conditions, caveats and corollaries which govern social action. In later chapters we will introduce his discussion of the transmission of knowledge within educational setting, a process which extends his analysis of transmission within the family. Evaluation of his work is correct in the judgment that the linguistic demonstration of Bernstein's thesis raises more problems than it solves, the concept of sociolinguistic code is ambiguous, and the identification of either restricted or elaborated speech variants does lack precision. The major importance of Bernstein's work lies, however, in his emergent analysis of social control, an exploration which is far from complete and which awaits a full empirical demonstration.

Much of the discussion of socio-linguistics has revolved around deficit and difference theories of disadvantage. That is, the extent to which inadequate performance is the result of a deficiency which the educational system can correct, or the extent to which inadequate performance is a consequence of different cultural styles being denied, or even ridiculed, within the school. Edwards (1976) stresses that we need to keep a sense of proportion in the discussion and suggests that if we removed all language disabilities, be these located in either a deficit or a difference explanatory framework, we would not significantly alter the class chances of success. Inequality in society is more complex and pervasive than is amenable to change as a result of improved language skills. Edwards also takes care to clarify what is being discussed and writes, 'Even for the "facts" we have, the notion of deficient linguistic *knowledge* is grotesquely simple' (his emphasis, 1976, p. 126). This is not to say that different children *use* speech to the same effect, but to stress that the difference in *use* has little relationship to their ability or potential for language development.

In a paper written with Hargreaves, Edwards (1976) is critical of the tendency within difference theorists, like Baratz and Baratz (1970), of being so relativistic in their account of variations within language styles as to ignore the difference 'between an "absolute" inferiority, and an inferiority relative to some communicative demands'. Edwards and Hargreaves point out that, 'Structurally insignificant differences in speech can still "locate" the speaker socially, provide stereotypical cues to other assumed attributes, and so create and maintain social distance.' There are different speech forms. Some are more appropriate to specific contexts than others and any evaluation of language use must recognize the socio-cultural environment. The danger which all teachers face is that of generalizing from an 'incorrect' speech form to a judgment about the child's overall abilities, thus treating a non-standard language speaker *as if* he were *intellectually* inferior. It is possible that this becomes part of a self-fulfilling prophecy so that the non-standard speaker performs less well in his academic work, thus confirming the teacher's suspicion that failure is a reflection of the child's 'poor' speech.

Let us conclude this section unequivocally; there is no evidence to show that non-standard English speakers perform less well at school as a *direct result* of their dialect or idiosyncratic language use. Their inadequate school performance may well be consequent upon the *social* use of language where their speech is judged by a teacher to indicate less ability. Such an assessment sets in motion a pattern of expectation which sees inadequate school performance confirming the deficits in the child rather than any inadequacy with the educational system.

Intelligence

One of the enduring debates within the social science is over the extent to which intelligence is the product of one's genetic background or the result of the environment in which one lives. An American journal, popular in the early part of this century, the *New Republic*, carried this debate sixty years ago between Terman and Lippman (reprinted in Block and Dworkin, 1977), and in 1969 the *Harvard Educational Review* published an article by Arthur Jensen which marked the opening shots in the most recent battle. One of the immediate features of the debate is the lack of consensus in the definition of terms, prompting Boring (1923) to write in the *New Republic* that 'intelligence is what intelligence tests measure'. This operational definition is supported by Krech, Crutchfield and Livson (1969) who cite a precedent within the natural sciences: 'Long before the physicists could agree on a sound definition of heat, they had invented reliable thermometers to measure changes in temperature.' The assumption made by such operational definitions is that IQ tests do in fact measure intelligence. In this section we shall examine this assumption and pose two further questions; even if IQ tests measure intelligence, and even if intelligence is strongly determined by genetic factors, how does this increase our understanding of the patterns of inequality within society; and second, why the resurgence of the nature (heredity)–nurture (environment) debate in the early 1970s?

When we use the term 'intelligent' in phrases like, 'Susan is intelligent', we may mean, 'She always agrees with me'; 'Can do a "quality" newspaper crossword in under ten minutes.: 'Does not panic and has a lot of "common-sense" '; or 'Is quick to see the point of an argument'. Here, speed, personality and skills are each part of what is meant by 'intelligent', each judgment relates to the particular interest of the speaker and not to an invariant attribute.

At the moment IQ tests tend to be validated against each other; a 'good' test producing results which are similar to those obtained from other 'good' tests which were originally validated against teacher assessment of intelligent behaviour. Given that teacher assessment of what is intelligent formed the original yardstick for the validation of tests, it is not surprising to know that IQ tests remain a strong predictor of school success. We could reinterpret Boring's definition of intelligence as 'intelligence is doing well at school', a definition which is tautological and which, incidentally, would assess Charles Darwin as being unintelligent, being someone who did not do well at school.

One of the most interesting explorations of the nature of the individual's response to the IQ tests has been provided by the anthropologist Thomas Gladwin. Gladwin (1970) was struck by the poor performance on IQ tests of navigators in the island of Puluwat in Polynesia (roughly lying 1,600 miles east of the Philippines and 1,000 miles north of Papua New Guinea). In common-sense terms the navigators had a highly developed skill which enabled them to travel across the open sea to reach their destination hundreds of miles away. There were some navigators who were better than others, but all showed a lack in the thought processes needed to do well on IQ tests, namely a lack of innovative thinking. Everything a navigator needed to know in Puluwat was already part of the collective knowledge of his society. There was no need to search for novel answers to new questions, no need to construct a hypothesis and give grounds for its acceptance or rejection. Yet IQ tests require innovative thought, require that the subject extrapolates from the known to the unknown; the ability, in short, to use a thought style which is much valued in Western society.

Cole and Gray *et al.*, (1971), after working with the Kpelle in central Liberia in West Africa, call for an understanding of 'local' thinking-styles and research into how those thought-styles might be used in the schools. The point is reinforced by Tulkin and Konner (1973) who write:

> Man is the only hunting mammal with a poorly developed sense of smell. He could only have come to hunting through intellectual evolution. If this argument is valid, the notion that different human groups have different inductive *capacities* [my emphasis] would be inherently illogical, since all groups have shared the same five million years of hunting, and whatever has happened since plays a relatively insignificant role in terms of time – and time is what is needed for brain evolution to take place.

Instead of working out how the Kpelle and the Puluwat navigators, or how Negroes, compare with other groups on tests of intelligence, we need to begin the much more difficult task of explaining why members of these groups make the response they do, having articulated what skills are embodied within the test. Occidental man is often said to be 'spiritually barren' when compared to Oriental man; his perception of the natural world is crude against that of African man; yet these skills are potentially available to all. Human beings need to be able to use the thought-styles which are appropriate to the problem being explored.

Brief history of intelligence testing

One of the clearest accounts of the development of IQ tests is that of Leon Kamin (1977). Kamin attributes the first test designed to measure the mental ability of an individual to the French physiologist, Alfred Binet, in 1905. Binet's test was intended to identify those children who were in need of special education and warned against 'this brutal pessimism' which saw intelligence as a fixed, unalterable quality.

The major development of testing was, however, in the USA. In 1916 Lewis Terman, then Professor of Education at Stanford University in California, published the Stanford-Binet Scale, and a year later, in collaboration with Robert Yerkes of Harvard University, the Alpha-Beta Group Tests (the Alpha Test was for literates, the Beta for illiterates). There are three important aspects to this rapid development of testing in the early part of this century. Kamin shows that in America and the UK there was considerable interest in the possibility of controlling the *quality* of the population through selective breeding. The Eugenics Movement under the influence of people like Sir Francis Galton, Herbert Spencer and Charles Darwin, pushed these ideas in the UK. In the USA, Indiana, in 1907, was the first state to pass a sterilization law in an attempt to control the evils of 'crime, idiocy and imbecility' (Kamin, 1977, p. 26). The second factor was the influx of immigrants into the USA and fears that if this were to be uncontrolled the 'stock' of the American people would be weakened. Kamin quotes Henry Goddard who in 1913 published the results of a Binet test which 'established that 83 per cent of the Jews, 80 per cent of the Hungarians, 79 per cent of the Italians, and 87 per cent of the Russians were "feeble-minded" ' (1977, p. 31). Goddard used a translation of Binet's scale into English and seemed to discount the language difficulties which would be faced by non-English-speaking immigrants.

The third aspect to the early development of intelligence tests was the use of the Alpha-Beta tests in selecting officers for the American army during the First World War. Gumbert and Spring (1974) have reproduced part of the instructions to be issued when administering the tests. These began (Gumbert and Spring, 1974, p. 94):

When everything is ready E. (examiner) proceeds as follows:
'Attention! The purpose of this examination is to see how well you can remember, think and carry out what you are told to do. . . .
The aim is to help find out what you are best fitted to do in the Army. . . . Now in the army a man often has to listen to commands and carry them out exactly. I am going to give you some commands to see how well you can carry them out.

As Kamin comments, 'The tests appear to have had little practical effect on the outcome of the war. They were not in fact used much for the placement of men' (1977, p. 33). However hundreds of the tests were produced and made readily available to school administrators after the war, thus underpinning a concept of intelligence which reflected the requirements of a large organization; what Spring refers to as the 'beehive mentality'.

Interpretation of IQ tests

Tests of intelligence are deliberately designed to produce a normal distribution. That is when used over a large, randomly selected sample the mean score will show an IQ of 100 and 68 per cent of the sample will score between 85 and 115, 98 per cent between IQs of 70 and 130. The difficulty with all such mathematical artefacts is that the numbers may give an impression of precision which the original data does not merit. It may be, for example, that in the 'real world' intelligence is not distributed normally; further, just because there is an equal interval between the numbers 70, 80, 90 and 100 does not mean that there is an equal interval between an IQ of 70, 80, 90 and 100. If intellectual abilities can be developed – a reasonable assumption held by many since Binet – then it may be that an individual will be able to increase his score on the test from 90 to 100 more easily than from 70 to 80. The 'intelligence gap' between 70 and 80 is not necessarily the same as the 'gap' between 90 and 100. Finally it is important to remember that an IQ score of itself means nothing; it is a *relational score* by which the individual can be compared to the score of other individuals on the same test. You do not have an IQ in the way that you sometimes have a head cold, but rather achieve a score on a test which may be better or worse than that scored by other individuals on the same test.

If IQ tests are to be used then the results obtained must be interpreted with great care; we have seen how Goddard's work was used to justify a strongly discriminatory policy by the USA at the turn of the century. There are, however, great variations in individual ability; some people are 'brighter' than others, better at mathematics, more gifted in language use, more agile, humane and so on. There is a wide variation in individual differences, which IQ tests attempt to measure. It is also a truism to say that the cause of these differences will be partly genetic, that unique pattern of characteristics, the genotype, which we inherit from our parents, and partly the result of our environment. Part of the difference will be the result of our genetic inheritance acting upon the environment, both changing and being inhibited by the environment. In other words, a child who appears to have a 'gift' for music may change, or cause her environment to be changed to enable the 'gift' to be developed; other children, however, will be unable to utilize their musical skills and thus to nurture nature. As is noted by Thoday (1965), 'Genotype determines the possibilities of an organism. Environment determines which or how much of those potentialities shall be realized during development.'

One of the most fruitless debates in the social sciences concerns how much of the difference in IQ is the product of genes or the product of environment. It is fruitless because even if we could achieve a perfect answer and give a precise figure for the strength of heredity over environment we would still be unable to explain why two *individuals* differed in their achievements, nor would we have any strategy for social policy. For at least four decades some psychologists have calculated the genetic component of IQ to be 80 per cent; that is 80 per cent of the variance in IQ scores over a *population* could be attributed to genetic factors. The evidence for such a prediction comes from a number of twin studies (including the now discredited contribution of Sir Cyril Burt, see Gillie, 1978) where the scores of identical twins reared apart, fraternal twins reared together and unrelated children reared together, are compared. After re-working the evidence, Kamin recommends that 'The prudent conclusion seems clear. There are no data sufficient for us to reject the hypothesis that differences in the way in which people answer the questions asked by testers are determined by their palpably different life experiences' (1977, p. 226).

The lack of precision in our estimates of the strength of heredity is demonstrated by Jencks (1973) who notes (p. 66) that

> our best estimate is that genes explain about 45 per cent of the variance in Americans' test scores, that environment explains about 35 per cent, and that the tendency of environmentally advantaged families to have genetically advantaged children explains the remaining 20 per cent.

But even Jencks is only providing a 'best estimate', indicating the possibility of error, which leads Bodmer (1973) to the conclusion that,

> We do not at present know the answer to the question of how much is the genetic component to the race-I.Q. difference; we do not have the techniques at hand to find the answer and the answer does not seem to matter anyway.

Turning to the last issue raised by Bodmer, does it matter whether or not we can provide a correct estimate of heritability? Herrnstein (1971) thinks it does on the grounds of the following syllogism:

65

> a. Since people inherit their mental capacities (as indexed, for example, in intelligence tests) to some extent, and b. since success in our society calls for these mental capacities, therefore c. it follows that success in our society reflects inherited differences between people.

It might appear that the qualifier 'to some extent' should also be a part of the second stage in Herrnstein's syllogism. Clearly we need people with high ability to run industry, social services, government and so on. High IQ is not a guarantee that the individual will have the diverse skills necessary for top responsibility, although a low score on an intelligence test may well denote the absence of such skills. More important than assessing the genetic component of intelligence is the assessment of the contribution which IQ makes to occupational success. Bane and Jencks (1977, p. 327) report:

> There have been more than a hundred studies of the relationship between IQ and people's performance on different jobs, using a wide variety of techniques for rating performance. In general, differences in IQ account for less than 10 per cent of the variation in actual job performance. In many situations, there is no relation-ship at all between a man's IQ and how competent he is at his job.

Using data from the US Census, Current Population Survey, in 1962, Bowles and Gintis (1977) present further evidence to show that Herrnstein's syllogism is far from a reflection of the role of IQ in the occupational structure. They calculate that the probability of someone in the top tenth of the IQ distribution also being in the top decile in economic success is 31 per cent; or approximately a three to one chance as against that of a randomly selected individual. However, success is not just the product of IQ, but also a feature of home background and length of schooling, as well as type of occupation, history of salary negotiations and so on. Bowles and Gintis tried to assess the strength of IQ, having controlled for the effects of these contaminating variables. With social class and schooling controlled, the probability drops to 14 per cent, or a 1.4 to one chance over that of a randomly selected individual. In short, they conclude, 'I.Q. is not an important intrinsic criterion for economic success.' Thus to turn back to the question we posed on the relevance of the heritability debate, even if the figure of 80 per cent were correct we would not have advanced our understanding of in-equality within society. In missing out the qualifier 'to some extent' in the second part of his syllogism, Herrnstein has neglected a most important link, that between IQ and success. The evidence presented by Jencks and by Bowles and Gintis suggests that IQ *of itself* has little influence on the existing patterns of inequality.

Finally, we need to turn to the reason for the resurgence of the nature-nurture debate in the late 1960s and early 1970s. The years following the Second World War had been years of educational expansion; there were more pupils in schools, partly as a result of an increasing birth rate and partly the consequence of a rising demand for education. The expansion had been coupled with the belief that through education the inequalities of opportunity which afflicted minority groups – either defined in terms of social class, race or sex – could be ameliorated if not eradicated. Programmes of compensatory education were started, such as Head Start, which began in the summer of 1965 in America, and in Great Britain there was positive discrimination in favour of socially disadvantaged areas. Despite this limited activity, Jensen felt confident enough to proclaim in 1969, 'Compensatory education has been tried and it apparently has failed' (p. 2).

In essence, the logic behind compensatory education programmes was that the failure of some children at school was because they had been insufficiently prepared for the educational system. Thus a programme of pre-schooling would make good the deficiencies in their home backgrounds and enable the child to obtain fuller benefit from school. The apparent failure of such programmes – that is the target children appeared to perform no better at school – might mean that either the preparation programmes were not long enough or, and this is the argument Jensen put forward, the failure reflected the genetic inferiority of the disadvantaged group. Putting on one side the issue of whether compensatory education had been attempted, intelligence tests became a convenient scapegoat for failure, directing attention away from the responsibilities of the educational system to that of the individual who failed.

Ability

In discussion of language and intelligence we stressed that the context within which either is observed or assessed affects the performance of the individual. Non-standard language speakers are not using an inferior speech form, though it may be a form which is inappropriate to its context. The score from an IQ test may reflect a skill which is of little relevance to the management of everyday life. Mehan (1973) shows how 'incorrect' answers to a test may well be 'correct' and display evidence of logical thought when judged by different criteria. For example, in a test for four- to six-year olds, children were asked to choose the 'animal that can fly' from amongst bird, elephant and dog. Many children chose the elephant as well as the bird, on the grounds that the picture showed Dumbo, Walt Disney's flying elephant.

In Mehan's words, 'The score sheet showing a wrong answer does not document a child's lack of reasoning ability; it only documents that the child indicated an answer different from the one the tester expected' (1973, p. 250).

The argument is that apparently individual attributes like ability are always part of a social context, whether or not this be recognized. Hextall and Sarup (1977) argue that unless we include the context, in their terms conduct a relational analysis, we distort the process of social reproduction. The apparently *individual* qualities of language, intelligence and ability hide the way in which existing social hierarchies are maintained. It is of relevance now to consider the part that examinations play in legitimating a concept of ability which reflects *individual* achievement.

The origin of examinations has been discussed by both Durkheim (1977) and Weber (1948), both agreeing that their creation was a consequence of the growth of bureaucracy. 'The bureaucratization of capitalism, with its demand for expertly trained technicians, clerks, et cetera, carries such examinations all over the world' (Weber, 1948, p. 241) and for Durkheim, 'the system of degrees and examinations is the result of the corporate organization' (1977, p. 129). Durkheim dates the beginning of examinations to about the fifteenth century, though Weber shows them originating much earlier, being extensively used during the Tang dynasty in China (that is the period from the year 618 until 907).

The Chinese Literati, the civil service of China until the establishment of the Republic of China under Sun Yat-sen in 1912, was selected not for the technical expertise of its members but according to their grasp of the nation's cultural heritage. Weber writes, 'The examinations of China tested whether or not the candidate's mind was thoroughly steeped in literature and whether or not he possessed the *way of thought* suitable to a cultured man and resulting from cultivation in literature' (1948, p. 428; his emphasis). Weber goes on to point out that even though the examinations were mundane – 'a cultural examination for the literati' – for the mass of Chinese people at the time, success in the examinations was interpreted as giving the candidate 'magical qualities' such that all his statements were treated with respect and deference. Thus the cultivated man, the Literatus, had far more than specialist knowledge, he had a particular stance towards the world, an attitude which made his judgment superior to that of the mere technical specialist. Weber argues that behind all discussion of education lurks the struggle between the specialist and the cultivated man, the technician and the gentleman. Wilkinson (1962) compares the Chinese system to the education received in British public schools at the turn of this century: 'Both systems helped to produce a governing group accustomed to social privilege and marked by a distinctive bearing; both tailored a classical curriculum to meet the requirements of civil examinations' (p. 236).

Behind the examination, therefore, was a particular concept of ability, in the case of China knowledge of the appropriate cultural style. The proliferation of examinations was not, Weber argues, because of 'a suddenly awakened "thirst for education", but the desire for restricting the supply for these positions and their monopolization by the owners of educational certificates' (1948, p. 241). In highlighting the growth in demand for educational qualifications Weber anticipates the work of Bourdieu and Boltanski (1978). They argue that there has been a change in the way in which the reproduction of economic and cultural advantages is maintained. The shift has been from the direct transmission of economic capital to its indirect transmission mediated through the school system. Educational qualifications appear to be a neutral, objectively achieved, indication of ability, but in fact are the new symbols of social reproduction. Whitty (1976) shows that within CSE level examinations there is a difference between Mode I exams, set and marked external to the school, and Mode III exams, set and marked by the school and externally moderated. It is the former which are seen as the unquestioned norm. Universities distinguish between 'A' levels which are 'academic' and 'non-academic' in selecting applicants, and within higher education it is better to get a degree from 'X' institution rather than from 'Y'. The formal qualifications are taken as indicators of *cultural intangibles*, that is assumptions are made by future employers, for example, that a person with a diploma from a certain institution will be the 'right' sort of person. He will be adjudged to have the style and manner, as well as the competence, to be able to work alongside existing colleagues and thus 'fit' into the firm. In summary, Bourdieu and Boltanski write (1978, p. 209):

It is known that the conversion of economic capital into certified cultural capital and the transition from the status of independent entrepreneur or owner to that of salaried manager can constitute a strategy which allows families who occupy the dominant positions in the ruling class to maintain their control over the field of business whilst ensuring for their children, through the intermediary of the school, the qualifications which authorize them to appropriate a part of the economic benefit of companies in the form of salaries, a better concealed . . . method of appropriating profits than rent.

Conclusion

In this chapter we have discussed aspects of the *process* of socialization and in doing so have shown that individual attributes also have structural dimensions. Thus talk of intelligence and ability is always talk which assumes a particular type of intelligence, or a specific form of ability. The importance of the work of both Bernstein and Bourdieu lies in moving beyond a recognition of the structural, to an exploration of how it is filtered through to individual consciousness. In his work on socio-linguistics, Bernstein argues that socialization through elaborated and restricted speech variants will influence our notion of who we are and will also imprint a view of the world as 'normal', hiding in whose interests that normality is preserved. For Bourdieu, social reproduction is validated through examinations, apparently objective indicators of ability. 'Apparently' is not used here in any perjorative sense suggesting that examiners are colluding in a plot to maintain the status quo; at the surface level examinations are objective and do distinguish between people on a range of skills. It is the proliferation of examinations which results in them being devalued as the real criteria for recruitment to the occupational structure. (Any glance at advertisements presenting the benefits to an individual's career from a short-service commission in the British army shows that the army well understands Bourdieu's point.) A full understanding of what appears to be the private act of an individual, such as taking an examination, requires the incorporation of the context of that act, the social structure, into the analysis. In the next chapter we continue the theme of structure, history and 'what varieties of men and women now prevail' through a consideration of what might be termed the hub of the educational system, classrooms in schools.

Chapter 5

Into the classroom

So far in this book, we have given scant attention to the educational system, having discussed the process of primary socialization and aspects of the child's home background. Throughout we have noted a classic dilemma for sociology, that of presenting an explanation of the social world so mechanistic as to deny any self-determination on the part of the individual, or so stressing the social construction of everyday life as to ignore the constraints on individual action. We suggested that in the work of Bourdieu and of Bernstein there are indications of theoretical perspectives which might encompass both the individual and the social structure, though the conclusion to the second chapter expressed the opinion that a tension between perspectives may well be most fruitful in enhancing our knowledge of educational processes.

In this chapter, we begin a discussion of schools by an examination of what for both pupils and teachers is the overwhelming reality – classrooms. We look first at the most frequently used perspective, that of interaction analysis, and then present two alternative approaches, interpretive and radical. The labels are fairly arbitrary; within interaction analysis are grouped those theories which use various observation schedules to discover a most efficient method for classroom teaching; interpretive refers loosely to those studies which tend to avoid any pre-emptive categorization and radical theories attempt to relate the daily activity of classrooms to a material base. One of the most puzzling aspects of classrooms is their resistance to change and we discuss some of the reasons for this. The chapter ends with two examples of attempts to relate the individual classroom to a wider social structure, an attempt which Parsons also made in 1961.

The school-class as a social system

The theme chosen by Halsey, Floud and Anderson (1961), for what was effectively the first British reader in the sociology of education, was the reciprocal relationship between the education system and advanced industrial society. The selection of readings was confined 'so far as possible, to studies of changes in the structure and functioning of schools and universities that can be traced . . . to economic pressures.' Attention was not on the school as an organization where interactions in their thousands take place daily, but on the larger scale of the education system itself. This neglect of classrooms can be partially excused by the intent to examine larger issues, but it also reflects the state of sociological knowledge at the time. Apart from Waller's discussion of schools published in 1932 and Becker's work in the 1950s, classroom research in 1961 had been dominated by social psychologists preoccupied by the nature of leadership and the influence of classroom climates on learning outcomes.

The article in Halsey, Floud and Anderson which comes closest to the classroom is Parsons's 'The School Class as a Social System'. He presents an exploration of the functions of the classroom which both extends Durkheim's discussion of education and anticipates some of the work of Bernstein. Like Durkheim, Parsons sees a necessity for children to learn their role within society, an idea which suggests each individual has a fixed role, the school just adding the polish and gloss to a pre-determined role occupant. Parsons suggests, as Bernstein also does subsequently, that the pattern of early childhood socialization will have consequences for the efficacy of later traditional or progressive teaching-styles (see Bernstein's 'visible' and 'invisible' pedagogies, discussed in Chapter 7). Parsons also puts forward an idea of a hidden curriculum at work in schools through which a child learns an evaluation of himself over and above the 'official' evaluation transmitted through the school's formal curriculum. Though an article which presents the classroom as the basic unit for the analysis of schools, a forerunner to much later discussion of classrooms, Parsons remains on the outside of the building looking in. He suggests a hypothesis to be tested but does not himself move into the classroom to examine its workings.

Antecedents to 'interaction' analysis

At the time that Parsons was working at a theoretical analysis of educational processes, a number of social psychologists were creating experiments and going into school classrooms to understand the different processes of interaction. Delamont (1976) has argued that one needs to locate this early social psychological work within the political context of its time. Lewin, Lippitt and White's work (1939) illustrates Delamont's point by stating that what lay at the heart of their analysis were questions like, 'What underlies such differing patterns of group behaviour as rebellion against authority, persecution of a scapegoat, apathetic submissiveness to authoritarian domination, or attack upon an outgroup?' (p. 271). The atrocities committed by Hitler outraged and perplexed many; how was it possible that within a democratic society a fascist state could emerge which was responsible for the slaughter of millions? Lewin was one of many intellectuals who fled from Germany in the 1930s to settle in America and whose work amounted to an examination of the nature of democracy.

An associate of Lewin, H. H. Anderson (1939), was one of the first to enter the classroom to explore the affects of *dominative* and *integrative* behaviour on children. Anderson was quite clear in his definition of dominative techniques: 'It is the technique of a dictatorship.' His research, however, did little more than show that teachers differed widely in their use of techniques, with little to support one over the other in terms of the consequence for learning outcomes.

Probably one of the most well-known studies of this period is the series of experiments conducted by Lippitt and White, both PhD students of Lewin. They were interested in the influence of different leadership styles on the behaviour of ten-year-old boys. The boys were in matched groups of five and performed a number of tasks like making masks and various models over a period of weeks, under the supervision of different adult leaders. The leaders adopted different leadership styles, either *autocratic*, *democratic*, or *laissez-faire* where the boys were allowed to please themselves as to what they did. The findings supported a democratic ideology; although the boys were more productive under an autocratic leader when the leader was present and generally unproductive and aggressive under a laissez-faire leader, they were content and consistently productive under a democratic regime.

Drawing on the work of Anderson and of Lewin, Lippitt and White, Withall (1949) also tried to detect the influence of the social-emotional climate in classrooms. He distinguishes between *teacher-centred* and *learner-centred* teachers with the presumption that the latter (Anderson's 'integrative' and Lippitt and White's 'democratic') would be the most effective. Withall's results were inconclusive but at least he strengthened the experience of those seeking to understand classroom processes. At Chicago University where Withall worked was a student who was to have a widespread influence on classroom research. Ned Flanders was completing his PhD at Chicago and ten years later it was he who produced the Flanders Inter-Action Categories (FIAC), the most well-known observation schedule for use in analysing classroom behaviour.

'Interaction' analysis

Having described, as had Withall, the teacher as learner-centred or teacher-centred, one still had to explain *why* the style was used and the consequences for learning outcomes. The assumption from which Flanders started was that the learning potential of pupils would be inversely related to their level of dependence upon the teacher. He argued that the more a student was dependent upon the teacher the less would that student develop her own learning strategies. Flanders's classification system is a tool designed to help test this assumption and is divided into two sections, teachers being either *direct* (lecturing, giving directions and justifying authority) or *indirect* (accepting feelings, ideas, encouraging students and asking questions). He also adds two categories of student talk (making responses and initiating activity) and a final category of 'silence or confusion'.

There are a number of hypotheses which can be tested by the Flanders system which relate back to the basic assumption from which he starts. For example, if the learning goals are unclear a teaching style which emphasizes *indirect influence* will be more likely to stimulate pupil activity. That is, where the children are unclear about what they are doing a teacher who spends a lot of time talking, giving directions and exercising authority, will increase the dependence of the children and reduce their reponsibility for their own work. An example might be a poor project in a primary school when neither teacher nor pupil may be clear about the nature of the task they face and simply reproduce appropriate sentences from resource material rather than genuinely making their own enquiries. Though Flanders's prescription is towards an indirect teaching style, he does allow that there are occasions where a direct style has benefits. It would be appropriate, for example, where goals are clear and pupils motivated towards attainment, the teacher's intervention being to push the children to the limit of their ability.

A fundamental problem with all research using pre-defined categories is that it becomes self-validating. In other words, the observer looks for information to fit the boxes which he already has; what Cicourel has called 'measurement by fiat'; rather than generating new categories to accommodate the data. Flanders directs attention to a further problem with one of his own ground rules; he suggests that, 'the observer must not be overtly concerned with his own bias or with the teacher's intent' (Amidon and Flanders, 1967, p. 127). He thus denies the 'indexicality' of speech (see chapter 1) or the recognition that all speech is an index for a wider meaning which is embedded in the shared relationship of the encouter. Walker (1972) provides an illustration:

> If the teacher asks one child, 'What are you doing?' when all the
> other children are playing an audience role, and it is clear that what

the child should be doing is listening, it has quite a different meaning from the same question asked of the same child during a science experiment when each child is engaged in his own task.

The observer must interpret 'intent' in coding teacher-talk, and in doing so he is on the same difficult ground as the interpretive researcher in attempting to reach an understanding of classrooms.

Flanders's observation schedule is biased towards a whole-class pedagogy and is more difficult to use in an informal classroom where the teacher seldom addresses the class. In focusing on 'public talk', it also ignores the powerful control element within a teacher's 'private' conversation. For example, a teacher may say to a particular child, 'Your handwriting is dreadful, I do not want to see such appalling presentation again'. In doing so the teacher is also alerting the rest of the class to the need to take care over handwriting and general presentation. Most observation schedules are also a-historical in that they do not account for the fact that each particular teacher–pupil interaction is part of the history of many such interactions. A science lesson immediately before games is not the same as the lesson with the same class first period Monday morning or following the excitement of Mr Chaos's third period on Tuesday. Finally, the schedules tend to ignore structural factors such as the teacher's status within the school, the evaluation given to different subjects and the resources available to support classroom activity.

Despite these limitations, observation schedules have been widely adopted. Simon and Boyer (1970) were able to list almost 100 different schedules and Biddle (1967) commented that the construction and testing of a schedule seemed to be becoming an obligatory requirement for a higher degree in education! In part, this popularity stems from their ease of use. Observers can be quickly trained, massive data is easily collected in a form which is assimilated by a computer. The results are not impressive, confirming that classrooms are talking centres and that it is the teacher who talks for 75 per cent of the time, even in so-called 'discussion' lessons, a result which confirms the work of Romiett Stevens published at the turn of the century in the USA. Stevens reported in 1912 that she had found that, 'On the average, teachers talked 64 per cent of the time ... about 80 per cent of the classroom talk was devoted to asking, answering, or reacting to questions; rarely did a teacher's question call for anything besides rote memory or superficial comprehension' (from Hoetker and Ahlbrand, 1969, p. 151). Observation schedules provide a research tool which is dependent upon a weak underpinning theory of classroom interaction; a theory built on a defence of democracy and containing a prescription towards child-centred methods. The roots of alternative theory, which we shall now

explore, take us back to the interpretive perspective and to the work of
Waller (1899-1945) in the early 1930s.

Antecedents to interpretive approaches to classrooms

When talking about the status of the teacher Waller wrote, 'A popular
epigram of a few years ago had it that teaching was the refuge of un-
salable men and unmarriageable women' (1932, p. 61). He pointed
out that any such epigram is unjust to many individual teachers, but
nevertheless it captured an element of teaching true of both the USA
and the UK. Many went into teaching either because they could think
of nothing else to do or with the intention of getting an insurance
against the failure of more ambitious plans.

Waller's analysis of classrooms is tangential to his concern with
teachers and their roles and draws its conceptual framework from
the work of W. I. Thomas. He uses Thomas's concept of 'definition
of the situation' as a means of looking at classrooms (Waller, 1932,
pp. 292-3):

> Strictly speaking, the definition of the situation is a process. . . .
> one person can greatly affect the definition of the situation which
> another arrives at, we are accustomed to say that one person defines
> a situation for another. The attitudes of others are in fact the most
> important limitations upon the behaviour of any one person.

Anticipating the work of Hargreaves (1972) and Hargreaves *et al.*
(1975) Waller points to the danger that once a situation has been seen
in a particular way, in a 'particular configuration', it is very difficult to
see it in any other way. An inherent problem to teaching is the premature evaluation of children as certain 'types' (as we shall see in the
following chapter), the 'definition of the situation' once made is difficult to change. This has been illustrated by Stebbins (1971, 1977) who,
after charting the 'definition of the situation' of a group of Canadian
and of Jamaican teachers, concludes, 'once our habitual definitions
are formed and stabilized through continuous use, they become more
or less immutable' (1971, p. 274).

Education, for Waller, 'is the art of imposing upon the young the
definitions of situations current and accepted in the group which
maintains the schools. The school is thus a gigantic agency of social
control' (1932, p. 296). Conflict is a necessary part of any model of
schools and classrooms, as Geer (1971) was to note almost fifty years
later. Waller saw that conflict arising from the competing interests
of the various groups seeking to exert some control over education:
teachers, parents and administrators. The 'talk' which is captured by

Flanders's interaction schedules is only a partial expression of the particular context within which teachers work; Waller's contribution lies in attempting to complete the parameters to that context.

In a similar tradition to Waller is the work done by Becker in the early 1950s. Arising out of interviews with sixty Chicago school-teachers, Becker introduces the idea of an *ideal client* (1952, p. 451) arguing that service occupations – jobs whose occupants do things for other people as against those which directly produce goods – worked within a framework of perceived client problems. These client problems are built into the knowledge of how the service is to be provided which is part of the receipe knowledge (to use Schutz's phrase) of each occupation. The framework revolves around a concept of an ideal client, that is an 'ideal hospital patient' for a nurse, an 'ideal customer' for a car salesman or an 'ideal pupil' for a teacher.

In discussing educational processes Becker suggests three areas in which the teacher will experience and have to manage client problems: the problem of actual teaching or bringing about an observable change in the skill and knowledge of the children which the teacher can attribute to her own efforts; the problem of discipline; and the problem of moral acceptability arising 'from the fact that some actions of one's potential clients may be offensive in terms of some deeply felt set of moral standards'.

A feature of any stratified society is that different cultural groups produce individuals who do not fit the model of an ideal client held by members of the service occupation. An aspect of the failure of many lower-class children in England is a result of their presenting values and patterns of behaviour which are not in accord with those held by the majority of teachers. The children do not value education as an intrinsic good, find lessons boring and irrelevant, and cannot see why they should hold the teacher in high esteem just because she is a teacher. Becker writes (1952, p. 465):

> All institutions have embedded in them some set of assumptions
> about the nature of the society and the individuals with whom they
> deal, and we must get at these assumptions, and their embodiment
> in actual social interaction, in order fully to understand these
> organizations.

The paths which Becker indicated in the 1950s have still only been rarely explored two decades later. Social scientists have been fascinated by interaction schedules, or by the technical problems presented in video-recording, tape-recording or other multi-media devices for capturing the interaction of children and teachers in classrooms. It has to be remembered that these techniques, whether set within a normative or or interpretive paradigm, are only tools whose efficacy is dependent upon the power of the underpinning theoretical model.

Differentiation within classrooms

Cicourel and Kituse (1963), in a case study conducted at Lakeshore High School in the USA, provide an early example of an exploration of the process of differentiation within classrooms. They demonstrate that in part, ability in Lakeshore High was socially constructed, in that the actual performance of students was interpreted by the school staff in terms of the expectations held for the *particular* student – in terms that is of an ideal client image. Thus two students could attain the same marks, but whether or not these marks indicated an 'academic problem' was contingent on the perceived intentions of the student, whether or not he intended to go from school to university, and the status of the university aimed for. The crucial decision was whether the student was 'of university material'; this influenced how his academic results were perceived and even provided a background against which the student's personal problems could be interpreted.

A related study on the effects of ideal client models on the nature of classroom interaction is provided by Lacey, (1966, 1970, 1976). He argued that within a school – in his case study a grammar school, Hightown Grammar – a twofold process of differentiation and polarization is taking place. *Differentiation* refers to the normal organizational practice of teachers whereby students are allocated to classes on some criteria, usually a conception of ability. But as the process of differentiation takes place so students come to evaluate themselves in terms of their organizationally defined status. Lacey shows in Hightown Grammar that even by the middle of the second year, in which students had been streamed according to their performance in mixed-ability first year classes, the bottom form was beginning to present behavioural problems for teachers. A process of *polarization* was taking place whereby students grouped themselves around either pro- or anti-school norms. Members of the lower streams began to seek protection against the norms of the school through the adoption of their own cultural values – popular music and wearing fashionable clothes. Members of the upper streams tended to reinforce school values of scholarship and hard work. Lacey points out that this model of differentiation and polarization is an oversimplification. There will be exceptions, the attitudes of children will not be consistent over time. Nevertheless it remains an important initial description of organizational processes.

Lacey links his work to the problems of the existence of differential achievement between social groups which Floud, amongst others, had demonstrated. The classroom is seen as a 'competitive arena' in which students are in competition for scarce prizes such as high grades in examinations. However the competition is not amongst equals, neither in terms of the knowledge that competitors have of the educational system, nor of the resources which each has to support him in the struggle. Lacey sees the contestants to be each child plus his parents; some teams have a good knowledge of the system and how it works and others have little knowledge, parents being easily deceived by a child who alleges, for example, that he has no homework because he was able to complete it all at school.

Interpretive approaches to classrooms

So far, then, we have seen something of the history of classroom research, having traced the development of the dominant strand of interaction analysis and the intermittent appearance of alternative strands based on a methodology of participant observation. As yet the perspectives which we outlined in the first chapter have had little part to play in our understanding of classrooms. Interaction analysis grew from a particular ideological stance and was influenced by the work of curriculum theorists like Tyler (1949), Bloom (1954) and Taba (1962). Each of these authors advocated the establishment of behavioural objectives as a prerequisite to curriculum planning. As Taba has it, 'Perhaps the most important [function of educational objectives] is that of guiding decisions about the selection of content and of learning experiences and of providing criteria on what to teach and how to teach it' (1962, p. 197). Implicit in this tradition is a belief in rationalism similar to that of Durkheim, the conviction that human affairs could be reduced to cause-effect equations, and that the best, most efficacious and efficient means to an end could be discovered by 'scientific' enquiry. Though it is important to remember that Durkheim was aware of the complex nature of school classrooms, writing, 'A class, indeed, is a small society, and it must not be conducted as if it were only a simple agglomeration of subjects independent of one another' (1956, p. 112). The purpose of interaction analysis, however, was to improve teaching effectiveness, to dissect teacher input so that the learning output of pupils could be maximized.

The alternative tradition of classroom research has a closer affinity to the work of Weber and the recognition of the nonrational (that is traditional and affectual) action which Waller sees as characteristic of schools: 'The school is the meeting-point of a large number of intertangled social relationships' (1932, p. 12). The search is less for a causal model than to identify and describe the process at work

79

within classrooms; Lacey (1976) refers to his own work as a 'spiral of understanding' whereby his observation inside the school suggested ideas and methods of analysis which increased his understanding of classroom processes which in turn affected the process of observation and so on. But through this critical description of the school the nature of the 'intertangled social relationships' within its classrooms becomes apparent and is caught by Lacey's twin concepts of differentiation and polarization.

If Lacey and Flanders work within theoretical perspectives which are not made particularly explicit by them, Keddie (1971) unambiguously works within an interpretive framework. Drawing from the work of Cicourel and Kituse (1963) and of Dumont and Wax (1969), Keddie argues that explanations of educational failure must take into account both, 'the defining processes occurring within the school itself and . . . the social organization of curriculum knowledge'. Keddie builds her discussion from empirical work with teachers and pupils following a fourth-year humanities course in a comprehensive school. She makes the distinction between teachers acting in an *educationist context* and in a *teacher context*; the former being the justification given for action which is located within educational theories and the latter to 'the world of *is* in which teachers anticipate interaction with pupils in planning lessons, in which they act in the classrooms and in which when the lesson is over they usually recount or explain what has happened' (Keddie, 1971, p. 135).

Central to the defining processes within the school is the knowledge which teachers have of pupils, a knowledge which stems from the particular school class of which the child is a member: 'The "normal" characteristics . . . of a pupil are those which are imputed to his band or stream as a whole.' Teachers make comments like, 'She's bright for a "B" ', evaluating the student against criteria which the teacher feels are appropriate to 'B' children. School knowledge is also differentiated according to what is felt to be appropriate for different children; for 'A's, theoretical and pure knowledge, for Cs, practical with lots of visual stimulus material. Keddie concludes (1971, p. 156):

> There is between teachers and 'A' pupils a reciprocity of perspec-
> tive which allows teachers to define, unchallenged by 'A' pupils,
> as they may be challenged by 'C' pupils, the nature and boundaries
> of what is to count as knowledge. It would seem to be the failure
> of high-ability pupils to question what they are taught in schools
> that contributes in large measure to their educational achievement.

There are three main problems with Keddie's study; the first is an example of what Halsey (1975) has called 'the fallacy of composition' or making generalizations about group attributes from the behaviour of an individual member. The fact that an individual is in a 'C' class does not preclude his saying something perceptive about school knowledge, but it is not sufficient to build on this comment in order to demonstrate different but equal intellectual competences of 'C'- and 'A'-stream children. Second, as Robinson (1974) has argued, Keddie presents little evidence by which one can assess her biases. In short, what model of the child does she hold, what of pedagogy, what counts as 'ability' for her? There is the necessity of making explicit the background assumptions she held as she began her research. Finally, Sharp and Green (1975), argue that Keddie ignores the societal context in which the teachers work, she fails to ask the question, 'Is it possible to conceive of the teacher, faced with material problems of classroom management, operating radically differently?' (1975, p. 13). Teachers are not free-wheeling individuals who have freedom to negotiate the nature of their classroom activities, but are constrained, to some extent, by the traditions, expectations and power which surrounds their position.

Keddie's work is part of 'new directions' sociology, or what Whitty (1974) calls 'possibilitarian' sociology which views people socially constructing their world, recognizing the taken-for-granted assumptions behind the labels used, but which fails to explore the structural constraints on action. Sharp and Green's work (1975) is an attempt to redress the balance by incorporating a Marxist perspective into their account of an infant school. Their intention is to establish a model whereby people are seen both controlling and in control of their world; or in the context of the classroom, where the teacher can both act out a personal identity but yet is constrained by the historical and structural contexts of her world.

Radical approaches to classrooms

The research undertaken by Sharp and Green is a case study of three infant classes in Mapledene Primary School, a new school which has established a local reputation for its use of 'progressive' methods. The study is exploratory in an attempt to suggest ways in which the structure of the teacher's world acts as a constraint on behaviour. In the operation of classroom activity, through day-to-day interaction, Sharp and Green observe a process of stratification occurring. The teacher differentiates between 'normal' pupils; those who correspond to her taken-for-granted assumptions about the sort of person who lives in the school catchment area; and 'problem' children or those who are 'really dim'. The stress is on 'really', for as every new teacher knows the danger of labelling children, the only way to note what the teacher interprets as actual 'dimness' is to preface the label with 'really'.

The pressing problem faced by teachers in the school is 'what-to-do' within the flexible space and time dimensions which is provided yet with the constraint of high teacher-pupil ratios. The solution adopted is summarized by Sharp and Green by the concept 'business'; children need to be seen to be occupied, the evaluation of what they are occupied doing becoming a secondary aspect. In theory the self-directed activity, the business of the children, should allow teachers to spend more time with the 'problem' children; in practice, Sharp and Green observe, teachers spend most of their time with children who are already working successfully under the progressive ideology. 'It appears that the latent function of allowing pupils choice is that the onus of responsibility for the child's success or failure in the classroom lies with the child' (1975, p. 125). Throughout the process of differential attention on the part of the teachers those children perceived as 'problem' children become confirmed in their status and the teacher, in monitoring classroom activity, is provided with an explanation for their lack of success; the children will not be 'busy', they cannot concentrate on the activity at hand. 'Thus, whilst the teachers display a moral concern that every child matters, in practice there is a subtle process of sponsorship developing where opportunity is being offered to some and closed off to others. Social stratification is emerging' (1975, p. 218).

Although Sharp and Green's study is a valuable discussion of the process of learning within classrooms, it does not in the end demonstrate how the nature of classroom activity is the product of the material base within which teachers work. One could not deduce from their work that any change in the social relations of production would influence the way in which teachers cope with classroom reality; 'problem' children would not disappear. Hargreaves (1978) doubts the extent to which they extend the work of interpretive sociologists, arguing that their criticisms misrepresent the work they find inadequate. Hargreaves asserts 'that man is and experiences himself as both free (in some respects) *and* constrained (in some respects)' (p. 11), and that Sharp and Green have recognized the constraints within which teachers work without presenting an empirical demonstration of how these operate..

The value of Sharp and Green's work is the exploration given to the nature of socialization within classrooms (1975, p. 225)

> Within child centred progressivism, far wider ranges of the child's attributes become legitimate objects of evaluative scrutiny and explanatory variables in the construction of success and failure. Not merely intellectual but social, emotional, aesthetic and even physical criteria are often employed in the processing of pupils in educational institutions, the social control possibilities thus being enhanced.

The paradox of this position is that it is also within the informal class-room that teachers find it most difficult to maintain their own dis-cipline, in Waller's terms (1932, p. 296):

From the fact that situations may be defined in different ways and by different groups arises a conflict of definitions of situations. . . . Many teachers have learned that it pays to spare themselves no un-pleasantness in order to establish and make secure their dominance in the first few days and weeks of school.

The paradox in Sharp and Green's work is that although the progressive ideology may allow for enhanced possibilities of social control the con-straints under which teachers work inhibit the full elaboration of that ideology.

Implementing changes in classroom practices

The tension between theory and practice has been noted by Hoetker and Ahlbrand, 'If the recitation (traditional teacher questions – pupil answers) is a poor pedagogical method, as most teacher educators have long believed, why have they not been able to deter teachers from using it?' (1969, p. 163). Westbury's answer to that question is that tradi-tional methods offer a *'coping strategy'* to teachers which optimizes the learning outcomes of pupils yet without placing excessive demands on the teacher. Progressive methods are expensive in their use of teacher resources and to be practicable must, Westbury argues, be introduced with sufficient technical support to enable the child to increase her control over the learning process; a move, as we shall see in Chapter 7, towards what Bernstein has called 'strong framing'. In a later paper (1978), Westbury, suggests that our present classrooms are built on four critical assumptions; that mass education provides basic literacy and numeracy while offering the chance of social mobility to the most gifted; that learning is the product of maturation and mental exercise; that it is also the result of the pupil being told and finally that the knowledge communicated is 'pre-ordained'. A change in the nature of classroom activities, such as from 'traditional' to 'progressive' teaching, presupposes a change in the basic assumptions which underpin that activity; to return to Waller, 'We can accomplish little by having teachers do something different, for they cannot do anything different without being something different, and it is being something different that matters' (1932, p. 453).

Classrooms are complex places; in Jackson's estimation 'we have found in one study of elementary classrooms that the teacher engages in as many as 1,000 interpersonal interchanges each day' (1968, p. 9).

The behaviour of teachers and children is neither consistent nor can it be adequately represented on a linear scale such as progressive-traditional. A. C. and H. Berlak (Berlak and Berlak, 1975; Berlak *et al*., 1975), working within a Meadian perspective and using data from a participant observation study of three English primary schools, see teachers facing constant *dilemmas* in their everyday action. An example is the view of children held by teachers as both unique beings whose life is qualitatively different from that of adults and who should be treated as such and as being quantitatively different, little adults who must be prepared for their future status in society. The origin of these contrasting views is the past experience, values and culture of the teacher, with the consequence that 'The diversity of these various experiences and ideas within the generalized other often results in multiple and *conflicting* beliefs about and evaluations of most schooling acts, within as well as among teachers' (Berlak and Berlak, 1975, p. 15).

Set alongside the complexity and multi-dimensionality of classroom life, the work of Flanders (1970) and of Bennett (1976) can appear jejune. The two questions which Bennett sets himself to answer are: do differences in teaching styles differentially affect the cognitive and emotional development of pupils, and do different types of pupil perform better under certain teaching styles: Bennett sent a questionnaire to teachers in 871 primary schools in the north of England in an attempt to discover the range of teaching styles in use. Using cluster analysis, a statistical method of grouping together people who made similar types of response, twelve teaching styles were identified ranging from teachers 'who favour integration of subject matter, and, unlike most other groups, allow pupil choice of work, whether undertaken individually or in groups' (p. 45), to the other extreme where 'none favour an integrated approach' (p. 47). At the second stage of the research, 37 teachers falling into 7 of the 12 categories of teaching style were chosen for closer study. Thirteen of the 37 were classified as 'informal' teachers, 12 'formal' and 12 'mixed'. The teachers administered attainment tests in literacy and numeracy, the research team gave a personality test to pupils within one month of entry to the fourth year of junior school, and two samples of written work were taken. The results showed that in reading scores children taught by 'formal' and 'mixed' methods did better than those taught 'informally'. In mathematics, children taught by 'formal' methods did the best, as they did in English, and children taught by 'informal' methods tended to do least well in both subjects.

In one of the informal classrooms, classified by Bennett as displaying 'cognitively orientated informality versus affectively or aesthetically orientated informality' (p. 99), children recorded high gains in every achievement area. The reason given for this success is the structure, organization and incentives to learning which the teacher provides. The existence of this case, plus the evidence of the Berlaks, suggests that the original conceptualization of classrooms in Bennett's study was not sensitive enough to accommodate the nuances and contradictions of classroom life as daily experienced by teachers. The assessment of teacher style which Bennett makes from questionnaire items was checked against descriptions of the classrooms written by research staff, the opinion of primary school advisers, and the accounts of their own school day written by the children. Nevertheless, the label 'informal' remains an umbrella term which hides any contradiction, dilemma or inconsistency in actual teacher behaviour. Bennett's study remains within the classic input/output model and gives no indication of the *process* by which children acquire knowledge in school classrooms. In Hargreaves's judgment, Bennett 'is unable to tell us of the nature or origin of the constraints to which progressive teachers are subject, nor is he able to inform us as to how educational failure is accomplished interactionally in informal classrooms' (1977, p. 591).

As we have seen, the range of perspectives of classrooms extends from Sharp and Green, Keddie to Bennett. There is a danger, as Delamont (1978) warns, of different perspectives merely substituting, 'one variety of a-theoretical "findings" – based mainly on observation and interview – for another – based mainly on test scores' (p. 66). The pendulum seems to have come full circle such that a recent reader in the sociology of education (Karabel and Halsey, 1977) is as empty of classroom research as its 1961 predecessor. Indeed in the 1977 volume, Rist sees a need for 'the detailing overtime of the interactional pattern ... within classrooms' (p. 302), apparently unaware of the work reported in, for example, Chanan and Delamont (1975), or Stubbs and Delamont (1976). It appears as if the pendulum has swung from the 'black box' of functionalism into the negotiations of everyday classroom encounters and back again to the 'black box' of political economy where classroom activity is seen as the mere reflection of the economic substructure, teachers and pupils the dupes of capitalist relations of production.

So far we have looked at the ranges of classroom studies from the point of view of the dominant theoretical perspective which informs the work. We need now to look at some examples of recent substantive studies, to chart what we 'know' about classrooms. For the purposes of discussion research on classrooms can be seen to coalesce around two major interests, the maintenance of order within classrooms and the nature of learning, an interest which has been expanded into a consideration of the language used in classrooms.

Classrooms and the maintenance of order

An early example of a study into the maintenance of order in class-rooms is Werthman's (1963, 1970) study of the behaviour of members of lower-class gangs in schools in the USA. Werthman argues that explanations of the failure of lower-class boys in school in terms of the boys rejecting the school as a middle-class institution is too simplistic. The fact is that some gang members receive high marks, and in this sense are doing well at school, and gang members only cause control problems in some classes and not others. The critical issue, Werthman argues, is the way in which authority is recognized by gang members as being legitimately exercised. He suggests that gang members use four criteria in judging whether or not the teacher's claim to authority is legitimate. These criteria are: the area of jurisdiction over behaviour – what a teacher has the right to comment on; the relevance of a teacher's critical remarks – 'under no conditions can race, dress, hair style and mental capacities receive legitimate official attention'; the style of authority – whether or not a teacher requests or commands obedience; and finally, of greatest importance, the basis by which grades, or marks, are given. Werthman shows that gang members recognize an impressionistic element in all marking, but do not accept as legitimate marks which are interpreted as reflecting a teacher bribing or being vindictive towards a student. Bad behaviour reflects an inappropriate use of authority by the teacher, but 'when gang members are convinced that the educational enterprise and its ground rules are being legitimately pursued, that a teacher is really interested in teaching them something, and that efforts to learn will be rewarded; then gang members accept the efforts made by the teacher and apparently behave appropriately.

Research which has affinities to that of Werthman is Furlong's (1976, 1977) observation and interview study of a class of fourth-year girls, most of West Indian origin, in the next-to-botton stream in an English secondary modern school. He argues that the subculture theories of Hargreaves (1967) and Lacey (1970) are limited to a relatively static view of behaviour, thus missing the extremely fluid nature of classroom activity. Furlong introduces the concept of interaction sets to refer to those pupils who 'come to a common "definition of the situation" by drawing on similar commonsense knowledge and who communicate their view to each other and define appropriate action together' (1976, p. 26). The point is that the membership of interaction sets is continually changing as individuals alter their definitions of the situation in accordance with their specific, and changing, purposes; thus, for example, working rather than 'mucking about' and hence for a time withdrawing from, even withdrawing approval from, any 'mucking about' set in the classroom. Interaction sets are linked to the pupil's *relevance structures*, or as Schutz has it, 'In order to master a situation we have to possess the know-how – the technique and the skill – and also the precise understanding of why, when and where to use them' (1970, p. 112). The process of classroom interaction, as Furlong shows, is the acquisition of this 'precise understanding', to be able to judge teachers, for example, as 'strict' or 'soft' by criteria accepted as relevant by the rest of the interaction set.

Furlong, in much the same way as Werthman, concludes that essentially what children demand from school is to learn something. This learning must be taken gradually, however, and be through language with which the class is largely familiar; children must also receive constant feedback from the teacher on their progress. The search for a 'relevant' and practical curriculum as a way of occupying reluctant fifth-year pupils may, according to Furlong, be misplaced. In his case study, the most successful teacher was a historian who, in the words of one of the pupils, 'If you had teachers like Mr. Marks, you'd get a good job when you left school with "O" levels and all that because they make you work' (1977, p. 179). Though, as Gannaway cautions, 'The ideal teacher . . . is a very difficult person to describe, both for pupils and teachers, as he represents a fine balance between conflicting oppoites, namely, freedom and control' (1976, p. 53).

One group of classroom studies, then, is primarily concerned with the not inconsiderable task of the maintenance of order within classrooms. Were we to write a programme for teachers from this work then words like 'strict', 'organized', 'respect' and 'humour' would indicate important dimensions to effective teaching. Children need to feel they are learning. Specific content is less important to them than the sense of accomplishment captured in the following brief dialogue reported by Quine (1974, p. 17):

> Interviewer asks three boys in a remedial class why they were put in that particular class;
> *'All three boys:* Because we are not very brainy.
> *Interviewer:* You sound very brainy.
> *Jim:* Well we are now because if we done something wrong, Mr. B. asks us about it – but some other teacher would do us.'

Learning and the problem of order are inextricably linked. Hammersley argues, 'Being able to produce "the answer" to the teacher's question requires knowledge of the conventions governing a particular kind of teaching and the ability to "read the signs" in the teacher's structuring of the lesson' (1971, p. 82). The socialization into the way of learning within school is also a socialization into the established order of the school where the authority of the teacher is ultimate and where knowledge is something which is received rather than actively sought after.

Studies of use of language in classrooms

The first group of studies, into the maintenance of order within classrooms, are both descriptive and speculative. They are an attempt to map out the negotiations which teachers and pupils undertake in pursuit of the reduction of conflict and the enhancement of learning. The second group also takes the nature of classroom learning as its theme, but recognizes that the prime vehicle for that learning is the language which is used, mainly by the teacher. Thus 'teacher-talk' becomes the object of enquiry. Both Barnes (Barnes *et al.*, 1969; Barnes, 1976) and Stubbs (1976) argue that to understand the nature of classroom language is to understand the process of education, a process characterized by Barnes as, 'The teacher teaches within his frame of reference; the pupils learn in theirs, taking in his words, which "mean" something different to them, and struggling to incorporate this meaning into their own frames of reference' (Barnes *et al.*, 1969, p. 29). In his later work, Barnes makes a distinction between 'school knowledge' and 'action knowledge'; the first being the objective knowledge of the teacher, the second the subjective or personal knowledge of the pupil. The central purpose of teaching is to enable the learner to make the objective knowledge personal; to make it his own.

In his study of classroom language, Barnes shows that the prevailing form of language is the recitation of one-word answers. The structure of the classroom militates against a pupil expressing his personal understanding of the topic under discussion. At the extreme would be the question of the type, 'Is Jakarta the capital of Indonesia?' Even a child who has heard of neither Jakarta nor Indonesia – even should he not have heard the question – still has a 50 per cent chance of being able to give the correct answer. Barnes shows that open-ended questions in which the teacher builds on the pupil's frame of reference and in which the pupil is given time to formulate his reply are a far less frequent event than the call for a single-word answer.

A more theoretically elaborate discussion of classroom language has developed from the work of Bellack and colleagues (1963, 1966). Building from Wittgenstein's metaphor of language games, Bellack sees learning to participate in the various kinds of language activities within the classroom as very much like learning to play a game. 'Players have to learn the rules, the purposes of the rules, and how the various parts of the game are related' (1966, p. 3). Having analysed the language in classes taught by fifteen teachers in seven high schools in New York, Bellack suggests that there are four components to the classroom language game, or four 'pedagogical moves'. The first is *structuring*, for example when the teacher directs the attention of the class to the topic for the lesson; the second is *soliciting*, as when a question is asked or a command given. Soliciting moves are reciprocally related to *responding* moves, as in answers to questions, and contrast to *reacting* moves that are 'occasioned, but not directly called out, by a preceding move'. An example which Bellack provides of reaction moves is in the following dialogue (Bellack *et al.*, 1966, p. 166):

Teacher (soliciting)   What do we import from Denmark?
Pupil (responding)   Modern furniture.
Teacher (reacting)   Right, and it's some of the best designed
furniture available any place in the world.

Here the teacher *reacts* by giving a positive evaluation to the pupil's response and by adding an opinion on the topic under discussion, in this case, on the quality of Danish furniture.

The various moves add up to a *cycle of teaching activity*, each cycle beginning either with a structuring move or with a soliciting move which is not following on from a structuring move. Bellack has found that in approximately 85 per cent of cases it is the teacher who initiates the cycle and that within the cycle almost 40 per cent of classroom discourse is taken up by reacting moves. Each of the three other moves occupy about 20 per cent of the time with again the teacher being the most active player in each case.

The difficulty with Bellack's analysis (and the similar work by Sinclair and Coulthard (1974) on classroom discourse with groups of English junior school children) is that it presents a system which is just as formal and static as that of Flanders and interaction schedules. The active, creative, dimension to classroom language is stressed by Edwards and Furlong (1978) who argue that, 'it is impossible . . . to separate the organization of classroom *talk* from the management of classroom *meanings*' (p. 11, emphasis mine). In short the two interests around which we have seen research in classrooms to be focused, the maintenance of order and the nature of learning, are in fact inseparable.

A synthesis between the individual classroom and social structure?

In their discussion of classroom language, Edwards and Furlong (1978) identify a central attribute to be that of *authority-talk*. By this they mean that built into the very nature of classroom discourse are the hierarchical relationships in which teachers and pupils are located. The various acts of teaching – telling, asking, explaining, directing and commanding, for example – both confirm the nature of the social relationships and are permitted by those relationships. 'It is through recourse to their sense of a structural relationship that teachers and pupils repeatedly reconstitute that structure, which is both the basis *for* their interaction *and* a product of it' (Edwards and Furlong, 1978, p. 154, emphasis theirs). Their work is an elaboration of Bernstein's central thesis that the form of the social relationship acts selectively on speech and that the speech in turn regulates the form of the relationship (see Chapter 4 above).

There is no suggestion in Edwards and Furlong's discussion that classroom discipline will be an inevitable corollary of 'authority-talk'. Probably Waller is correct in his assertion that it is not sufficient to point out that the school is a despotism; 'It is a despotism in a state of perilous equilibrium' (1932, p. 10). It is this sense of flux, of potential disequilibrium, that leads many teachers to feel that they are sitting on top of a distinctly 'live' volcano. Given this continual tension the dominance of the teacher 'is both an extraordinary fact and a remarkable achievement' (Edwards and Furlong, 1978, p. 11). Ultimately the teacher is in control, her vocabulary, her orchestration of events underlines that control and defines for pupils the parameters of what is 'normal'. In their role as pupils children in turn confirm the teacher's authority.

The division within the sociology of education into what is often labelled 'macro' and 'micro' perspectives is a division eschewed by Edwards and Furlong. Their discussion of the specifics of classroom language is located within a wider structural dimension of social control. The reciprocal relationship between micro and macro perspectives is taken further in the work of A. Hargreaves (1977, 1978, 1979). He argues that a critical factor in the shift towards 'progressive' methods within education is a shift in the *mode* of control. Though on the surface of progressive methods pupils appear to have more autonomy, to be able to exercise greater discretion in their activities, in fact the teacher retains power. The shift (which has also been discussed by Bernstein through concepts of 'visible' and 'invisible' pedagogy, see chapter 7), is one from explicit to implicit modes of control. That is from the child being told clearly and precisely what is expected of her in behaviour and attainment, the shift is to the child having to interpret what is appropriate from her understanding of the intentions of the teacher.

This shift in the mode of classroom control is more than just a perverse action on the part of the teacher. A full understanding requires that the detail of classroom interaction be linked to wider structural constraints. Teachers do take a major responsibility for the nature of their classrooms, but this process 'occurs perhaps in situations not of their own choosing' (1978, p. 75). For A. Hargreaves, the central concept linking classrooms to social structure is similar to that used by Westbury (see above), namely the notion of *coping strategies*.

Coping strategies are, for A. Hargreaves, constructive in that they represent a response by teachers to the various ideological and practical pressures under which they work. In so far as the various strategies adopted enable the teacher to cope with the demand upon her, so will they tend to become institutionalized as 'successful teaching', as *the* strategy to adopt within school. A. Hargreaves suggests that there are three general constraints upon teachers for which a solution is required. First, 'it can be argued that *in contemporary capitalist society the goals of the educational system are fundamentally contradictory*' (1978, p. 78, emphasis his). The contradiction is implicit in the requirement of responding to the child as a unique individual yet at the same time having to select and allocate children for the occupational structure. One coping strategy for this constraint is that of 'guided choice', where ostensibly the pupil is able to choose which option she wishes to follow, but in reality is 'guided' to make the choice which the school staff judges to be most appropriate to her perceived abilities. It is difficult to see how else school staff could function given that not all pupils are equally fitted for the different areas of the curriculum.

The second general area of constraint identified by A. Hargreaves is one he labels 'material constraints'. He argues that 'gradualism, pragmatism and economy are the characteristic stamp of the British approach' to the provision of educational facilities. Educational considerations have tended to follow economic expediency rather than whatever is educationally desirable. Finally there is the constraint imposed by different educational ideologies which 'contain definitions of "correct" practice and provide routes for career advancement for those who attach themselves to such a body of ideas and approaches' (1978, p. 87). An adequate account of classroom interaction needs to transcend the idiosyncrasies of the unique event to reach an evaluation of social structure, an initial task being to confirm the web of constraint which impinges on action and to which teachers must constantly adapt their coping strategies.

Conclusion

This review of the literature on classrooms does not lend itself to an optimistic assessment for the future of such work. The formalized approach of Flanders and Bellack, for example, seem to have produced little beyond the observations of Romiett Stevens at the turn of the century. The interpretive approaches are in danger of becoming a-theoretical descriptions and the radical an opportunity for their proponents to confirm what they already 'know', that somehow the classroom corresponds to the relations of production within capitalist society. Part of the problem is the complexity of classrooms, reflected in the dilemma identified by both Bellack and A. Hargreaves of seeing children as unique beings and also future members of the occupational structure. Part of the problem, I suspect, arises from viewing classrooms as isolatable units of analysis; because classrooms are an administrative unit within a school they are assumed to be an appropriate unit for research. However, classrooms are so dominated by teachers, pupil identities, and the knowledge which is transmitted, and are as such so embedded within the school as an organization, that it may be inappropriate to assume that what are administrative boundaries can be equally clearly drawn for the purpose of research. We shall return to this line of argument in the final chapter, having discussed those aspects from which the classroom is constituted. We begin this discussion in the next chapter in a consideration of teachers and teaching.

Chapter 6

Teachers and teaching

Until now we have tended to use the child as the focal point for our discussion, his socialization at home and in the classroom, his acquisition of language and the nature of his ability and intelligence. In this chapter we turn to discuss the teacher and the process of teaching. Teaching is both an activity and a status; the term 'teaching' may refer to what teachers actually do at work within educational institutions but may also refer to their membership of an occupational group. Halmos (1970) has called such occupations as teaching, social work and nursing, the 'personal service professions', each having in common the 'principal function . . . to bring about changes in the body or personality of the client' (p. 22). We begin this chapter by a consideration of some of the implications of labelling the occupation of teaching a 'profession'; we then explore the process of becoming a teacher, the process of professional socialization, including an assessment of 'what teaching does to teachers'. Finally we examine the activity of teaching within classrooms, sometimes referred to as the 'role of the teacher', and the related processes of labelling and identity formation within schools.

Teaching as a profession

In popular discussion, teaching is often referred to as a profession; but then so is medicine, estate agency and some football playing. In 1925 Carr-Saunders suggested, 'A profession may perhaps be defined as an occupation based upon specialized intellectual study and training, the purpose of which is to supply skilled service or advice to others for a definite fee or salary' (reprinted 1966, p. 4). For Cogan, 'professional practices are refined by science and corrected by wisdom' (1953, p. 47). Both definitions would seem to exclude football players but still lump together doctors, estate agents and teachers. In arguing that

93

there is a distinction between professions and other occupations, Wilensky (1964) lays great stress on the need for the practitioner to adhere to a service idea, that is 'devotion to the client's interests more than personal or commercial profit should guide decisions when the two are in conflict' (p. 140). Now the claims of the estate agent may seem less strong as it could be argued that the prime motive behind dealing in property is to make commercial profit, the interests of the client coming second.

The presupposition behind these attempts at definition is that there is an 'ideal type' profession; a set of essential attributes common to occupations so labelled which may be studied as 'social facts'. There is, as we shall see, a clear functionalist perspective in much of the discussion; professions have, it is argued, a necessary role in advanced industrial society, the existence of professions being one of the characteristics of such a society. Greenwood (1957) provides a clear example of what has been labelled the 'trait' approach (Johnson, 1972) or the 'attribute' approach (Dingwall, 1976) to the study of professions. Greenwood maintains that occupations can be grouped along a continuum from 'the well recognized and undisputed professions' to the 'least skilled and least attractive occupations'.

Having noted that there is a distinction between profession and non-profession, Greenwood then proceeds to identify five distinguishing marks of a profession. The first of these is a *systematic body of theory*; that is, the skills which characterize a profession arise from a body of theory which is developed and refined and which, hopefully, extends the professional's understanding of the grounds of his own practice. The second distinguishing mark is that the professional 'knows' what is in the best interests of his client, in contrast to the non-professional who has customers who 'know' what they require; in short, the professional has *authority* within his sphere of competence. This authority is reinforced by the control the profession exercises over the *admission* of new members and its stipulation of acceptable criteria for membership. As well as control over admission, the professional body also exercises control over the conduct of members and has the power to withdraw the licence to practise from members judged to have breached the accepted *code of ethics*. Finally, according to Greenwood, what is unique to a profession is its set of values, norms and symbols; its *culture*. One of the aspects of the professional culture is the notion of a career, and, 'At the heart of the career concept is a certain attitude toward work which is peculiarly professional . . . professional work is never viewed solely as a means to an end, it is the end in itself' (1957, p. 51).

Towards the conclusion of his article Greenwood considers the nature of social work as a profession. He argues that it is a profession and that claims by social workers for professional status are really claims to move higher within the professional hierarchy. If we adopt his model it can be seen to provide a basis upon which groups may aspire to be accepted and to strengthen their position within the professions. However, Millerson (1964) argues that analysis such as that by Greenwood is weak, in that it starts from the author's interest in promoting the claims of a particular occupational group for professional status. Millerson presents a table showing twenty-one different attempts to classify the 'essential' attributes of a profession. The three traits most commonly identified are: 'adheres to a professional code of conduct', and 'organized', each specified by thirteen authors; and 'skill based on theoretical knowledge', specified by twelve of the twenty-one authors. The other traits ranged from 'requires training and education', identified by nine, to a number of traits each identified by a single author.

The major weakness of the attribute/trait theorists is that their argument is tautological. An ideal-type profession is constructed based on what is generally considered to be an established profession and other occupations are then judged by their similarity to the ideal type. Medicine is an established profession because medicine is the base for the ideal type; teaching is not so established because teaching is not like medicine. Hughes suggests that we pass from, 'the false question, "Is this occupation a profession?" to the more fundamental one, "What are the circumstances in which people in an occupation attempt to turn it into a profession, and themselves into professional people?' (quoted in Vollmer and Mills, 1966, p. v). It may appear, therefore, that teaching should be generally accepted as a profession, not for the semantic niceties of social science, but because it then legitimates the control teachers can exercise over the curriculum and organization of schools, their authority over children and parents and, by no means least, their claim on the public purse for an adequate salary. Here adequate means a salary which is commensurate with that paid to other 'professionals'. The Report of the Houghton Committee contains the somewhat gratuitous statement, 'Teaching is a profession. That is the status claimed for it by teachers themselves', and in recommending increased pay for teachers continued, 'But if the community shoulders the increased cost, teachers must also accept an obligation to use their professional power and expertise in the community's service' (1974, para. 194).

By convention, then, teaching is regarded as a profession, though one without the status of either the medical or legal profession. Etzioni (1969) uses the label 'semi-profession' to refer to teachers, nurses and social workers; Leggatt (1970) prefers bureaucratic profession', arguing that the particular characteristics of teaching arise from work within organizations: 'The outstanding characteristics of teachers as an occupational group are the large size of the group, its high proportion of female members, its lowly social class composition, its small measure of autonomy as a group and its segmentation' (p. 161). In developing our understanding of teaching as an occupation we will take each of the characteristics identified by Leggatt and examine them further by examining the structure of teaching.

The structure of the profession

In maintained primary and secondary schools in England and Wales in January 1976 there were 448,000 teachers, of whom 60 per cent women and 40 per cent men. The distribution of men and women between headteachers and deputy headteachers makes an interesting comparison, as shown in Table 6.1. Also in 1976 the average salary

TABLE 6.1 *Percentage of men and women head and deputy-headteachers, England and Wales, 1976*

	Men (%)	Women (%)	Total
Headteachers			
Nursery/Infant/First	13	87	7,422
Primary	77	23	16,485
Comprehensive	86	14	2,990
Deputy-headteachers			
Nursery/Infant/First	8	92	6,275
Primary	52	48	13,198
Comprehensive	58	42	4,676

Source: DES *Statistics of Education*, vol. 4, Table 22, 1976.

for all teachers was £3,959; in primary schools the average was £4,393 for men and £3,620 for women and in secondary schools, £5,357 for men and £3,789 for women. In short, though 60 per cent of teachers are women, men dominate the senior posts and, consequently, on average, are paid more than women teachers. Leggatt argues that as a result of the large size of the teaching profession there is a high annual wastage (in 1976 this was about 9 per cent of all teachers leaving the profession) therefore a high annual recruitment will be necessary to maintain the current level of the profession. Towards the end of the 1970s about 35,000 new teachers were being recruited annually, an intake which made it difficult to impose any stringent criteria on the quality of applicants, thus weakening the claim that teachers possess esoteric knowledge and skills which may be used in the service of their clients.

The stereotype of teaching as a women's occupation has, according to Leggatt, a basis in fact; 'it is an occupation with a predominance of women members and it involves work, at least in the primary schools, for which women are especially fitted' (1970, pp. 164-5). Deem, on the contrary, argues that 'it is not justifiable to assume that because women often have responsibilities for carrying out domestic labour and caring for children, their commitment to any other task is necessarily lower than that of men' (1978, p. 116). She goes on to attack arguments such as Leggatt's which assume some essential attributes of women which make them 'especially fitted' for the world of the primary and infant school. For Deem, this is a symbol of the 'sexual division of labour, or to the manner in which capitalist societies organise and reward productive and non-productive work'.

TABLE 6.2 *Social origins of teachers in maintained primary and secondary schools in England, 1955*

Father's occupation when teacher left school	Type of school in which teacher works			
	Primary	Secondary modern	Grammar	All teachers
	Men (%)			
Middle-class	6	8	16	10
Intermediate	48	46	26	51
Working-class	46	46	26	39
	N = 1251	1178	1763	
	Women (%)			
Middle class	9	11	24	15
Intermediate	52	55	60	56
Working-class	39	34	16	24
	N = 1149	1083	1833	

The third characteristic of teaching as an occupation identified by Leggatt is the 'lowly social class' origins of its recruits. The major source for this assessment is still evidence from a postal questionnaire study undertaken by Floud and Scott, on a sample of teachers in service in May 1955. The Table 6.2 has been adapted from their work (Floud and Scott, 1961, p. 540).

This table shows that most teachers – 51 per cent men and 56 per cent women – are recruited from families classified as 'intermediate', that is from families where the father is, for example, a teacher or

97

clerk or draughtsman. It also suggests that teaching is a more marked avenue of social mobility for men than for women, 39 per cent of male teachers and 24 per cent of female coming from working-class homes. When the social class background of teachers is compared across schools the proportion of those from working-class homes declines as the social status of the school increases; 42 per cent of primary school teachers come from working-class homes but only half that percentage, 21, of grammar school teachers. Leggatt quotes data to show that this picture of the social class background of teachers is also true of the USA, and Balloch (1974) presents similar findings for teachers in France.

The next characteristic of teaching as an occupation is 'its small measure of autonomy as a group'. Teachers do not regulate who is to be admitted to membership, nor do they ultimately judge what counts as acceptable professional conduct; both these functions belonging to the Department of Education and Science. But, as Tropp (1957) has demonstrated, the teaching profession, although created by the state, has, as the result of prolonged effort, negotiated some autonomy, 'and has reached a position of self-government and independence that is a source of continual envy to teachers in other countries' (p. 3). As an organized group, teachers have more autonomy than Leggatt suggests, though as a group teachers are hampered by the segmentation of the profession. Within teaching there is a division between teachers in different types of school, between graduate and non-graduate and even between teachers working in high-status areas like mathematics and science and those working in low-status areas like PE and art. As Leggatt comments, 'These cleavages preclude any but a fragile unity, leaving effective power . . with administrators' (1970, p. 168).

The struggle for enhanced professional status

One attempt to overcome the segmentation within the profession, and increase its autonomy, has been the long struggle to form a General Teachers' Council, a professional body like the British Medical Association. The story has been told by Baron (1954), Tropp (1957) and N. and J. Parry (1974). The attempt to establish a Council failed as a result of the divisions within the profession and the implacable opposition of the government. As Tropp puts it, 'There was . . . a fundamental difference between the motives of the middle-class teachers and the motives of the elementary-school teachers in supporting scholastic registration' (1957, p. 100). The former, in the main teaching in the endowed grammar and private schools, wanted a licence which would exclude the teachers of 'the industrial poor'. On the other hand, to quote Tropp again (1957, p. 100):

The reasons the elementary teachers gave for supporting scholastic registration were (in rough order of importance) that it would raise their social position; that it would drive the unqualified teacher from the profession; that the 'Scholastic Council' would represent the profession as a whole and act as an advisory council to the government on educational policy; that scholastic registration would promote the science of education and the training of teachers and thus induce men of a higher class to enter the profession. Lastly it would defend the child against untrustworthy teachers.

It is clear from this list that the motives of exclusiveness and the desire to enhance status, and thus presumably salary, were predominant. It is interesting to note the 'pecking-order'. The grammar-school teachers wanted to exclude the elementary who in turn wanted to exclude the unqualified. The segmentation within the profession prompted Carr-Saunders and Wilson to observe, 'The teachers in elementary schools occupied humble positions, and between them and the headmaster of Eton there was a gulf fixed, the impassability of which can only be appreciated by those who understood Victorian exclusiveness' (1933, p. 252). The 'gulf' was increased in 1902 when the Teacher's Registration Council established that year immediately started two registers, Column A and Column B; 'the first was for certificated teachers in elementary schools and the second for teachers in secondary schools who could fulfil certain specified conditions' (Baron, 1954, p. 136). Baron shows that it was the intention that jobs in secondary schools should be open only to those registered in Column B, those that is, who had a degree together with proof of training specifically related to secondary schools: 'Thus no elementary school teacher would be able to cross into the other branch of the profession, since, even if he had a degree, his training qualifications would not be acceptable' (1954, p. 136).

As a result of pressure from the National Union of Teachers, the two-column register was discontinued in 1906. The struggle for an effective professional body continued, however; its failure being interpreted by N. and J. Parry as evidence of the state's control of education. 'The stark fact now is that the state, having become the most powerful force in education, has a vested interest in opposing the ideal of the teachers' registration movement; that is in blocking the establishment of a self-governing teaching profession' (1974, p. 183).

The search, albeit unsuccessful, for general recognition of high professional status was a search for the power that status gives. Bledstein (1976) argues that the rise of professionalism is related to the growing belief in the application of scientific knowledge to human affairs, a belief which we saw in the last chapter to be a feature of research in classrooms and which we shall see influencing the development of the curriculum in our discussion in the next (Bledstein, 1976, pp. 90, 94):

> For middle-class Americans, the culture of professionalism provided an orderly explanation of basic natural processes that democratic societies required. Science as a source for professional authority transcended the favoritism of politics, the corruption of personality and the exclusiveness of partisanship . . . now clients found themselves compelled to believe on simple faith that a higher rationality called scientific knowledge decided one's fate.

Balloch doubts if the 'organization or relationships typical of the traditional profession present wholly desirable targets for present teacher policies' (1974, p. 524). She particularly refers to the 'exclusive' status of the professions where social and ideological homogeneity is preserved through self-recruitment and professional socialization and whose skills are only available to those who are members of the profession. Balloch argues for an 'open' or 'responsive' model of a profession as being more appropriate to teaching; and occupational identity which sees teachers facilitating learning rather than guarding 'sacred' knowledge which is to be distributed to those who qualify.

In her analysis Balloch reflects the concern shown by Johnson (1972) who says of the professions, 'Janus-headed, they promise both a structural basis for a free and independent citizenry in a world threatened by bureaucratic tyranny and at the same time themselves harbour a threat to freedom' (p. 17). For him, the emergence of professions is the emergence of a form of social control; to be understood, this event needs to be explained in terms of why some occupational groups at specific points in time are able to exercise sufficient control over their clients to establish the autonomy of the profession. As we have seen, the teachers' move to establish a General Teachers' Council was an attempt to establish such autonomy. As Grace (1978, p. 42) puts it:

> As a weapon in this struggle, the teachers used the ideology and rhetoric of professionalism. They claimed with increasing confidence, expert knowledge on the nature of 'true' education and with a sense of professional authority, condemned much of the curriculum, pedagogy and evaluation of the elementary school.

Grace goes on to show, however, that implicit in the autonomy won by teachers is a series of paradoxes. Although teachers have achieved much autonomy, and thus far more control over both the manner and contents of what is to be taught, many of their pupils remain bored and feel a sense of estrangement from school. Thus a critique has been developed – by Sharp and Green (1976), for example – which asserts that teacher autonomy is not in fact real but illusory, masking the real constraints of capitalist relations of production. Yet, Grace asks, if teacher autonomy is not real, why has there been a growing attack on teachers from the political 'right' under the slogans of 'accountability', 'core-curriculum' and 'greater parental choice'? Following Bernstein's argument (see Chapter 7), Grace concludes that what has happened has been 'a movement from essentially visible and centralized control to essentially invisible and diffused control' (1978, p. 218). There has been a change in the nature of social control (Grace, 1978):

> This invisible control is constituted among other things, by the activities of examination boards and of their definitions of válid knowledge; by the constraints of the work situation and, crucially, by what 'being a good teacher' and 'being professional' are taken to imply.

The process of professional socialization

In order to explore further what is implied by 'being professional' and 'being a good teacher', we need to consider the *process* by which the individual becomes a teacher, a discussion not of how one passes certain examinations, goes to college, passes other examinations and then obtains a teaching job, but of how one acquires the identity of a teacher. As Waller puts it, 'Teaching does something to those who teach. Introspective teachers know of changes that have taken place in themselves. Objectively minded persons have observed the relentless march of growing teacherishness in others' (1932, p. 375). Our concern then, is with the process of *secondary socialization*, with explaining what happens to people as they pass through initial teacher training courses into the ranks of established teachers. For Berger and Luckman, secondary socialization is 'the internalization of institutional or institution-based "sub-worlds". Its extent and character are therefore determined by the complexity of the division of labour and the concomitant social distribution of knowledge' (1967, p. 158).

As the dominant perspective informing the discussion of professional status was functionalist, so the perspective dominating the discussion of becoming a professional is interactionist, largely influenced by the work of G. H. Mead. Bucher and Sterling (1977) have developed a general model of professional socialization which is based on fieldwork they undertook with various kinds of medical specialisms. Their basic thesis is that the professional characteristics which new recruits possess are the product of the interaction of *structural* and *situational* aspects of the training programme; that there is a 'programming effect' which the training programme has on the professional identities of the new members of the occupation.

101

By structural variables, Bucher and Sterling mean the social structure within which the training takes place, suggesting that the social scientist should answer questions such as, 'What is the nature of the organization housing the training programme and what sort of affiliation does it have with other institutions?' (1977, p. 21). It would be extremely valuable to our understanding of the changing pattern of higher education in England and Wales to ask this question of the various organizations in which teachers are educated. One could hypothesize that before the reorganization and mergers of the Colleges of Education in the mid-1970s staff had greater freedom to pursue their own views of preparation for teaching and construct courses which reflected that view. After reorganization, where teacher education was brought closer to non-teacher training higher education, it was important that teacher education was seen to be legitimate by colleagues in non-teacher training departments, and thus the courses have become more 'academic' and possibly of less relevance to the needs of teachers.

By situational variables, Bucher and Sterling mean, for example, those opportunities which have been established on a course within the framework provided by the structural variables, such as, 'to what extent do trainees have an opportunity to perform the roles, or do the work, associated with the profession?' (1977, p. 24). Central to every course of initial teacher training is teaching practice, a critical question being the extent to which this is monitored by the college staff so that any potentially 'negative' socialization of the trainee by the school staff is ameliorated. Bucher and Sterling conclude that there is evidence of a *programming effect* and that 'for the most part, the trainees emerged from their respective training programmes much as one might have predicted' (1977, p. 264).

It might appear that Bucher and Sterling are following a passive, over-determined model of secondary socialization. They suggest, however, three factors which work against the total indoctrination of recruits: where the trainee already has a strong orientation towards the field, where she is able to support that orientation during training, and where she is able to minimize contacts with the staff of the training department. All factors which suggest, as does Lortie (1975), that courses of initial teacher training will have a relatively weak programming effect. The trainee already possesses a strong orientation to the field, namely that which she acquired during her own thirteen years of schooling, and thus will be able to 'resist' the influence of college tutors. The programming effect is further reduced by contact with school staff during teaching practice as well as through contact with staff not directly concerned with teacher training during her college course.

In becoming professionals, trainees are not just responding to events but (Bucher and Sterling, 1977, p. 275):

1. the subjects moving through the system are actively evaluating themselves and others, 2. that they get better at this process, and 3. they acquire a sense of mastery and can more confidently pick and choose from among the elements provided within the structure of the program and validate their own choices.

As the neophyte gains in confidence, so is she able to assess the relevance to her own values and purposes of the training received; she is also better able to evaluate the 'worth' of the criticism received from the tutors on the course. This is an *active* model of socialization, and one, as Mardle and Walker (1979) argue, which takes into cognizance the biography of the individual teacher. One which reflects 'the sociological imagination' (Mills, 1959) and recognizes not only structure and identity as components but also the historical background to both. Part of our understanding of teacher socialization is an understanding of why the training organizations came to be as they now are and also why the individual came to be a member of that organization.

Identity and commitment

The recognition that there are antecedents to both identity and structure – that teachers have a biography and schools a history – was also made by Gouldner (1957) in his discussion of latent identity. He argues that each organization exercises some constraint on individual behaviour; for teachers this would be, for example, on the language that was thought to be appropriate, or the familiarity in the relationship with children. But as members of organizations we each have *latent identities*, features of our person or biography which though not strictly relevant to how we behave in a school or college, nevertheless influence both our acts and the responses to those acts. The fact of being either male or female, young or old, affects the pattern of interaction within the organization. Gouldner ties in the concept of latent identity to his distinction between 'cosmopolitan' and 'local'; a distinction which, incidentally, may be traced through Merton (1949) back to the work of the German sociologist Ferdinand Tönnies (1855–1936) who made a distinction between 'gemeinschaft' (localistic) and 'gesellschaft' (cosmopolitan). 'Cosmopolitans' would have a strong latent identity in that, unlike 'locals', they have a major commitment outside the organization; for example, the music teacher who sees recognition by fellow musicians to be of greater importance than his evaluation in the school as a teacher. As Becker and Geer state, 'People carry culture with them; when they leave one group setting for another they do not shed the cultural premises of the first setting' (1960, p. 305).

Associated to the idea of latent identity in the discussion of secondary socialization is the notion of 'commitment'. For Becker (1960, 1964) commitment refers to the way 'in which externally unrelated interests of the person become linked in such a way as to constrain future behaviour' (1964, p. 41). Throughout life we accumulate what Becker calls 'side bets' – Geer (1966) calls them 'valuables' – which may have the effect of increasing commitment to our job. A teacher may decide not to leave her present school because she enjoys the colleagueship in the staff room, has a part-time job in the evening classes which are run at the school, and normally can be home at the same time as her own children. These side bets, or valuables, enhance her commitment to her job even though they are not directly related to teaching. Geer argues that a characteristic of teaching is the ease with which the accumulation of 'side bets' can begin to be detrimental to the activity of teaching; the possibility of being able to work comparatively short hours together with long holidays allows teachers to 'moonlight' in such a way that some may become more attached to their suplementary activities and view their teaching simply as a means of allowing them to do other things.

For Kanter (1974) commitment is the process 'through which individual interests become attached to the carrying out of socially organized patterns of behaviour which are seen as fulfilling those interests, as expressing the nature and needs of the person' (p. 127). The concept of commitment represents for Kanter the interface between the individual and the organization. To continue to exist, the latter must solve three problems which are analytically distinct: continuance, cohesion and control. The individual in following his own projects, or intentions, will also be variously committed to each of these three problems. An example provided by Kanter is, 'a rebellious teenager may reject his parent's control but be unwilling to withdraw from the family system', he has a commitment to its continuance but not to the form of control exercised.

Woods (1979) develops Kanter's discussion, relating it specifically to the secondary socialization of teachers within a school, Lowfield Secondary School. He views teachers continually accommodating to the constraints of the organization by adopting a number of *survival strategies*. Woods identifies eight such strategies – domination, negotiation, socialization, fraternization, absence or removal, ritual and routine, occupational therapy and morale-boosting. An occupational problem identified by Woods is that these survival strategies do not necessarily facilitate teaching (1979, p. 168):

They often take the place of it, and even assume its guise. Success ensures the establishment of a strategy, but many outlive their usefulness and turn into problems themselves. New teachers are quickly initiated, and so the system perpetuates itself. If there is a 'hidden curriculum', there is also a 'hidden pedagogy'.

Woods shows how the *hidden pedagogy* of survival strategies can dominate teacher activities so that the necessity to keep control in classrooms begins to blot out any educational development of the children. Webb (1962) suggests that 'Self respect for the typical teacher (as a teacher and inside the school) is a simple function of degree of control. This is why his attitude towards control is obsessional' (p. 268). Fuchs (1968) clearly demonstrates the effectiveness of a hidden pedagogy in charting the early socialization of a new teacher in an inner-city school. Initially, the teacher gave accounts of her activities in terms of how she could improve and adapt her teaching style to meet the demands and needs of her pupils. Within a year however, she had adopted the explanation of teaching given by the existing staff; in essence, failure was the responsibility of the child, one could not expect 'children from this area' to appreciate what school was about. As Waller recognized, 'Teacher and pupil confront each other in the school with an original conflict of desires, and however much that conflict may be reduced in amount, or however much it may be hidden, it still remains' (1932, p. 195).

Initial socialization of teachers

The only British study of teacher socialization which incorporates similar theoretical perspectives to Bucher and Sterling, Becker and Waller, is that of Lacey (1977) on students taking a one-year postgraduate certificate in education course. Lacey's central concept is that of *social strategy* by which he means the intentions and acts of an individual within a social setting. He argues that on beginning their course, students have already internalized a view of the world which has been embedded in their different degree subjects. In other words, the priorities, view of knowledge and of the nature of teaching held by a physicist, will differ from those held by a student who has a degree in English. These different views of the world, or 'master patterns', form *latent cultures* which, 'provide the basis for but also limits the number of strategies available to an individual in any given situation' (1977, p. 70). The subjects in which the student has been socialized provide a range of social strategies which are potentially available to her in negotiating her passage through training and into the profession of teaching.

It is important to note that Lacey interprets latent culture as a basis for social strategies; he is not putting forward a determinist position whereby each physicist or historian acts in the same way. He allows for individual choice and introduces three sub-types of social strategy to accommodate this. The first is *strategic compliance* where the student goes along with the prevailing definition of how things are managed, though holds to her own view of the 'real' nature of things. Next is *internalized adjustment* where the student fully accepts the prevailing view, and finally its *strategic redefinition*, where the student, although without any formal power, is able to change the prevailing definitions of the situation by, for example, using a teaching method which challenges the existing view of the curriculum within the school and which becomes adopted by the school staff.

Lacey's work is a beginning, an attempt to chart the processes of becoming a teacher starting from the assumption that teachers have their own purposes, idiosyncracies, values and particular orientations. Schools are not homogeneous entities which allocate 'roles' to incoming teachers, but, 'institutions penetrated by a flow of individuals who hold divergent views as to how the institution should be run, indeed as to what the purpose of the institution is!' (1977, p. 136). The return of teachers from the 'progressive' ideals of the initial-training institution to the more traditional values of the school has been well documented by Fuchs (1968), Taylor and Dale (1971) and Cope (1969). As Waller suggests, 'Most of the programs for the rehabilitation of the schools founder upon the rock of teacher resistance' (1932, p. 457); less pessimistically Lacey argues that in many cases the return is the adoption of strategic compliance, the 'radical' (and one must presume in some instances the 'traditional') is dormant until the structural prerequisites which support it are appropriate.

When and how change is made in schools is barely understood; the process of implementing and sustaining innovation in education is complex, difficult and uncertain. To return to Westbury's argument (1973, Chapter 5), before we can begin to understand change we must understand why teachers use the coping strategies they presently adopt. For Woods (1979) their prime task is one of survival; for Grace (1978) teachers face a 'crisis of validity' in what they do. In our discussion of becoming a teacher we have identified some of the constraints on their actions, but in understanding teachers we must also recognize the wider set of values, the cultural expectations, within which they work. It may well be that the 'demand' that schools produce a particular type of competence in pupils – technically efficient, achieving maximum marks in formal examinations – is a major constraint on teachers. That is, teachers are expected to manufacture a particular form of the intellect, which acts as a major constraint on the teacher's interpretation of her task.

The role of the teacher

We have examined the status of teaching as an occupation and looked at the theoretical perspectives which surround explanations of the process of becoming a teacher. The latter is still a relatively unexplored area within the sociology of education and, if one discounts Lacey's work on initial secondary socialization, there is even less discussion of the affects of teaching on teachers. Studies like those of Hilsum (see for example, Hilsum and Strong, 1978) provide a description of the teacher's day from which one appreciates the range of the tasks under-taken but gleans little understanding about the effectiveness of teachers, the management of different expectations, nor the consequences of this for both teachers and pupils.

The discussion of the activity of teaching has tended to be couched in the vocabulary of the 'role of the teacher', for example, Wilson (1962), Westwood (1967), Biddle (1970), Grace (1972) and Goble and Porter (1977). It is easy to criticize the concept of 'role' (as we saw in Chapter 3) for reflecting a passive, static view of human action which fails to capture how real teachers negotiate 'survival' each day. The criticisms are valid, but at this stage in our limited understanding of teachers and teaching I do not think it appropriate to argue for the total abandonment of the concept.

It is possible to distinguish two strands in the literature on the 'role of the teacher', one is prescriptive, the other descriptive. An example of the first is Floud's assertion that the teacher in the affluent society 'is to be not only a missionary in the slum but a *crusader* in the suburb, dedicated to the war against mediocrity and to the search for excellence' (1963, p. 388, her emphasis). Floud is not claiming that this is what teachers are but prescribing what she feels their role ought to be in an affluent society. In this lies a benefit of the concept of role in that in its *prescriptive mode* it indicates some of the values and expectations, the ideological framework, from which teachers may be judged. Similar views are contained in the Preface to Goble and Porter (1977):

> Teachers are a critical factor in development: they are in a privileged position to break the circle of poverty, ignorance and prejudice in a manner likely to be accepted by the populations concerned; while the multiplier effect of their occupation singles them out as a valuable investment at a time of crushing demand and limited resources.

It is naive to believe that teachers could have the multiplier effects envisaged; every teacher is constrained by, for example, the structural reality of limited opportunities for many of their pupils. These limits may be on their opportunity to grow crops in the face of exploitative rents and restricted markets in the Third World, or on their chance to obtain employment in the Developed World.

The *descriptive mode* of role also emphasizes the web of circumstances in which teachers work. As well as the conflict arising from the many different expectations and values held of teachers, Wilson (1962) indicates four other broad areas of conflict and insecurity. The first stems from the diffuse nature of the occupation; it is difficult to know when a teacher has fully discharged her obligations, when the job is done. Many teachers tend to over-extend themselves in their role in the continual search for novel approaches and alternative methods to keep alive the interest of the class. Conflict and insecurity also stem from conditions where the role is inadequately supported, or is indeed marginal to, the institutional framework. For example, the liberal studies teacher in a college of further education may feel her contribution to be marginal to the prime goals of the organization and all teachers have much less control over the running of educational institutions than do doctors over hospitals or lawyers over the workings of the courts. Finally, Wilson argues, 'Because of the diffuse, affective character of the teaching role there is, in contemporary society, a most significant role-conflict arising from the divergence of role-commitment and career orientation' (1962, p. 29). This is really a tension between what Gouldner has called 'locals' and 'cosmopolitans', between staying at school where the teacher knows and is known by the children and following a career-line; that is, moving to enhance prospects for promotion. To quote Wilson again, 'There is an inducement in this situation to make right impressions on the significant people rather than significant impressions on the right people – the children' (1962, p. 30). It is important to remember, however, that Wilson was writing in the early 1960s when the educational service was expanding. Two decades later the opportunities for rapid career mobility are much reduced.

Discussion of the role of the teacher, then, tells us something about how teachers are perceived in society and also describes some of the conflicts, albeit somewhat mechanically, that teachers are alleged to experience. In general the discussion of the role of the teacher tells us little about how individual teachers manage their own survival, or what teachers actually do in schools. In sum, located within a functionalist perspective, teachers have been conceptualized in passive terms, responding to social structure and not actively contributing to the building of that structure.

Labelling in schools

Given the unease with the discussion on the role of the teacher and the paucity of work using any form of interpretive perspective, one can appreciate the enthusiasm which greeted research whose purport was to show the teacher as an essential part in any model of educational success or failure. Snow (1969) quotes a review of such research in the *New York Review of Books* which claimed, 'Maria, moved . . . from "slow learner" to "gifted child" . . . . The implications of these results will upset many school people, yet these are hard facts' (p. 199). The research, by Rosenthal and Jacobson, was published under the title *Pygmalion in the Classroom* (1968), a title which picks up Eliza's plea in G. B. Shaw's *Pygmalion* that 'the difference between a lady and a flower girl is not how she behaves, but how she's treated'.

Rosenthal and Jacobson did their research in Oak School, an elementary school of 650 pupils in south San Francisco. All the children, ages six to twelve, were given a 'relatively nonverbal' test of intelligence; however, the teachers were told that the test would allow the researchers to predict those children who were likely to 'show an unusual forward spurt of academic progress' in the near future. At the beginning of the next school year the teachers were given the names of from one to nine children in their class who had attained high scores on the test; in fact the names given had been selected at random. Thus Rosenthal and Jacobson claimed that any difference between the 'special' children and the rest was not based on any tangible evidence, but rested in the minds of the teachers. All the children were re-tested six months, twelve months and again two years after the original test. The results led Rosenthal and Jacobson to conclude, 'After the first year of the experiment a significant expectancy advantage was found, and it was especially great among children of the first and second grades' (1968, p. 176). In other words, a favourable teacher expectation towards a child seemed to have a positive influence on her attainment. In the first grade at Oak School the 'experimental' children gained on average fifteen points over the scores of the 'control' children, and in the second grade a gain of nine points.

After the initial enthusiasm for the research, more careful evaluation such as Thorndike (1968), Claiborn (1969) and Snow (1969) showed it to have serious methodological flaws. For instance, the 'relatively nonverbal' test of intelligence was not suitable for children in the first two grades; where in fact the only 'significant' gains were recorded for the experimental children; Rosenthal and Jacobson record (1968, p. 189) that the mean IQ of the nineteen children in class IC was 30.79, a score which if accurate implies that in a public elementary school there are children who are severely educationally sub-normal. Further, the authors comment on the children in the second grade, 'Of the twelve children originally alleged to be potential spurters who remained in the school for the entire year of the experiment, not a single one was recalled as a potential spurter by any second grade teacher' (p. 155).

It would seem crucial to any hypothesis that claims that teacher expectations have an effect that teachers can actually remember the
names of those towards whom they hold expectations. This second
weakness is related to a third, namely the study gives no indication of
the *process* of labelling – how in practice teachers responded to children for whom their expectations differed.

This absence of process variables in Rosenthal and Jacobson's work
is similar to its absence in interaction analysis which we discussed
in the previous chapter. Rist (1970) is critical of such mechanistic
approaches to classroom processes as (p. 413),

> although the studies may establish that a teacher has differential
> expectations and that these influence performance for various
> pupils, they have not elucidated either the basis upon which such
> differential expectations are formed or how they are directly mani-
> fested within the classroom milieu.

Working within an interpretive perspective akin to that of Becker,
Rist's own study was a longitudinal observation of an inner-city,
'urban ghetto school' in the USA. Twice each week he spent an hour
and a half in the kindergarten (reception) class and the same amount of
time when the children were in the second grade (aged eight). His thesis
is that teachers have an image of an 'ideal client' – a concept of the 'sort
of child' who does well – and relates to children in her class on the
basis of this ideal client. Rist observed that within a week of starting
school the teacher with whom he was working had grouped the children
so that as one moved from the nine children seated around the table
nearest the teacher to the ten furthest away, there was an increasing
difference between them. The latter group were all poorly dressed and
generally unkempt, they did not take the initiative in classroom activities, were less adept at the use of 'school language' and were more
likely to come from homes with low income, large families and whose
parents had had little education.

The children on the table nearest the teacher, we must assume, were
also the children who came closest to the teacher's ideal type of pupil.
Not only were the children segregated, but the teacher also responded
to each group in different ways, tending to favour the high-status and
ignore the low-status children. By the end of the year the differences
became 'objective' as the teacher recorded details of the child's achievements on a record-card. The information on this card was used by
the teacher of the next grade as a basis for allocating the children to
appropriate work groups.

The dimensions of the ideal type of pupil held by the teacher, her
ideal client, are not explored by Rist. Using classroom observation and
the repertory grid technique, Nash (1973) and Blease (1978) are able

to fill in some of the parameters of the ideal client. By the repertory grid technique, the teacher is presented with the names of three children in her class and asked to specify the way in which one child differs from the other two. In this way the teacher gives the attributes which are important to her, rather than those assumed to be important by the researcher. Both Nash and Blease show that 'ability' in a classroom is related to an affectual dimension – whether or not the teacher likes the child – and confirm Rist's finding that teachers treat children whom they view favourably in different, more positive ways than children who are viewed negatively.

Having conducted a study into labelling in two secondary modern schools, Hargreaves, Hester and Mellor (1975) clarify what they mean by the process of labelling by the question, 'How do teachers make the transition from X pupil is a person who commits Y deviant act(s), to X is Y type of deviant person? (p. 40). Hargreaves and colleagues identify three stages to the process; 'speculation', where the teacher first meets her class and forms initial impressions of it as a collectivity and of its individual members against the background the teacher has acquired from teaching other classes. Then follows 'elaboration', or the verification that the child really is as first impression suggests. This is a process of hypothesis testing in which the teacher may also change her initial impression if the child's behaviour does not correspond to the initial judgment. Finally comes the third stage of 'stabilization' where the teacher has a relatively clear and stable conception of the identity of her pupils. She 'knows' the child, has little difficulty in making sense of the behaviour of the individual and is not puzzled or surprised by interaction within the classroom. The difficulty with such stabilized conceptions is one of changing one's assessment of the child; once we 'know' that someone is of a certain type, it is difficult to shift this belief.

Labelling is an example of what C. Wright Mills (1940) has called 'vocabularies of motive'. The labels are a part of the framework within which teachers work. 'As such', Apple (1979) argues, 'they must be treated as historically conditioned data, not absolutes . . . categories that developed out of specific social and historical situations which conform to a specific framework of assumptions and institutions' (p. 134). There is a tendency for the person to 'become' the label so that the assessment, 'John is stupid' is such that 'stupidity' is the overwhelming, all-embracing summary of what John is which remains inviolate and unalterable for all time. As Apple puts it, the label 'has an *essentializing* quality in that a person's . . . entire relationship to an institution is conditioned by the category applied to him. He or she *is* this and only this' (1979, p. 135, emphasis Apple's).

A clear example of the way in which a label envelops a person is provided by Coard's (1971) discussion of the plight of West Indian children in English schools. Numbers of West Indian children far in excess of their proportion in the schools were labelled 'ESN' (educationally sub-normal), and allocated to special schools. Coard's point is that to understand why this has happened it is crucial to know how the label has come to be applied, an understanding which at best shows English schools to be insensitive to the problems which West Indian children face in accommodating to a new environment. The shift has to be away from the individual problems of the child to an examination of the structural factors which produce the assessment.

The argument is quite complex. There are some West Indian children who have acute learning problems for whom a place in a special school may be very appropriate; it is the numbers so allocated which suggests an institutional problem. The same issue was observed by Sharp and Green (1975, Chapter Five) with the teachers of Mapledene Primary School. Aware of the dangers of labelling, teachers used the epithet 'really' as in 'really dim' to indicate that even despite the labels, some children had problems. There can be an assumption in the discussion of labelling that as the label is imposed by teachers it can also be removed by teachers and thus the underlying 'problem' will also disappear. Clearly to refrain from labelling does not of itself eradicate the condition.

A solution to the problem of distinguishing between label and condition is indicated in the Report of the Committee of Enquiry into the Education of Handicapped Children and Young People (Warnock Report). The committee advocates abandoning the labels used to designate various 'handicapped' children and instead to use the general term 'children with special educational needs'. This is more than just a semantic change in that the proposed designation begs the question, 'What sort of special need?' Thus the Committee is making an attempt to overcome 'the assumption of homogeneity' (Apple, 1979, p. 145) by which all people given the same label are assumed to be the same, by requiring a precise definition of what the need is and how it might be met. The implication is that we avoid blanket phrases like 'John is stupid' and instead indicate precisely the problem which he faces. His 'stupidity' might have more to do with the way in which we teach and the organization of our schools than being some essential attribute of John which is apparent in all circumstances.

Conclusion

In our consideration of teachers and teaching we have again noted the interrelationships between the individual, social structure and the historical background to both. We began this chapter with the assertion that teaching was both an activity and a status. An appreciation of the status of teaching took us into a discussion of professions and the continuing struggle for autonomy which has characterized teaching. The occupation is full of paradox; freedom yet restraint, responsibility yet a proliferation of specialist teaching tasks such as counselling, which reduces the authority of the individual teacher. The belief that teachers have too much autonomy is apparent, for example, in calls for a 'teacher-proof' curriculum; that teachers have too little, in the struggle to establish a General Teachers' Council. The complexity of the currents moving through the profession casts doubt on any simple correspondence theory which sees teachers as mere agents of a dominant class reproducing the conditions of oppression. Rather, as Bernstein has argued (1977) teachers are a part of an 'interrupter class', engaged in the reproduction of cultural capital, transmitting forms of resistance as well as aspects of the master culture.

In our discussion of teaching as an activity we picked up the theme of individual and structural factors in looking at secondary socialization. It may well be that the dominant structural variable over the next decade will be a contracting pupil population resulting in the closure of some schools and a reduction in career mobility for teachers. A situational consequence may be that individual teachers will increase their 'side bets', seek personal satisfaction away from the school rather than in developments within teaching. Structural variables will thus have a negative influence on the commitment of teachers such as to affect the transmission of knowledge, the curriculum, within schools. In the next chapter we discuss the social organization of knowledge advocating the adoption of a 'relational model' of the curriculum which reflects individual, structural and historical variables.

Chapter 7

Social organization of knowledge

We have noted on several occasions that much sociology of education has used a 'black box' model of educational institutions thus failing to look at processes within schools and colleges. Of major importance, both to an appreciation of schools as organizations and in evaluating the nature of social reproduction, is an understanding of how knowledge is defined, transmitted and evaluated within educational institutions. This lacuna in sociology of education stems from the neglect of some of the leads which Durkheim and Weber provided almost a century ago.

In his lectures on the history of French education, Durkheim (1977) constantly related what was taught in schools to the political and moral climate of the age. He argued that the dialectics – instruction in logic – given in medieval universities served to create a body of knowledge whose end was the unambiguous proof of religious belief. Durkheim's thesis was that 'Educational transformations are always the result and the symptom of the social transformations in terms of which they are to be explained' (1977, p. 166). He therefore depicted the curricular changes in the sixteenth century, the Renaissance, as the consequence of economic changes in French society. The greater wealth of the society stimulated 'a taste for the easy, elegant life of luxury', the rise of the nation state and a spirit of independent enquiry could not be contained within the existing intellectual tradition of scholasticism. The result was a new curriculum designed to develop 'taste'; literature and not logic or dialectics, became the heart of the educational process. Durkheim comments, as we saw in the first chapter, that an undesirable consequence of the change from the old curriculum was that, 'Neither Erasmus nor Vives had any awareness that beyond this small world, which for all its brilliance was very limited, there were vast masses who should not have been neglected, and for whom education should have raised their intellectual and moral standards and

114

improved their material condition' (1979, p. 206). (Note: Vives and Erasmus were both philosophers having a considerable influence on early sixteenth-century educational thought; both were at the Catholic University of Louvain in Belgium, 1519-21.)

The importance of the curriculum in developing attitudes towards the world, in providing frameworks through which the world is interpreted, were also recognized by Weber. As we saw in Chapter 4, the Literati of Imperial China were schooled in a way of thinking based on classical literature which was judged to be more than an adequate preparation for government service and administration.

Both Weber and Durkheim saw the organization of knowledge within educational institutions responding to changing social structure. They recognized that the decision as to which knowledge should be transmitted in schools had no *a priori* validity but reflected the partial resolution of the conflict between different views of the world. This aspect of their work tended to be ignored by sociologists interested in education; basic texts written in the 1960s, like those of Banks and of Musgrave in the UK and of Brembeck in the USA, either ignored or only briefly mentioned the topic of knowledge. (Note that both Banks and Musgrave devote a chapter to the topic in later editions of their respective works.) The shift in perspective to the 'new' sociology of education in the late 1960s was marked by a return of interest in the social organization of knowledge. This move was parallel to the rise of the curriculum renewal movement within education, symbolized in England and Wales by the creation of the Schools Council in 1964. Although the publication of *Knowledge and Control* in 1971 is often seen as the start of contemporary sociological interest in the organization of knowledge, this ignores the work of sociologists working within a functionalist perspective such as Musgrove, Hoyle and Musgrave.

System theories

Musgrove (1968a) viewed the curriculum, 'first and foremost as an artificial device, a contrivance, in some sense an unnatural arrangement' (p. 100). The task of the sociologist was to explore 'the systematic social relationships on which this artificial contrivance depends'. Musgrove identified five tendencies within modern society which would influence the curriculum; these were, 'the declining demand for unskilled labour; the greater expectation of life; the rapid obsolescence of knowledge; the earlier physical (and perhaps emotional and intellectual) maturing of the young; and even less distinction between the roles of men and women' (1968b, p. 16). Whatever form the curriculum takes it will influence the socialization of both teachers and students. The curriculum is not just made up by a number of subjects each giving 'facts' about molecules and atoms, rulers and government, but also carries a hidden agenda which teaches the child, 'the kind of person he is' (1968b, p. 14). Musgrove holds to the view that the knowledge transmitted in educational institutions will influence the personality of the learner. However, this assertion does not show *how* knowledge and personality are linked or how the social structure influences the formation of individual identity. Trapped within a systems perspective, schools are seen adapting to societal needs and pupils internalizing a view of the world and themselves without either process being explicated and discussed. A list of the external factors of the school which may well impinge upon the curriculum is not of itself a theory of cultural transmission. One has not explained why the curriculum has taken the form that it has nor the implications this may have for the development of human consciousness; to explore these issues further we return to the work of Bernstein.

Bernstein and the organization of knowledge

We have already discussed Bernstein's socio-linguistic theories in Chapter 4. His work on the organization of knowledge is an extension of this earlier work and has been running parallel to the language theories since 1964. The essential problem that he addresses is common to both aspects of his work, namely the reproduction of the conditions through which social control is managed, how consciousness is structured by the pattern of class relationships in which the individual is located. As we have seen, this theme is explored in his socio-linguistic work through the pattern of socialization within the family. In his work on the organization of knowledge he states that, 'How a society selects, classifies, distributes, transmits and evaluates the educational knowledge it considers to be public, reflects both the distribution of power and the principles of social control' (1971, p. 202). In other words, educational transmission is part of the wider process of cultural transmission which, if ignored, trivializes the study of socialization.

Educational knowledge is a mould which has a major contribution to play in the structuring of our identity; part of our own account of ourselves as people is that which has been provided by the school. We see ourselves as someone who is 'good' at history, 'bad' at mathematics or without any 'ability' at art or music and so on. This concept of identity is realized through what Bernstein terms, 'three message systems' of curriculum, pedagogy and evaluation. These are the three dimensions to the process of educational transmission: what counts as valid knowledge, what counts as valid transmission and valid evaluation. The knowledge which is transmitted in schools, content, or the curriculum, is only a part of our available knowledge. Some knowledge is seen to be appropriate to schools, such as accounts of the reigns of various kings and queens, and other to be inappropriate, such as the analysis of the genealogy of race-horses. The mode of transmission of that knowledge – its form, pedagogy or mode of teaching – may also be valid, as in a conventional lecture, or invalid as in the use of behaviour therapy or techniques of 'brain-washing'. In Bernstein's model the third message system, evaluation, is dependent upon the other two; the style of evaluation is constrained by the content of the curriculum and the form of its transmission.

Turning first to the curriculum, or what counts as valid knowledge, its most immediate characteristic, Bernstein argues, is that there are boundaries around that knowledge. The content is grouped into units which reflects some underlying principle of organization. At the extremes, the grouping is marked by boundaries which are strong, the emphasis being on 'things that must be kept apart' which Bernstein labels *strong classification*; and at the other extreme, things that must be put together, there is a reduced boundary strength or *weak classification*. Strong classification is the hallmark of a school curriculum whose underpinning principles Bernstein calls a *collection code*, and weak classification is the hallmark of a curriculum whose underpinning principle is an *integrated code*. Neither the collection code (strong classification) nor the integrated code (weak classification) are as yet empirically demonstrable phenomena. One could not walk into an educational institution holding a 'Bernstein Inventory for School Curriculum, Evaluation and Transmission' or BISCET, and rapidly assess the boundary strengths implicit in its processes. Collection and integrated codes are theoretical constructs, conceptual tools created by Bernstein to gain some purchase on the nature of educational transmission.

As already stated, the essence of Bernstein's work is an exploration of the nature of the reproduction of conditions through which social control is managed; the strength of classification has, he argues, implications for the nature of this reproduction. Strong classification signals strong boundaries or separateness; the student studies mathematics, physics and chemistry as discrete subject areas with no attempt being made to interrelate one with the other. Consequently, socialization is into a subject loyalty, the labels 'physicist', 'sociologist', 'mathematician' carry assumptions on the part of the speaker about 'the sort of people who do sociology', etc. Lacey (1977) shows how students taking a one year initial teacher education course grouped themselves into subject sets. Their attitude towards educational issues in general and to the statements made by other students in discussion varied as to whether they were amongst their subject peers or in a multi-subject tutorial. Socialization into a subject identity reveals *difference from* rather than *community with*; we emphasize how different science is from humanities at the expense of demonstrating where their procedures and problems are similar.

The experience of many children, however, is one of having an inferior educational identity; not, 'I am a physicist', but an 'early leaver', a ROSLA child' or a 'non-examination' pupil. This indicates a lack of status which is reflected in the low status of the content transmitted as, for example, social studies, community studies, housecrafts and games. Thus the collection code carries as part of its message a measure of status. Bernstein is not entering a debate about the intrinsic merit of, for example, social studies as against physics, but rather pointing to a consequence of strong boundaries. Young (1971) has taken the point further and argued that high status knowledge will reflect principles of exclusion, as does any elite, and will be theoretical, stressing the remoteness from everyday things. There will also be a tendency for high-status knowledge to be taught to those who are identified as the most able.

There is, however, a logical flaw in Bernstein's argument. He begins with a definition of strong classification, then gives an example of this as in the traditional curriculum presented within an English grammar school. He then takes *other* aspects of that grammar school curriculum as if they were necessarily contingent upon strong classification. His assertion that 'Any collection code involves a hierarchical organization of knowledge, such that the ultimate mystery of the subject is revealed very late in the educational life' (1971, p. 213) reflects a prevailing *method* of teaching (framing in his model), the accumulation of facts at the expense of principles, rather than being a *necessary* dimension of strong classification. Thus one could, theoretically, have within a strongly classified curriculum an intellectual discourse which adumbrates the transient and changing nature of man's understanding of the physical world.

The existence of boundaries implies the existence of boundary maintainers, those who define what is to count as the legitimate activity within the field. As these boundary maintainers have been socialized into the world view of their subject, they are likely to resist changes in the strengths of classification as a threat to themselves. The movement towards general science in schools in immediate post-war England was resisted by physicists and chemists who saw in the move a threat to their professional identities. One can be a chemist, but what is a general scientist, or in more recent times an integrated scientist? The point is important and worth empirical exploration in the context of the problems of implementing curriculum innovation. A major problem in curriculum change is to socialize teachers into an acceptance of a new identity, to reiterate Waller, 'it is the being something different that matters' (see Chapter 5 above).

The polar extreme of strong classification is weak classification, or a curriculum which embodies the integrated code, the principle that things must be put together. For Bernstein, integration requires the subordination of previously insulated subjects to some relational idea which blurs the boundaries between subjects and which acts collectively on what is to count as knowledge. What is taught, the content, is no longer pre-defined but dependent on this relational idea, an umbrella concept, which links the discrete subject areas. For example, one such concept which might be chosen by science staff is that of *movement*. The integrated science for this unit requires that the physicists, chemists and biologists explore 'movement' in each of their subject areas. In making this exploration there are no longer any tightly prescribed limits to where such a journey might lead, in consequence the pupils are more able to suggest possibilities. They are able to push their own work into new areas and may be felt to threaten the professional competence of the teachers. Within the curriculum based on the integrated code, therefore, there is a shift in the power relationship between teacher and taught such that more of each is likely to enter the pedagogical relationship. We will return to look at some of the implications of this shift in power when we examine Bernstein's second message system, that of pedagogy.

As the content is more open to negotiation so, Bernstein argues, will there also be a shift in emphasis away from the surface to the deep structure of knowledge. In a science syllabus which reflects the collection code, where knowledge is taken-for-granted, a topic like 'movement' may appear on many occasions, in discussion of gravity, propulsion or capillarity. Each instance is the surface manifestation of a deeper phenomena of the cause and the nature of scientific movement. Under the integrated code these principles become the essence of the enquiry, it is these which are illustrated in different forms in physical, chemical and biological movement, and it is the principles of movement which selects out of physics, chemistry and biology that which is relevant to the enquiry being made.

Interrelated with curriculum is the form of its transmission, pedagogy or mode of teaching. As the basic principles of curriculum are realized through classification, so that of pedagogy is realized through *framing*, an altogether more ambiguous concept. Bernstein defines it as 'the degree of control teacher and pupil possess over the selection, organization, pacing and timing of the knowledge transmitted and received in the pedagogical relationship' (1971, p. 206). His discussion of this concept is described in a more recent paper, 'Class and

Pedagogies: Visible and Invisible' (1975), in which he suggests three factors which regulate the teacher-pupil relationship. These are the factors of hierarchy, sequencing rules and criteria, each having an explicit and implicit dimension. Hierarchy refers to the power within the relationship, either unambiguously explicit as in 'I am in control because I am the teacher', or implicitly where there are no *overt* rules. The stress on 'overt' is crucial – the paradox of implicit hierarchies is that although on the surface there may appear to be no rules nevertheless rules exist. In the infant classroom the teacher may invite the children to 'do your own thing', to take responsibility for their own learning. The children quickly come to appreciate, however, that 'doing your own thing' does not include setting fire to the Wendy House or throwing sand across the classroom! Under the apparent freedom there is control and the child must learn the markers to that control.

The second aspect to the teacher-pupil relationship is the sequencing rules which regulate the order in which transmission takes place. If the rules are explicit, there is a clear recognition of what is appropriate to the child at any particular stage. Every teacher has experienced, for example, going into a noisy classroom and saying, 'What class is this?' and, on being told a fourth-year class, responding, 'I thought it was the first year, the amount of noise you were making.' There is appropriate behaviour at appropriate stages; if the rules are implicit, 'the sex and chronological age of the child do not become strong marking features of the sequencing rules'. In this case only the teacher will be aware of what is appropriate, picking up cues from the child's behaviour as to his reading readiness or developmental stage.

Finally the transmission realizes criteria of accomplishment which also may be explicit or implicit. If explicit the teacher on asking, for example, the child to draw a house will criticize the production if it does not have windows, or if the windows are in the 'wrong' place. If the criteria of accomplishment are implicit, the child is invited to 'Tell me all about your painting'. The criteria are apparently the child's. However the paradox reappears when at the end of the lesson not every picture is put on the wall for all to see; or if we had given the example of a piece of written work, not every piece is typed-up and placed in the class story book. Under the openness of the relationship there are criteria, there is control though its nature changes. Where the hierarchy, sequencing rules and criteria are *explicit* Bernstein labels the form of transmission one of *visible pedagogy*; where they are *implicit* he labels the form of transmission one of *invisible pedagogy*.

We have seen that Bernstein argues that under an integrated code, more of the pupil and teacher enter the pedagogical relationship. This can now be expanded by linking to his discussion of visible and invisible pedagogies. As the strength of classification weakens, so what counts as knowledge becomes more open to negotiation, the child may bring more of his world into the classroom. But in doing so he introduces more of himself as a unique person. Within a visible pedagogy (that is strong framing and strong classification) the teacher need not know her pupils as people; symbolically she enters the classroom through one door and the pupils through another and the two need never meet. This type of relationship is epitomized by the mass lecture in higher education – the personal biography of both lecturer and student is not relevant to the occasion. Within an invisible pedagogy, (weak framing and weak classification), the teacher knows more about the child as a person and must also reveal more of herself, if only to admit ignorance in answer to a pupil's question. But as more of the pupil is available so less of his unique self is protected from the school's influences, hence the paradox that although the invisible pedagogy appears to be the open, liberal pedagogy, it is also more pervasive in its control, the child begins to internalize the requirements of the classroom.

Bernstein is talking about the curriculum at a high level of theoretical abstraction, necessarily so if we are to begin to understand the place of education in the process of social reproduction. The curriculum is not a neutral package of knowledge which responds to the natural demands of the wider society. It is a vehicle both for increasing the child's knowledge of the world but also for moulding her stance towards that world, as Wylie puts it, 'From the attitude of teachers, from the way in which school work is presented, from the textbooks, the children learn to make basic assumptions concerning the nature of reality and their relationship to it' (1973, p. 73).

Bernstein has begun an exploration of how children might come to make basic assumptions about the nature of reality; the strength of his model lies in bringing together content and form, curriculum and transmission, and linking both to the process of social reproduction within society. Its weakness is that some of the links in the argument are ambiguous and await further development. For example, in Bernstein's analysis of the invisible pedagogy lies the problem noted in Chapter 5 when discussing Sharp and Green's work, that is, the practical difficulty of operating within an invisible pedagogy. As Bernstein argues, the invisible pedagogy is expensive in terms of human, physical and time resources. Thus it would appear that even despite its alleged greater potential for effective social control it is rarely found within educational institutions. Bernstein does recognize the inter-relationship between content and form such that attempts to reduce classification strength will also influence framing; the failure to appreciate this inter-relationship has been an important factor in the failure of attempts to change the curriculum over present decades.

Models of the curriculum

Probably the most distinctive aspect of the 1960s in education was the rise of the curriculum renewal movement across the world. There are several factors which stimulated this renewed interest in the curriculum. In England, the Reports of the Central Advisory Council (Crowther, 1959; Newsom, 1963) pointed to the irrelevance of much of the extant curriculum to the perceived needs of the latter part of the twentieth century. On 4 October 1957 the Russians launched 'Sputnik', an event which became a symbol to those in America and England who advocated the reform of the science curriculum. If the Russians had gone into space first, surely, the argument went, this indicated a lack of effectiveness in the way in which science and mathematics was being taught. Reform was essential. Also many countries became independent of colonial rule and anxious to establish a curriculum in schools which reflected their national identity rather than the interests of the former colonial power.

In both the developed and in the developing world educationalists were addressing the same problem: the reconstruction of the school curriculum. Over twenty years after 'Sputnik' it is easy to form the impression that the hopes of the curriculum planners have not been realized. The overwhelming fact is not how much schools have changed, but how similar they are to those of the pre-'Sputnik' or to the colonial era. In 1973 SAFARI (the acronym stands for Success and Failure and Recent Innovation) was launched at the University of East Anglia in an attempt to chart what had happened to four curriculum projects in England. Evaluations of curriculum innovation projects, like Shipman (1974), illustrated that the practice of the new curriculum was often very different from, and often contradictory to, the intentions of the original developers. In the developing world, Ibrahim Saad (1976) reached the conclusion that 'most of the curriculum changes have been ameliorative, thus the core of the curriculum is still based on former colonial models', a judgment which led some at least to propose that 'Implementational measures of new curricula need to be improved to avoid sabotaging by teachers' (Fatimah, 1977, p. 47). If only technologists could invent a teacher-proof curriculum then innovation could be assured and the school curriculum regenerated.

Rationalist models of the curriculum

The perspective which has dominated curriculum innovation is the same as that which we saw dominating research in classrooms in Chapter 5, that of *rationalism* or behaviourism; what Reid (1978) calls 'rational managerial'. Eggleston (1977, p. 53) writes:

In its fundamentals the perspective is *received* by the teacher and by his pupils as part of the given order. Associated with it in the school are established standards, norms of behaviour, rituals and hierarchical social divisions. Beyond the school it is part of an established social order in which the nature and distribution not only of knowledge but also of power is seen to be given and, for the most part, unchanging.

It is the *factory model* of education which Apple (1979) sees supporting 'the widespread interests in technical control of human activity, in rationalizing, manipulating and bureaucratizing individual action, and, in eliminating personal style and political diversity' (p. 128). Cooper's (1971) comment on the quality of the information received by the US government from Vietnam in the 1960s could equally apply to the 'received perspective', 'It was all very quantitative, very scientific, and very misleading' (p. 202).

The roots of this perspective may be traced back to the late nineteenth century to what Shroyer (1970) has called 'scientism'. Scientism is an ideology in which, 'spheres of decision-making are constructed as "technical problems" requiring information and instrumental strategies produced by technical experts' (p. 212). An ideology which assumes that knowledge is neutral, thus neglecting what ought to be the prior question of whose interest knowledge serves. In the study of the curriculum this 'scientism' is represented in the work of E. L. Thorndike (1874-1949) who in Franklin's assessment, 'more than any other individual . . . was responsible for the behaviouristic psychological perspective that has dominated the curriculum field since its formative years' (1976b, p. 298). The ideology of 'scientism' was also basic to the concept of 'scientific management' as developed by F. W. Taylor (1856-1915).

Callahan (1962) has traced in detail the influence of Taylor's theory of scientific management on educational ideas and planning. In essence, Taylor argued that there was always a best method of doing any job, a method which could be determined through scientific study. Given that management wants to maximize output in the industrial setting, then, by rationally analysing the tasks needed and specifying what each worker should do, the optimum working conditions could be created. Taylor's ideas were adapted to education by J. F. Bobbitt (1876-1956), Professor of Education at the University of Chicago from 1918 until 1941. In his 'The Elimination of Waste in Education' published in 1912, Bobbitt rehearsed the principles of scientific management and advocated their use in school planning. In a more extended study published in 1924, *How to Make a Curriculum*, Bobbitt reduced the goals of education to 180 objectives, one of which was the 'ability to make one's sleep contribute in maximum measure to the development and maintenance of a high level of physical vitality' (quoted in Eisner, 1967, p. 34). It was possible to construct the curriculum in accordance with 'scientific principles': analyse what society needs (objectives), specify the content which will achieve these objectives, determine the method by which the content will be transmitted and, finally, draw up a quality control chart (evaluation) to assess the extent to which the objectives have been met.

One of Bobbitt's students, R. W. Tyler argued (1949) that in designing a curriculum four questions must be answered; what educational purposes should the school seek to attain? What educational experiences can be provided that are likely to attain these purposes? How can these educational experiences be effectively organized? How can we determine whether these purposes are being attained? The causal chain is Bobbitt's: objectives, content, method, evaluation, an efficient way of turning raw children into educated products honed to serve the needs of society. With Tyler's help, Bloom *et al.* (1956) produced a handbook which listed the educational objectives which could be attained in schools. Curriculum design was now a science, the blueprint had been provided, all that was required was the rational planning of the curriculum of each school in order to fit the grand, scientifically determined, design.

The rationalist school - the 'received perspective' in Eggleston's terminology - did not pass unchallenged, and by the mid-1970s it was becoming clear that the precision with which objectives and tasks had been formulated had a less than precise relationship to the actual implementation of curriculum innovation. However many of the early Schools Council projects in England had adopted the rationalist approach to curriculum renewal, the attraction of the approach being, in Inglis's words, that, 'It appeals to a model of reason whose terms derive from the coarse utilitarianism developed for the administration of social welfare in a mass competitive and consumer society' (1974, p. 3). Typically, a team of experts was gathered together at a university - the symbol of legitimate knowledge - where a package of curriculum material was assembled, tried in schools, reassembled and finally released onto the market. This *centre-periphery* model of curriculum development failed because of the lack of understanding of how schools receive and implement innovation. Further, as Gleeson has commented, 'Such a hierarchical conception of "development" not only assumes a split between "experts" and classroom teachers, but also implies a clear ascendancy of curriculum "theory" over school "practice"' (1979, p. 195).

Under the guise of scientific neutrality, Bobbitt failed to realize that implicit in every curriculum are values as to what is considered appropriate. The questions of who is to decide what the needs of society are, or how one would determine the worth of one objective as against another, remain underdeveloped in the work of Bobbitt, Tyler and Bloom. The extant curriculum is not the neutral sample of human knowledge to be transmitted in schools, but the product of a long process of political decision reflecting the distribution of power within society. As Reid has it, 'The question of how decisions on the curriculum *can* be reached is just as central to curriculum research as the question of what *can* be taught' (1978, p. 31, his emphasis). Second, the very existence of objectives as goals to be attained is a misleading model within education; to be educated means to travel rather than to arrive at some 'educated destination'. No one is ever a completely educated individual, we can continue to explore our world and our relationships with it so that it is inappropriate to conceptualize a 'finished' product. Third, the very existence of objectives precludes the openness of much educational enquiry which is an exploration of 'what will happen if'. Many students only write the introduction to their essay when it is completed, for only then are they able to say where they intended to go in the essay. Finally, there is no evidence to show that teachers in school actually plan their work in terms of pre-specified objectives. All teachers will have some long-term aims, be these the desire that children will enjoy literature, develop a critical awareness of scientific methods or reach an appreciation of their historical and geographical location. These long-term aims become the guiding principles which teachers use to select the activities of each day. What is covered in a lesson is also determined by the mood of the class, the enthusiasm of the teacher on that day, and is governed by the constantly changing pattern of interaction within the class. Actual curriculum, that which is taught in each lesson, is not the mechanical following of the pre-defined path to pre-specified objectives.

The rationalist model of the curriculum has been dominant in both developed and developing countries, attractive because of its neat logic, its seeming objectivity and its correspondence with an 'efficiency' conception of education. But in Kliebard's judgment, 'The bureaucratic model, along with its behaviouristic and technological refinements, threatens to destroy, in the name of efficiency, the satisfaction that one may find in intellectual activity' (1971, p. 91).

Reflexive models of the curriculum

An alternative perspective on the curriculum is that which Eggleston labels 'reflexive', Apple 'the socialization approach' and Reid 'the humanistic'. This perspective, which like the rationalist model is also part of a long intellectual tradition, 'is one in which curriculum know-ledge . . . is seen to be negotiable. . . . Essentially it is dialectic and manifestly subject to political and other influences; a construction of those who participate in its determination' (Eggleston, 1977, p. 52). It is allied to what we have called the interpretive perspective and draws much of its inspiration from the sociology of knowledge.

The term *sociology of knowledge* is generally attributed to the German philosopher Max Scheler and refers to the relationship between thought and the social context in which that thinking takes place. For Marx and Engels, 'The ideas of the ruling class are in every epoch the ruling ideas. . . . The class which has the means of material production at its disposal, has control at the same time over the means of mental production' (1970 edn, p. 64). In this view there is a danger of being unable to see any reality other than that which serves the interests of the ruling group, as the very concepts by which we make sense of the world are the creation of the dominant class. Mannheim is saying some-thing similar when he writes, 'Strictly speaking it is incorrect to say that the single individual thinks. Rather it is more correct to insist that he participates in thinking further what other men have thought before him' (1936, p. 3). What counts as knowledge is always knowledge from a particular point of view (though Mannheim excluded mathematics and science from his discussion), thus what counts as school knowledge reflects the interests of particular groups within society.

The power to define what counts as knowledge is for Young (1971) a discussion about the status of knowledge. That is knowledge is high-status, like mathematics and pure science, or low-status such as PE or technology. There are two contingent features to Young's notion of the stratification of knowledge; the first is that changes in the curricu-lum will tend to be resisted in high-status areas as endangering the 'sacred', such as the prolonged struggle to change the 'A' level examina-tion in England and Wales or the preponderance of innovative curricula in low-status areas. Second, Young argues, pupils will also tend to accept the prevailing definition of knowledge and will resist change which is seen to be a change in status, such as the movement from geography to humanities, or Afro-Caribbean children taking 'Black studies'.

In his discussion of the curriculum, Young is talking about actual knowledge-in-use: the conventions, prejudice, traditions and practice of the knowledge which is negotiated and presented in school classrooms. For Young, this knowledge-in-use is socially constructed; it is the result of human decision, the reflection of class interests and the ability to mobilize resources to support claims for time within the formal curricu-lum of the school. These issues are separate from a discussion about the *status* of knowledge itself, a discussion of the final truth claims of dis-tinct areas of knowledge or a discussion of epistemology.

It would be possible to agree with Hirst (1974) that there are logically distinct ways of knowing about the world which are independent of our own relative stance and also agree with Young that the curriculum *as taught* is a social construct. What is sometimes seen as a debate between sociologists and philosophers about knowledge and the curriculum is in fact another version of the is-ought dilemma. Establishing what *is* the status of knowledge, or presenting an *a priori* division of knowledge into different forms does not, of itself, prescribe what *ought* to be included within the school curriculum. Thus, for example, Hirst sees religion as a distinct form of knowledge; whether one agrees or not with his assertion does not provide sufficient grounds for the inclusion, or exclusion, of religion in the curriculum as taught in school. Young's position is close to that of Berger and Luckmann (1967), who argue that the sociology of knowledge ought not to concern itself with the ultimate status of knowledge but 'with everything that passes for "knowledge" in society'.

In exploring what passes for 'knowledge' in the school, Young (1977) makes the distinction between 'curriculum-as-fact' and 'curriculum-as-practice'. The former sees the school transmitting a body of facts, it 'presents education as a thing, hiding the social relations between human beings who collectively produce it' (p. 242); the latter, 'how men collectively attempt to order their world and in the process produce knowledge' (*ibid.*). The difference between the two is not one of epistemology but of power: curriculum-as-facts presents the learner without power in the learning exchange, he must memorize what others present to him, in contrast to curriculum-as-practice where he begins to search for answers to his own questions in collaboration with teachers. Young is careful to point out that the weakness of the latter view is that 'Teachers are . . . given a kind of spurious autonomy and independence from the wider contexts of which their activity is a part, and thus have no way of understanding their own failures except in terms of personal inadequacy' (p. 234).

Curriculum-as-fact is ultimately a curriculum of control as knowledge is presented as an independent, imperious entity, beyond the range of human influence; on the other hand curriculum-as-practice can delude by giving an appearance of responding to human intention yet masking the reality of political power. For Young, as well as for Whitty (1977), both perspectives need to be transcended by a critical theory based on a political commitment to social change which incorporates control of the curriculum. Such a theory remains to be fully elaborated and explored. In the meantime, Vulliamy cautions against a rejection of the reflexive, curriculum-as-practice model, and demonstrates that, in the case of music, 'prevailing conceptions of educational knowledge play a significant role in maintaining traditional patterns of educational success and failure' (1978).

Relational models of the curriculum

So far we have identified two major perpsectives on the curriculum. The first we labelled rationalist and was linked with behaviourism and organizational theories such as scientific management. It was criticized for its passive, dehumanized view of the individual and for maintaining a conservative view of knowledge. The second, reflexive or interpretive, view of the curriculum, was criticized for being too relativistic and for maintaining a naive view on the possibility of teachers being able to change the prevailing definition of knowledge within educational institutions. There is a third view which attempts to relate what is taught in school to the socio-political context of the time; this view has been labelled 'the restructuring' perspective by Eggleston, the 'relational model' by Apple, and is the product of what Reid has called 'practical reasoning' in the curriculum.

The central feature of the *relational* model is the attempt to link what is taught in school to the social structure; to ask of the educational knowledge transmitted in school, 'Why is *this* taught? And why is it taught in *this* way? And to *this* group?' (Shaw, 1973, p. 285, emphasis his). Or, as Apple puts it, 'To begin to grapple with the ways of understanding how the kinds of cultural resources and symbols schools select and organize are dialectically related to the kinds of normative and conceptual consciousness "required" by a stratified society' (1979, p. 2). The relational model takes us back to what Bernsetin is attempting to do (as discussed at the start of this chapter), an exploration of social control recognizing that schools process knowledge as well as people. That is, embedded within the differentiation of pupils into different teaching groups, usually on the basis of ability, is a set of assumptions about what knowledge is deemed to be appropriate to those different groups. The challenge is, to quote Apple again, to explicate, 'the *interplay* between curricular knowledge – the stuff we teach, the "legitimate culture" – and the social relations of classroom life' (1979, p. 40). Work on articulating the nature of this 'interplay' has scarcely begun; for Wexler (1976) the most fruitful direction lies in combining work in the tradition of Bourdieu (see Chapters 2 and 11) and the ethnographic work on the 'meanings and rules which comprise the cognitive routines of everyday classroom life' (p. 53).

An important dimension of the relational model of the curriculum is the recognition that what counts as knowledge in school grows from a particular historical background. This is seen in the work of Layton (1973) on the emergent science curriculum in nineteenth-century England, Davie (1961) on the mathematics curriculum at Edinburgh University, and Johnson (1976) and McCann (1977) on the way in which the nineteenth-century elementary school was used as a vehicle for social control. This is illustrated by McCann through a quotation from a sermon by the Rev. D. Wilson in March 1819: 'In every country, but especially in this free state, the mass of your Poor, like the base of the cone, if it be unsteady and insecure, will quickly endanger every superincumbent part. Religious education, then, is the spring of public tranquillity' (quoted in McCann, 1977, p. 1). Each of these authors demonstrates that the actual curriculum, that which was taught in school, had little to do with any *a priori* view of knowledge, but was the product of a struggle, at times acrimonious, to legitimate a particular view of the world as the established, 'natural', curriculum. Davie shows how the victor in the struggle, to consolidate a position, must rewrite the textbooks, legitimating a particular stance towards the world.

Those working within the relational model of the curriculum go beyond the rationalist theorists to incorporate an active theory of the individual (see Chapter 3), drawing from the phenomenological work of Schutz and of Cicourel. Relational theorists also extend reflexive theorists in recognizing the pervasiveness of social structure; in this the dominant influence has sprung from the work of Marx. Though, as O'Keeffe (1977) notes, 'little has been done to elicit determinate relationships between curricular forms and socio-economic structures' (p. 101). He suggests that such relationships are either assumed to exist or the determinants of the curriculum are not given extended analysis. O'Keeffe proposes that the curriculum be viewed both as an *investment* good, as for example, in the provision of courses to provide skilled manpower or human capital, and also as a *consumption* good ministering to human preferences such as the demand for courses in sociology in the early 1970s. He argues that consumption has been ignored by both traditional and by Marxist writers such as Althusser or Bowles and Gintis, 'where an exclusively investment stance is adopted' and 'education in a capitalist society is seen as providing the skills and social docility necessary for the reproduction of the social relations of production' (p. 102). In short, there is also a strong consumption element at work in influencing the curriculum which will not easily be reduced to the 'charge of bourgeois manipulation'.

Hidden curriculum

An important component in relational models of the curriculum is the notion of the hidden curriculum. The idea of a hidden curriculum is contained in Parsons's discussion of the school class as a social system. Parsons uses the label 'moral component of the curriculum' to refer to pupils learning such things 'as respect for the teacher, consideration and co-operativeness in relation to fellow-pupils and good "work-habits" ' (1961, p. 440). The term 'hidden curriculum' was coined by Jackson to refer to the lessons which pupils learn from being part of a crowd, thus learning to bear with equanimity, 'the continued delay, denial, and interruption of their personal wishes and desires' (1968, p. 18). For Dale (1977) the basic function of schooling is the reproduction of the social relations of production, a function which he sees being achieved predominantly through the hidden curriculum, 'Of central importance in the hidden curriculum is the authority structure of schooling. Specifically, the hierarchical nature of both the structure and the process of schooling carries lessons of subordinacy and hierarchy which are essential to the potential worker in an industry or a bureaucracy' (1977, p. 46). For Dale, it is the *form* of schooling, the messages transmitted as a result of its organization and practices, which is more powerful than the *content*, or the overt curriculum, in maintaining the established order; and the essence of the form of schooling is contained within the hidden curriculum.

Apple picks up a theme which we have identified in the work of McCann when he argues, 'We should be aware that, historically, the hidden curriculum was *not* hidden at all, but was instead the overt function of schools during much of their careers as institutions' (1979, p. 49, his emphasis). There is little 'hidden' in the Rev. Wilson's claim that religious education was 'the spring of public tranquillity'. In the nineteenth century the control aspect of education was much more apparent, the prevailing 'visible pedagogy' rendering explicit the relations of power and hierarchy. Eggleston observes that, 'The hidden curriculum is only hidden, if at all, to the teacher; it is clearly visible to the students' (1977, p. 18). He goes on to suggest that 'It identifies the students with "their place" in the social system, brings them into compliance with its norms and values and with the structures and the sanctions with which they are imposed' (1977, p. 117). It is through the effects of both the hidden and the overt curriculum that we can begin to see the salience of Musgrove's comment to which we referred at the start of this chapter, 'The curriculum teaches a pupil the kind of person he is, it shapes his conception of himself' (1968b, p. 14).

The process of curriculum change

We can now begin to link together threads which have appeared in this and the last two chapters. Schools are places where children are socialized into adult identities, though this is not a mechanistic process whereby children are perfectly moulded to the requirements of society. Children are active participants in their own socialization, they take different messages from the school and respond in different ways to the same message. In our discussion of the curriculum, we have shown that the processing of knowledge is an important component in the school's influence, it works alongside the labelling process which we discussed in the last chapter and the structure of classroom learning in providing the framework within which children develop. Any strategy for curriculum change must begin with a recognition of what has been labelled in this chapter as the relational curriculum (after Apple); curriculum change begins with teachers and children in specific educational contexts, and requires an understanding of 'the intricate relations between biography, social interaction and social structure' (Eggleston and Gleeson, 1977, p. 25).

An example of a study which is moving towards the adoption of a relational model of curriculum change is that by Hamilton (1973, 1975, 1977) on the implementation of the Scottish Integrated Science Project. Hamilton makes the point that, 'Every school has a distinctive network of institutional and social variables that interact in complicated ways and influence much of what takes place there' (1975, p. 205). He shows, as does Shipman (1974) for the Keele Integrated Studies Project, that no matter how 'teacher-proof' the curriculum, in its implementation in Simpson and Maxwell schools it is changed in many and often unexpected ways.

In Simpson school, where the innovation was assimilated and then redefined in terms of what Hamilton identifies as the dominant collection code within the school. The worksheets, for example, intended as support material to the Project became the syllabus for science teaching. Such were the organizational problems of the school that ten teachers taught science to the first year where four full-time teachers would have been sufficient. Some classes had more than one science teacher so that communication between teachers became crucial to effective work. There was a lack of apparatus and laboratory accommodation and teachers commuting from the upper school had no opportunity to develop the additional material recommended by the designers of the Integrated Science Project. In short the structural conditions within which the project was launched at Simpson school was both inimical and antipathetic to the objectives of the planners.

Maxwell school, on the other hand, was a new, purpose-built comprehensive, though, like Simpson, there were organizational problems which militated against the Project. The science department in the school was organized into teams of subject specialists – physics, chemistry and biology – with the Head of each team taking a turn each term to act as Head of Science. The structure of the department, therefore, was one that supported a collection code and undermined attempts to achieve integration. Hamilton makes the judgment that at Maxwell the teaching of integrated science became too organized; topics to be covered by each class were tightly scheduled in an attempt to keep the whole year at the same stage and able to take the same assessment examination at the same time. Though each class had the same time for science, five periods per week, the distribution of that time was different. Some classes had an uninterrupted double and an uninterrupted triple lesson for science, others had a double lesson with the mid-morning break in the middle, yet other classes had two double periods for science followed by a single period. The management of time is a constraint on how the teacher is able to cover the material prescribed by the Project team. Hamilton concludes that at Maxwell the innovation had taken, albeit precariously, but in a context where there were pressures to return to the more traditional curriculum. It was difficult to maintain the innovation when organizational arrangements reflected a different, and contrasting, style of curriculum, pedagogy and evaluation.

Conclusion

The value of Hamilton's work is that it describes what happened when an innovation in the curriculum was introduced to particular schools. The future for research on the curriculum would seem to lie in the accumulation of evidence from such case studies, which have attempted to identify the constraints and possibilities for change. We know that there is no 'blue-print' for change; we know that individual teachers are constrained by the organization in which they work, the expectations of their pupils, and the pressures of other legitimate claims on the time available within school, as well as the limits to their own energy and enthusiasm. We also know that many teachers are successful in implementing change, in providing a curriculum which excites the intelligence of their pupils, develops their powers of judgment and evaluation while increasing their skills. We are less certain of how that curriculum was initiated, introduced and sustained, how constraints were overcome and resources mobilized to achieve success. The thesis of this chapter has been that our understanding of curriculum change will be best advanced through the adoption of a relational model. Such a model carries the recognition that knowledge is only one component alongside classroom interaction and teacher characteristics all of which come together as part of an analysis of the school as an organization, an analysis to which we turn in the following chapter.

Chapter 8

Schools as organizations

In the last three chapters we examined different aspects of the school: its classrooms, teachers and the knowledge that is transmitted. We now put these together, stand back a little, and consider the school as an organization. As usual in sociology, the title to the topic is deceptively simple; what is meant by an organization? Etzioni (1964) defined organizations as 'social units (or human groupings) deliberately constructed and reconstructed to seek specific goals' (p. 3). Schools have been 'deliberately created' in that at some point a decision was made to establish a school to facilitate the teaching of a range of subjects as diverse as the Koran to Trade Union Legislation. Schools are also reconstructed, in that each day people relate to one another in the context of the school; some teach, others struggle to learn, yet others clean, serve food or administer the school's various activities. The goals, however, are more complex than Etzioni's definition suggests. Goals may vary from those of Shakespeare's 'whining school-boy . . . creeping like snail unwillingly to school', whose goal may be to pass the time as quickly and painlessly as possible, through those whose goal is the desire to instil a love of learning, to those who want the opportunity to make a little 'pin-money'. Each member of the organization will want different things from his involvement, many of these goals being far removed from the purposes behind the deliberate construction to found the school. As Davies has it, 'Within any given institution, the only thing we may be sure about in advance of investigation is that what different individuals and groups of individuals are working towards will be partly common but often different' (1973, p. 256).

Schools are an example of a *formal* organization, and in 1958, Parsons wrote, 'An immense amount of work will be required before we can have anything that deserves to be called a theory of formal organization.' Bidwell (1965) and Davies (1973) have reiterated Parsons's comment in relation to education; Davies judges that, 'While schools are familiar objects to us all, and colleges to many, our ability to explain and generalize about how they work in any degree of depth is still severely limited by the shortcomings of organizational analysis itself and by the paucity of worthwhile empirical studies within education' (1973, p. 249). The continued lack of any coherent, generally accepted theory of the school as an organization is probably indicative of a sociological chimera. The complexity of educational institutions is such that no general theory could represent the nuance and idiosyncracies of unique institutions without sounding banal and trivial. What has been developed are different ways of looking at the school, perspectives which illuminate some aspects and obscure others. As we shall see, the best are built around case studies, discussions of specific institutions through which an attempt is made to relate biography and structure to a historical context.

Weber and bureaucracy

A claim could be made that much of the work in the sociology of organization has been a debate with Weber and his theory of bureaucratization. In Chapter 1, we saw that Weber made a distinction between 'power' and 'authority', and that the latter could be legitimated in terms of a belief in either tradition or the charismatic appeal of some 'outstanding' person or in the legal/rational procedures which prescribe the rights and obligations of members of society. The bureaucracy is the embodiment of this legal/rational authority. The benefits of bureaucracy lie in the increased efficiency and justice which may develop, though there is always the danger of what Marx referred to as 'the sordid materialism of bureaucracy', that is, the tendency within the bureaucracy for it to become an end in itself. Bureaucracy is the master rather than the servant, such that instead of enjoying the benefits of increased efficiency we become trapped in bureaucratic procedures as satirized, for example, by Joseph Heller in *Catch 22*.

Weber identified six principles of bureaucracy:

1 Fixed rules and procedures through which the bureaucrat completes his task.
2 Hierarchy of offices with an associated structure of command.
3 Files which document the action taken.
4 Specialized training for the various functions within the bureaucracy.
5 An identifiable career structure.
6 Impersonal methods of dealing with both employers and clients within the bureaucracy.

Probably the civil service in any country has the closest fit to Weber's ideal type. Bidwell (1965) argues that schools are characterized by a 'structural looseness' which tends to mitigate the pressures towards bureaucratization. By structural looseness, Bidwell means the tension within schools between the autonomy of the teacher and the requirement to meet the universal needs of the students. Each teacher has considerable freedom over *how* she teaches within her own classroom; nevertheless, the content of what is taught is laid down by a syllabus, be that the construction of members of the school staff or the requirements of an examination board. Teachers also have some latitude in how they respond to the individual within a class yet ultimately must use universal criteria in any public assessment of the individual's performance. There is also a structural looseness in the way in which the school is articulated to the rest of the educational system. Head teachers have some freedom and a deal of responsibility for what happens within their schools, yet the evaluation of what happens is subject to the opinions of parents and local politicians and is also circumscribed by the rules and regulations of the Education Department.

Elements of Weber's ideal type can be seen in most schools. There is a hierarchy of offices supervised by, and stemming from, that of head teacher, though in many large schools the role of the head is diffused through a small executive committee of senior staff. Files are kept on student progress and, as we saw in Chapter 6, there is the danger that students 'become' the file; their identity is the description contained within the files. There is specialized training which in secondary schools tends to be along subject divisions and one could argue that primary school teachers, though not specialized in the sense of secondary specialists, are nevertheless specialists within the educational system. There are career lines within schools, albeit rather squat, as teachers becomes heads of years/houses or heads of departments, then deputy heads and finally head teachers.

The school has some bureaucratic tendencies though there is a 'structural looseness' which reduces the appropriateness of Weber's concept. The greatest problem, however, lies in fitting the children, the students, into the Weberian model. Students are an essential part of every school yet individual students probably spend less time, fewer years, in the school than individual teachers. As an organization, the school is continually faced with the task of socializing new recruits, often with little choice over who those recruits will be. The need to incorporate recruits will also tend to detract from the formation of a tight bureaucracy. Schools need to continually adapt to their clients if they are to accommodate their idiosyncracies, whims and different needs. An organization cemented into 'correct' rules and procedures of bureaucracy would be less flexible to the needs of clients than a more open, less bureaucratic, structure.

Management approaches to organization

In Chapter 7, we saw how a rationalist model came to dominate curriculum theory, the origins of this perspective being assumptions about the nature of science prevalent in the nineteenth century. Miller (1973) shows how the concept of school organization was related to another nineteenth-century invention, the factory. The prime concern behind the establishment of schools was that it be done cheaply and with maximum efficiency – hence the popularity of the monitorial system of Joseph Lancaster and Andrew Bell. The former was able to report in 1803 that, 'due to his reorganization of the system and the introduction of new methods of tuition in spelling and arithmetic, "proficiency" in these areas had been "more than doubled" with "individual scholars spelling 20,000 words and working 2,000 sums . . . per annum; whereas, the same space of time, in the common modes of tuition, would have been . . . irretrievably lost in idleness' (quoted in Miller, 1973).

Like the factory, then, the monitorial system, whereby the 'master' taught the lesson to certain monitors, who in turn taught it to other children, was cheap, efficient and made considerable economies of time and labour. The form of the school organization dictated what was to count as education, the domination of 'facts'. This domination is reflected by Dickens through the words of Mr Gradgrind in *Hard Times*, 'Facts alone are wanted in life. Plant nothing else, and root out everything else.' The monitorial system did not allow that facts are conditional, that there are conflicting facts about the same event, or that circumstances may well alter facts; it only permitted the regurgitation of facts. Where one master supervised the activities of a thousand children it was inconceivable that individuals be allowed to discuss, let alone argue against, the facts being presented. The principle is clearly expressed by Bentham for his model school, Chrestomathia, where the primary objective was to attain 'the union of the maximum of despatch with the maximum of uniformity; thereby proportionably shortening the time, employed in the acquisition of the proposed body of instruction, and increasing the number of pupils, made to acquire it, by the same teachers, at the same time' (cited in Miller, 1973, p. 19).

Scientific management

In the USA, Frank Spaulding, superintendent of schools in Newton, Massachusetts, used the principles of *scientific management* in the organization of schools. Like the monitorial system, or the factory, scientific management was an attempt to obtain the most rational and efficient form of organization for the tasks it had to fulfil. Callahan

(1962, p. 68) summarizes the essentials of scientific management as:

1　The measurement and comparison of comparable results.
2　The analysis and comparison of the conditions under which given results are secured – especially the means and time employed in securing given results.
3　The consistent adoption and use of those means that justify themselves most fully by their results, abandoning those that fail so to justify themselves.

The implication is clear; there is a 'best' organizational form for schools which will maximize learning outcomes and at the same time minimize cost. Reminiscent of the claims of Joseph Lancaster, Spaulding calculated that, 'twelve pupil-recitations in science are equivalent in value to 19.2 pupil recitations in English and that it takes 41.7 pupil recitations in vocal music to equal the value of 13.9 pupil recitations in art' (quoted in Callahan, 1962, p. 73). Presumably if one wanted to increase the cost effectiveness of schools one concentrated resources on science and strongly discouraged 'vocal music'. This bizarre calculus would seem to have no relation to the educational grounds for an activity, but simply to reflect a dubious notion of efficiency.

In essence, scientific management claims that there is a best form of organization for each task and, despite its limitations and dehumanizing aspects, it continues to be used. Perrow (1970) argues that most of the criticism is a consequence of scientific management being the first attempt to understand the large corporations and government agencies which were being created at the turn of the century. Many of the prescriptions which stem from scientific management – like a command structure where subordinates only receive orders from one source, or a control structure where no more than five people report to one supervisor – have an intuitive 'good sense'. They are also prescriptions which are frequently ignored such that some groups receive contradictory orders from different superiors.

Socio-technical systems

Perrow's own analysis of organizations is labelled *socio-technical*, that is, the distinguishing characteristic which differentiates between organizations is the work for which each organization was established. All organizations have a raw material on which they must act to produce a finished product. This holds whether the organization is a factory producing manufactured goods or a school producing educated individuals. The technology used by the organization is dependent on what is known about the raw material; either a lot is known, in which case the organizational processes will be predictable, or only a little is known, and consequently the processes will be less predictable. As socio-technical systems, schools may well cover the range of organizational forms. In some schools the staff will 'know' the nature of its clients, will have a clear conception as to where pupils intend to go on completing school, and therefore the organization will have a predictable structure. An example would be a traditional 'public' school in England where the raw materials are relatively homogeneous and the intended outcomes well defined and accepted by the clientele.

Other schools will have such a range of clients that it is impossible to specify the nature of the raw material. Such schools will tend also to have a wider range of goals, reflecting the diverse nature of the raw material, and hence will have a less predictable organizational structure; reverting to Bidwell's analysis, there will be a greater structural looseness within the school. An example would be a secondary comprehensive school serving a heterogeneous neighbourhood. Such a school would tend to have a well developed pastoral network as well as its academic structure, and would offer students a multitude of options in an effort to match the requirements of each individual.

The advantage of socio-technical approaches towards organizations is that they move beyond the unitary, 'best form', or organization so assiduously sought after by scientific management theorists. However, there is still the suggestion in socio-technical theories of a most appropriate organizational format. Schools may differ, but each ought to strive after an optimum form to best serve its raw material. The difficulty with this view is seen in answer to the question, whose organization? Both scientific management and socio-technical approaches to organizations adopt an explicit managerial perspective, that is, in the case of schools, what is good for the head teacher is necessarily good. If we were able to construct a general theory of formal organizations we would need to recognize that the management perspective is a partial perspective which complements but does not override other view points.

Systemic approaches to organizations

The earliest theoretical perspectives on organizations were those of scientific management. The most widely adopted, however, are various forms of systems theories. The hallmark of such approaches is the recognition that the parts of the system are related to the whole. Such an inter-relationship necessitates that we can specify what the parts are, as well as the 'whole' to which they relate; it also implies that we can identify the *boundaries* of the parts, in other words that we can distinguish what is, and what is not, the part, be this the classroom, the pastoral system, the school or the educational system.

Gray (1979) suggests that boundaries can be classified as 'psychological, temporal and physical' and points out that membership of one does not necessarily include membership within others: 'A pupil who day-dreams may have physical and temporal membership of the school but not psychological' (p. 35). As boundaries exist, so each organization has what Gray calls a 'boundary-spanning function', that is the task of managing who crosses and who maintains the boundary. He argues that it is the regulation of various boundaries which gives an organization its identity, delineating what is and what is not the organization. Given a conception of organizations as interlocking parts, each part can also have sub-parts, or internal boundaries. Thus schools consist of departments, departments of year groups, year groups of classes and classes of sub-groups of friendship systems, work groups and 'anti-social' groups. The teacher normally maintains the boundary-spanning function of what is, and what is not, the classroom, allows access and exits and strives to keep her pupils within the 'psychological' boundary of the classroom.

Organizations do not just exist, they were created for some purpose; that is they have *goals* or what Miller and Rice (1967) label a *primary task*. In order to fulfil its primary task an organization needs *inputs*; for schools these would be pupils, teachers and materials. These inputs are processed within the organization (*throughput*) to become the *output* of the system; an output which presumably corresponds to the organization's goals or primary tasks. In the case of schools, children learn something which has been taught to them. The evaluation of the output, whether or not the system is meeting its primary task, acts as a *feedback*. The continual monitoring of the 'feedback' will result in the adaptation of the 'throughput' such that the 'output' corresponds to the 'primary task'. Such a mechanistic conception of the school is an example of the 'scientific-economic-technological' (SET) approach to the social sciences of which Yee (1972) expresses the fear that 'the ultimate outcomes of the strict SET approach to social policy will be totalitarianism and irrespect for individuality' (p. 22-3). This is not a call for the abandonment of systemic approaches, but for a recognition that embedded in all decisions are values and intuitions as well as rationality.

Part of the social system within which schools operate, part of their environment, is the complex of values and expectations. Each school must accommodate legitimate and conflicting demands, from parents, local industry, professional opinion and educational policy. The notion of 'boundary' has an empirical aspect in that it is relevant to ask of each school which demands it recognizes and the priority given to each. This recognition need not entail an assumption of a uniform, homogeneous institution, responding as a whole to outside pressures, but can allow that within the school there may well be contradictory values. The mapping of the school's ideological environment presents some of the constraints within which the school has to function.

A second area of constraint for all schools lies with the nature of their input. Some comprehensive schools may recruit predominantly from the lower end of the ability spectrum, have teachers who are inexperienced with low-ability children and lack the capital and material resources to mount a wide range of courses. Others will have a 'balanced' intake, a staff committed to the idea of comprehensive education and a range of specialist rooms and equipment to cater for the needs of its pupils. There is a clear affinity here to socio-technical systems: the nature of the raw material can have an influence on the structure of the organization. There is, however, nothing deterministic; schools with similar inputs may well have a range of different organizational forms. At best, system theories are an economical way of describing organizations, they do not explain *why* a particular school has the structure that it has.

There is a danger in the search for an all-embracing explanatory theory of schools as organizations that the critical features of specific schools will be lost. Davies makes the point that 'the urge to generalize between organizations has usually tended to depress the importance of focusing on differences stemming from the relatively unique tasks of organizations' (1973, p. 285). In his paper, Davies argues that educational institutions are so pervaded by the values of teachers, parents and pupils that any single model of organizations will be too mechanistic and partial to capture the complexity of schools. His prescription is for empirical work which recognizes that organizations have histories (it is important to disentangle how the organization came to be) and work within a series of constraints, the complexity of organizations being such as to require the strengths of many perspectives in their analysis rather than the slavish adoption of a single approach.

Individualized approaches to organizations

Both management and systems approaches to organizations tend to reify the organization; that is, the organization is discussed as if it were a real active agency, independent of the purposes and intentions of its members. Individualized approaches resist this tendency having in common the recognition that organizations consist of people. There are differences within this tradition, however, between those who adopt a passive view of the individual and those who adopt an active view.

140

Passive theories

In a much-quoted paper published in 1973, Argyris argues that there is
an incongruency between the needs of a mature personality and those
of formal organizations. For the purposes of his discussion he constructs an ideal type model of both a mature personality and a formal
organization. His characterization of personality, which he attributes
to American culture, is seen as evolving, for example, from a passive
state in infancy to increased activity as an adult; from dependence
to relative independence; from erratic, capricious interests as a child
to pursuing interests in depth and accepting challenges; and from a
lack of awareness of self to developing a sense of integrity and self-
worth as an adult. Argyris argues that in the struggle for maturity,
individuals will tend to strive for the optimum expression of their
personality. On the other hand, the ideal-typical formal organization
will, in the drive for efficiency, tend to institute a chain of command
and increase the specialized nature of work. These developments will
inhibit the evolution of a mature personality in that the increased
specialization of work fails to offer a challenge to the individual and the
prescribed roles within the organization will inhibit the expression
of initiative. In this way the organization person will experience frustration, failure and conflict and will be unable to develop identity
through work. Argyris ends his polemic with the challenge, 'How
is it possible to create an organization in which the individuals may
obtain optimum expression and, simultaneously, in which the organization itself may obtain optimum satisfaction of its demands?' (1973,
p. 314).

The problem facing schools is that they span the years from infancy
to maturity and must therefore have an organizational form which
facilitates the struggle for maturity of its student recruits; we return
to this issue below. The difficulty with Argyris's approach rests with
the notion of the 'needs of the mature personality'; it suggests what
in Chapter 3, we called a passive model of individual socialization, with
a uniform path being taken to an unclear goal, maturity. Maturity is
a prescriptive, not a descriptive concept, its designation probably saying
more about the values of the person using the concept than the attributes of the person so labelled.

Active theories

An *active theory* of organizations is that proposed by Silverman (1970):
'The action of men . . . stems from a network of meanings which they
themselves construct and of which they are conscious' (p. 129). An

organization then, is among other things, the active creation of its members; the stock of knowledge about the organization must be continually reaffirmed by the actions of others. Like Davies, Silverman stresses the importance of also conducting a historical analysis of organizations, in his case to identify why the particular definitions of the situation have emerged. He recognizes the importance of Berger and Luckmann's aphorism that 'He who has the bigger stick has the better chance of imposing his definition' (quoted in Silverman, 1970, p. 138), that, for example, a head teacher has more power in ensuring that his meanings are accepted and sustained within a school than has a probationary teacher. Organizations exist, then, in the sense that they are an expression of the meanings which people attach to their world; they are objective in so far as these meanings become 'sedimented', or laid down and accepted over time as 'normal'.

The implications of alternative perspectives to the study of schools such as Silverman's 'action frame of reference' have been pointed out by Barr Greenfield (1975). He argues that 'organizations are cultural artefacts which man shapes within limits given only by his perception and the boundaries of his life as a human animal' (1975, p. 65). The existence of conflict within organizations is seen to be a crucial problem, not in terms of whether order is maintained, 'but rather who maintains it, how and with what consequences' (1975, p. 72). Barr Greenfield urges that we remain sceptical of any claim that a general theory of organizations is obtainable. Thus one must treat with caution those models of organization developed in one cultural setting, usually that of the USA, when applied to other settings. A corollary of this view is that 'the possibility of training administrators through the study of organization theory has been seriously overestimated' (1975, p. 76). There is no universal blueprint, most efficient model or ideal organizational framework for Barr Greenfield; organizations are definitions of social reality and 'some people may make these definitions by virtue of their access to power while others must pay attention to them' (1975, p. 75).

Any understanding of what goes on in school must start with a description of what happens within the school; the different images and meanings people experience. For Barr Greenfield, the image of the school is not the factory of scientific management, nor the natural system, but, 'the public utility which produces a service which people use for their own ends' (1975, p. 78). For P. and J. White (1976), this is a 'grotesquely inadequate model', as it neglects the purpose of the school to change pupils and, paradoxically, suggests a passive view of the pupil. In the end, it is difficult to see Barr Greenfield reaching C. Wright Mills's injunction that an adequate social science will entail structure, identity, and the delineation of the historical background to each.

Not surprisingly, arguments such as those of Barr Greenfield provoke much comment. In a symposium published in response to his paper, P. and J. White (1976) also questioned the status of 'objectivity' within phenomenological perspectives. Members of organizations may have different experiences and views as to what the nature of the organization is. The point, however, is that there is still something common to all to which these differing views refer. The argument is rather similar to that we made in discussing Durkheim in Chapter 1: the form of the organization may be culturally and historically relative, but it is still possible to identify what is, and is not, the organization or school. What counts as a school is *not just* the collected meanings of its members. Other authors in the symposium saw a danger that benefits would be lost in rejecting systems theories. Reiterating a point which reflects Perrow's socio-technical model, Bone commented, 'there can be good and bad structures for particular purposes, and that analysis of the effectiveness of different structures is not wasted' (1976, p. 13).

The curriculum and organizations

For socio-technical models like Perrow's, the critical factor which determines the form an organization takes is the nature of the raw material. For schools, this may be thought just to include children, teachers and the material resources used. Bernstein (1975) added another dimension, namely, the nature of the knowledge transmitted. In the last chapter, we examined Bernstein's concepts of classification and framing; the former may be either weak or strong, strong classification indicating strong boundaries and separate subject identities and weak classification the bringing together, under the aegis of some relational idea, previously insulated subjects. We looked at the consequences of Bernstein's model for conceptualizing the process of socialization, and in this section we discuss its relevance for the structure of educational organizations.

Where the curriculum reflects strong classification, a collection code, the school will tend to be organized into well insulated subject departments. Bernstein suggests that such a structure points to a management pattern where the institution is controlled by an oligarchy of head and senior heads of departments. Such staff will have both strong horizontal work relationships with other subject heads, and strong vertical work relationships within their own department. Junior staff, however, are likely to have only vertical work relationships, that

143

is they will probably only have working allegiances within their own department. This tendency is reinforced by the socialization of staff into specific subject identities as mathematicians, scientists or geographers. Each subject department is also often in competition with other departments for scarce resources, thus staff are more likely to feel secure within their departmental enclaves rather than risk the hostile comments of non-departmental colleagues over the efficacy of departmental work. In schools, for example, science departments receive greater resources per child than other departments, a fact which may attract critical comment from non-science colleagues even to the point of putting in jeopardy some future developments in science teaching.

This departmental competitiveness is further exacerbated by the career structure within schools whereby promotion is within departments and thus more likely in an expanding rather than a contracting department. Bernstein concludes, therefore, that horizontal relationships of junior staff will tend to be limited to non-task-based contacts. It is worth noting that in most comprehensive schools the departmental career structure is supplemented by the pastoral structure, such as head of year/house, school counsellor, deputy head (pastoral), which could be as strongly classified as any subject department. Bernstein concludes, 'This is a type of organizational system which encourages gossip, intrigue and a conspiracy theory of the workings of the organization, for *both* the *administration* and the *acts of teaching* are *invisible* to the majority of staff' (1975, p. 103, emphasis Bernstein).

According to Bernstein's models the move towards an integrated code, weak classification, where subjects are interrelated, will also affect the organizational structure. The nature of the task, which is now the integration of subjects, requires that staff share teaching and co-operate in both the planning and execution of the curriculum. The consequences are that the power structure of the school will become more open and both administration and acts of teaching shift from invisibility to relative visibility. Thus, for example, a junior member of staff may be the co-ordinator of a topic area and over the year the co-ordination function will be held by different staff as the topic changes. It will therefore be important that each member of staff is equally informed as to the use of resources within school. Within this management pattern, students are also more likely to be active participants in decision-making as against the collection code where there would be a clear divide between staff and student.

The empirical exploration of this aspect of Bernstein's work is as yet limited, thus his thesis must be seen as an ideal type model awaiting confirmation. Using data drawn from his study of seventy-two secondary schools in the south-west of England, King (1976) suggests that the relationship between the curriculum and the organizational structure is not as clear as Bernstein implies: 'Put simply, it is suggested that the introduction of one "open" innovation into a school is not necessarily associated with moves to "open up"other aspects of the school, and may sometimes be associated with the closure of others' (King, 1976, p. 440). Organizational forms may persist which correspond to past curricular arrangements but which reflect the present demands on the school, the diverse and conflicting demands to which all schools accommodate results in a structure more complex than Bernstein's modified socio-technical approach would suggest.

An attempt to reflect this complexity is Smith's extension of Bernstein's work. Recognizing that 'Cultural transmission within educational institutions is located in a mosaic of highly differentiated groupings' (1977, p. 4), Smith argues that Bernstein's model has two inadequacies. The first is a failure to explore the interrelationship between school and wider structural variables, the second, to encompass the heterogeneity within student sub-cultures. In meeting and responding to its ideological setting, every school faces two orders of problem. The first is the technical one of how to *implement* decisions, the second and more fundamental, is how to *legitimate* those decisions. Like Bernstein, Smith sees a general drift away from the strongly classified curriculum and its concomitant organizational form, but also sees this move challenging the ideologies of legitimation, the basic rationale of the organization.

Smith identifies three dimensions to the drift away from the collection code. One he labels 'egalitarian collection', or a shift towards greater democracy *within* a subject department. Another is the instance where a head forces an innovation, such as team teaching or interdisciplinary enquiry, through the existing hierarchical structures; as Smith puts it, 'Such reforms remove many trappings associated with the old academic hierarchy; taken to extremes they undermine the very power structure within which they are carried out' (1977, p. 13). Finally there is the dimension identified by Bernstein as the integrated code, which Smith labels 'co-operative integration' and which bestows upon the whole group control over all its members. The dilemma which staff face is that having lost a subject identity they have not gained a purpose. Schools are not isolated, so that staff having gone to the extremes of democracy and student participation are still caught in a net of external legitimacy, a mesh consisting of certificates, diplomas and degrees. Smith comments on the change to co-operative integration that, 'Such a change simply alters the *conditions* of competition, giving new advantages to those who still recognize the competitive character of the educational system' (1977, p. 13, his emphasis).

The importance of the 'conditions of competition' has also been recognized by Bourdieu (see Chapters 2, 9 and 11). At a time of greater democracy within school without a parallel shift in the mode of selection and allocation in the wider society, *cultural intangibles* - like style of speech, background and 'taste' - will increase in importance. Smith emphasizes that understanding the organizational form of a school requires an understanding of its historical and of the ideological framework within which it is located, but, like Bernstein, his theoretical discussion awaits empirical exploration.

Case studies of schools

Schools as organizations

Given the lack of an adequate general theory of schools as organizations, it has been suggested above that the most useful work has been case studies of individual schools. However, such case studies must meet two major requirements; first, to identify how the organization came to be, or a *historical* requirement; and second, to identify the social structure within which the organization must work, or a *structural* requirement. A part of the structural requirement is what Smith identified as the ideologies of legitimation and implementation, the constraints of different values and expectations to which schools must accommodate. With these requirements in mind, in the remainder of this chapter we will look at two case studies of schools and in the final section consider case studies into schools as agents of socialization. The two case studies of schools represent different perspectives, that of Richardson (1973, 1975), an open systems model whose central concept is that of boundary; that of Woods (1979), in the symbolic interactionist tradition of Mead, Blumer and Becker.

From September 1968 until December 1971, Richardson worked as a consultant with the head teacher and staff of Nailsea school in south-west England. She described her role as consultant as being to help the staff of the school to understand the problems involved in the management of change. The school has a primary task made up of an 'import-conversation-export' process, that is, 'a school can survive only if it fulfils its primary task of taking in children, providing an educational programme that . . . will enable these children to grow and learn, and sending them out after a number of years as more mature persons than they were when they came in' (1973, p. 18). As well as the task system within the school there is also the sentient system, or the emotional, personal attachments which people make within an organization. Richardson argues that one of the functions of leadership in a school is to bring the task and sentient systems together so that both staff and pupils derive personal satisfaction from the work that has to be done. There are boundaries to both systems; as there are to the inner and outer world of the individual; acting as a kind of membrane which separates one group from another, and indeed one institution from another. Much of Richardson's analysis is an exploration of these boundaries – how they are created, sustained and changed, how the individual negotiates a path across and protects his own and the institutional boundaries. It must be stressed, however, that Richardson is using boundary as a heuristic device, that is, as a means of explaining the pattern of interaction within schools, and is not suggesting their existence as some objective category.

Within this framework, Richardson's study is of the changes in the form of management within the school as it moved from a grammar to a comprehensive. The study does not present 'findings' as such, which one might transfer to other settings, but rather records the processes of a school coping with change. For example, the problem faced by the head teacher in the creation of a standing committee of senior management in terms of his own role within the school. The problem is not one which leads to an apt solution valid for all time, but is a continual source of tension more intense at some periods than others. This tension involves the extent to which the head teacher should take responsibility and initiative or follow the lead of other colleagues, a problem of being too autocratic and creating too much dependency on the part of staff, or being too democratic and leaving colleagues with the impression that the school lacks leadership.

At the end of her study, Richardson has produced a description of the management of authority within a school. She presents a view of the interplay between personal biography and a changing structure; of individuals taking responsibility (or failing to do so) for their acts, and the consequence for the school's pursuit of its primary task. The weakness of the case study is a relative lack of emphasis on social structure, on the social class of the pupils, and the related opportunity structure which they face. The world of pupils, classrooms and of teachers managing their identities in the face of groups of children receives scant attention. In terms of the two requirements which we suggested case studies ought to meet, Richardson's work does include a history of Nailsea school including a discussion of how its present structure evolved. The structural requirement, however, is not developed; conflict is recognized but as something which is resolvable given the individual's complete understanding of his responsibilities within the school or a more appropriate management style. The fundamental conflict which can question the legitimacy of the school, challenge its primary task, such as that between the value of encouraging the

child to develop her own interests as against the expectation of employers for workers who are obedient and who will 'fit-in', is a conflict
which goes unremarked in Richardson's study. Ultimately, Nailsea
school is viewed from the position of management and not from that
of the clients it serves.

A contrasting case study is that of Woods (1979), to which we made
reference in Chapter 6. Rather than acting explicitly as a consultant
he was an 'involved' observer at Lowfield secondary school. As such he
worked with pupils as well as staff, shared the humour of the staffroom
as well as the jokes of the classroom, involving himself in most aspects
of the school's life over a period of a year. The study draws from a
symbolic interactionist perspective in that Woods attempts to present
a picture of the school through the shared meanings of its members.
The central concept which evolved during his study was that of 'division' (1979, p. 256):

> division of the 'self' and of 'consciousness' on the part of both
> pupils and teachers, division of public and private spheres of life,
> between choice and direction, of laughter and conflict, pleasure
> and pain, as well as divisions between and within groups of pupils,
> teachers and parents owing to their different social locations, both
> in regard to the school and to the social structure.

Woods's portrayal of Lowfield school captures the complexity of
the organization. His figures are active in that they make decisions
and respond to events as they occur in creative ways, but also their
acts become routine. Part of all teachers is what Woods refers to as the
'teacher bureaucrats', where the individual concentrates on the rules
and rituals of the school as a response to the pressures of the job.
Under-resourced, maybe facing 200 different pupils each week, the
teacher cannot develop 'warm' relationships with everyone; for her
own 'survival' she has to use routines. The danger, as Woods, following
Waller, points out, is that the routine can take over; the teacher's
individuality becomes lost in the school bureaucracy. As well as being
a problem for teachers, the maintenance of individuality is also faced
by children, 'Pupils are engaged in a continual battle for who they
are and who they are to become, while the forces of institutionalization work to deprive them of their individuality and into a mould
that accords with teachers ideal models' (pp. 247-8).

The way in which social structure impinges on the everyday life
of the school is partially explored in Woods's study. He demonstrates
the weakness of any mechanistic view of structure which sees the
school as simply reproducing the conditions of wider society. However,
he does not fully explore the ideologies which surround Lowfield;
the views of local industry or the school's governing body could have

provided an additional dimension to the constraints within which the organization must work. Also, the historical requirement to case studies is under-developed, such as how the school came to have its present form or the aspirations and background of its staff. These criticisms must be seen in relation to the immense task facing any attempt to present a case study of a school, an immensity which lends support to the assertion made at the beginning of this chapter, that a generally accepted theory of the school is probably a sociological chimera.

Effects of school

Both Richardson and Woods have presented case studies which attempt to describe the processes, the pattern of interaction within schools as organizations. A further group of studies examines the effects that schools have on children, as it were, the consequences of the organization for the child. Himmelweit and Swift (1969) recognized that it was not sufficient to regard the school environment as being equivalent for all pupils but that the *same* school could have different effects on different children. This was important for, as we shall see in the next chapter, research like that of Coleman (1966) had been read to conclude that schools had little influence on their pupils; that, in short, schools did not matter, a conclusion which indicates more about the limitations of social research and the inability of large-scale surveys to tap the intricacies of the school than making a valid assessment of school effects.

An indication that schools do matter came from Himmelweit and Swift (1969), who concluded that where a school is a 'strong system' – that is, has a clearly defined 'input' and 'output' – so it will have a strong influence over pupils. Power *et al.* (1967) and Phillipson (1971), using data from a London borough, show a range in the annual average of boys making a first appearance in court from 0.9 per cent in one school to 19 per cent in the school at the other extreme. This range could not be explained by obvious characteristics such as the size of the school, the nature of its recruitment, variation in police practice or the influence of differing catchment areas. Phillipson concludes that 'Some schools apparently protect their pupils from delinquency while others may put them at risk of it' (1971, p. 245). Unfortunately, the local education authority would not allow the research team to collect organizational data from the twenty schools involved to enable this conclusion to be elaborated.

The challenge made by Phillipson has been taken up by Reynolds (1976a, 1976b; Reynolds and Sullivan, 1979). The intent of his

149

research in a relatively homogeneous community in Wales was to see if 'some schools are managing to prevent – and others promote – the growth of deviancy amongst their pupils and to see what it is about the successful schools that may help them excel' (1976b, p. 220). Like Power and Phillipson, Reynolds found large differences in indices relating to boys in the nine secondary modern schools in the area. Rates of attendance ranged from 89 to 77 per cent, the number of boys going to the local technical college on leaving school from 52 to 8 per cent, and the proportion being found guilty in court from 10 to 4 per cent. With the co-operation of the local education authority, Reynolds was able to explore possible school organizational factors related to the different rates of success. The more successful schools tended to be smaller, though by national standards *all* the schools in Reynolds's sample were small, ranging in 1974, from 136 to 355 pupils as against the national average of 600 for maintained secondary schools in Wales. The successful schools also had a lower staff turnover, smaller classes, and tended to be housed in older and less adequate buildings. It is important to remember that Reynolds is exploring associations between two variables and is not implying any causal connection such, for example, that poor school buildings 'cause' successful schools.

Initially, all the schools appeared to be similar in their internal organization, all 'rather "unprogressive", traditional working-class secondary modern schools, closely modelled on the grammar schools that have had such high prestige within the educational system of Wales' (1976b, p. 224). On closer observation, however, subtle differences became apparent; the more successful schools, for example, tended to have school prefects. In one school 30 per cent of final year pupils were prefects, 12 out of 40; to obtain the same participation ratio in an average sized school would entail 45 prefects from a year group of 150. It is unlikely that members of the 45 would feel as special and have the same commitment to the school as the fewer number in the smaller school. The most significant difference, however, was in the relatively high degree of autonomy, what Reynolds calls 'the truce', which characterized relationships between staff and pupils. Though not condoning activities like smoking and eating in class, staff at the more successful school were less punitive in enforcing school regulations. Reynolds summarizes the point as (1976b, p. 226):

> It is worth saying quite simply that the evidence from these schools suggests that the more a school seeks high control over its more senior pupils by increasing organizational compulsion and decreasing pupil autonomy, the more these pupils may regard their schools as maladjusted to their needs. Rebellion within and delinquency without will be the result of the failure of the pupils and their teachers to declare a truce.

Without doubt school organizational factors are associated with differences in pupil outcomes. What is less clear from Reynolds's study, despite his statement that the schools serve 'a relatively homogeneous former mining community, with very small differences in the social class composition of the people', is how much the difference is a function of variation in the nature of each school's input. As he recognizes, we also need to know why teachers use the different management styles they adopt, how 'the true' is manifest in classroom interaction, and the effects of the pattern of expectations held by teachers; in short further empirical work is required.

In a later paper (Reynolds and Sullivan, 1979) explanation is sought from the adoption of a Marxist perspective. In this paper, the successful schools are seen to be adopting an 'incorporative' strategy and the less successful a 'coercive' strategy. Both types of school are vehicles for the implementation of social control which is seen to be the legitimation of 'the ideology and values of the dominant class in society'. There is a danger of the analysis sinking to 'romanticism' and ignoring the fact that all education has a control element, be this in Cuba or Canada, the USSR or the UK, China or Chile. The forms of control will differ in each society but it is essential to remember that a paradox of education is, as Johnson notes, that 'schools reproduce forms of resistance too' (1976, p. 52). In this later paper there is a resurgence of a passive model of the organization where teachers, pupils and parents are, by implication, the dupes of the state. 'Basically, teachers in these incorporative schools attempt to tie pupils into the value system of the school and of the adult society by means of developing "good" personal relationships with them' (1979, p. 50). This is a denial of the intention of members of the organization and a return to the assumptions of clearly defined and unitary goals which are a part of some functionalist models of the organization.

Ostensibly, the most 'scientific' British investigation into the effects of schools is that by Rutter and his colleagues (1979). Having reviewed the research in the area, including that of Power and of Reynolds, Rutter concludes that any evaluation of school effects needs to consider *both* the characteristics of children on entering the school as well as organizational variables. Rutter's team was able to do this; from earlier research, Rutter had data on the ability and behaviour characteristics of a sample of ten-year-old children in a south London borough. Similar data was collected from the *same* children when they were in the third year in twenty comprehensive schools in three areas of south London. At that time, 1974, similar data was also collected from the other third-year pupils in the twenty schools, data which confirmed that the original children did not differ from their peers. Twelve of the twenty schools were then chosen for detailed investigation into

151

school effects; the twelve covered the range of organizational forms from boys only, girls only, mixed, Roman Catholic and Church of England as well as local authority controlled.

Like Reynolds and Power, Rutter's team found significant differences between the schools on four 'outcome measures'. These were attendance, behaviour (such items as, 'skipping lessons', damage to school property, late arrival in lessons and disallowed chatting and calling out in class), delinquency amongst boys, and attainment in school examinations. These differences were not the result of variation in any of the intake measures for each school, such as ability at eleven, parental occupation or the child's behaviour in primary school. This is not to say that the schools admitted identical children but rather than knowing the characteristics of the school's intake would not allow one to predict the nature of its outcomes.

The differences in the four outcome measures were not associated to either the size of the school – in this case ranging from about 450 to about 2,000 pupils – the quality of buildings or to variation in size of classes. What the research team report is a positive and significant association between academic, or instrumental, values and school outcomes. What is meant by academic values, or the school 'ethos', seems to correspond to what might be called professional good sense. That is, a successful school is one where teachers prepare their work in advance, turn up promptly to lessons, set homework, mark books regularly and where the senior staff 'know' what is happening in the school.

As Rutter continually emphasizes, the causal relationship between school variables and pupil outcomes still awaits exploration. Thus the association between homework and success must not be read causally but rather that homework probably has 'symbolic importance in emphasizing the schools concern for academic progress' (p. 110). Homework is part of a set of expectations that children will work, will succeed, that seems to mark out the successful schools. This study supports Reynolds's conclusion that successful schools are also schools where pupils are given responsibility. 'The findings suggest that there are likely to be benefits in ensuring that a high proportion of pupils have opportunities to hold some kind of post of responsibility' (Rutter *et al.*, 1979, p. 130).

Apart from confirming 'professional good sense', however, it is not possible to demonstrate from Rutter's work *how* or *why* school processes influence learning outcomes. Corbishley and Hurn (1979) argue that the research provides 'no overall model to enable us to summarize more precisely what school process is' (p. 50). They go on to show that the method of constructing an overall school process score used in the research – that is adding together such discrete component variables as number of friends a student has in the same year, whether teachers have adequate clerical help, the percentage time teachers spend on the topic of the lesson and the percentage of lessons ending early – does little to increase our understanding of organizational processes. In Corbishley and Hurn's assessment, 'Their combination to form an overall school process score makes the interpretation of why this combined score should predict school outcomes almost impossible' (1979, p. 51).

Conclusion

We have now discussed four aspects of educational transmission: classrooms, teachers, knowledge and, in this chapter, organizations. Viewed overall the scene is messy, uneven and in many areas illdeveloped. There is, however, a thread, a leitmotif passing through our discussion of the school and its processes, that is the theme of *differentiation*. This may be seen in the formation of sub-groups within classrooms, in the use of labels, the assumption of certain kinds of knowledge for different types of children and in the divisions within the organization as identified by Woods. Each example reflects, though by no means in a unitary way, a moral concern with equality. At the beginning of this book we argued that the many perspectives within sociology were a necessary feature to an understanding of education. The search for a common, consensual sociology of education which held on to the 'best' features of functionalism, interpretive and Marxist sociologies, is misplaced. Tension between perspective is normal, conflict in approach is natural in a subject whose essential problem is moral, the promotion of equality. In whatever guise it appears, sociology of education is addressing the fact of differential achievement between groups of people – most frequently between different social classes, but also between sex, region and racial groups. In our discussion of school processes this fact has always been present. Exploration of it has taken us through topics as diverse as classification and framing, social and coping strategies, hidden curriculum and school effects. Always the ultimate issue is the explanation of differentiation, a moral issue. Not all equalities are even, not all are possible, the pursuit of equality is not always in accordance with justice, there are unresolvable contradictions within education. In the next chapter we give further consideration to these issues as we step outside the school to look at the opportunity structure within which it is located.

Chapter 9

Education and the structure of opportunity

Until now, we have looked at children, their socialization, classrooms and schools, as well as their teachers and the curriculum they experience, always within a tacit assumption that education is a good thing and that it will benefit all children in their future lives. We now turn to look more closely at the assumptions which support schools and, in almost every society, a policy of at least a period of universal education. Ultimately the basis of that policy is that education will help to bring more equality of opportunity and for some, that education will bring an egalitarian society. The two are not the same, the advocate of equality of opportunity may also support an increase in inequality within society and the egalitarian see the pursuit of greater opportunity as contradictory to his aims of a classless society.

The debate about equality is fundamentally a discussion about values and secondly about means. Whatever his perspective, the sociologist explores the mechanics of equality and though we may never be able to agree as to what equality is, we can at least reach some consensus as to how inequality is created, sustained and reproduced, whether or not it is necessary to the working of society and, more particularly, how schools affect the dynamics of equality.

Many things have been meant by equality; for Ellen Wilkinson, the first Minister of Education in the British post-war Labour administration, her operational concept was 'parity of esteem'. By this she meant that the three divisions in education – secondary grammar, secondary technical and secondary modern – were to be separate but equal. The intent was that the secondary selection examination taken when children were eleven years old (the 11 plus) would not just be a device for picking future grammar school pupils but an assessment of each child's abilities so that children could be placed in the educational setting best suited to their aptitudes and abilities. In theory the selection examination provided *equality of access*: each child had access to a secondary school place and the test used to allocate him was 'objective' and thus fair to all. The lack of fairness, however, soon became apparent as 'In some Welsh education authorities, two in five children at eleven would be sent to grammar school, some English authorities catered for fewer than one in five' (Bellaby, 1977, p. 10). The tests themselves were not a perfect predictor of eventual academic success, selecting some able children for secondary modern schools as well as some less able for grammar.

A consequence of the failure of equality of access was to shift the definition of equality. Instead of equality of access attention began to focus on *equality of outcome*; it was not enough to seek equality in the admission of children to the educational system, one had to work towards the achievement of equality at the end. It is important to clear up one common misunderstanding. Equality of outcome is not the same as identity of outcome; it does not mean that each child should leave the school with identical grades in identical subjects. Equality is not identicality, a monotonous mediocrity where the weak are supported and the strong repressed. The aim of social policies in promoting equality of outcome is that if the population were divided into groups along non-educational criteria then the achievement of those groups would be the same. In other words, if one took the achievement of children born north of Manchester this ought to be the same as that for children born south of Guildford; or if one took children with blue eyes they should match the achievement of those with brown.

If children are divided into groups on the basis of their father's occupation, all children of bus-drivers together and all the children of lawyers, for example, one might expect that the achievements of each group would be the same. Clearly *within* each group there would be a range of different achievements – just as some individual children are better at ball-skills than others so some are better at solving mathematical problems than others. However, examining the educational achievements of children so grouped we would discover one of the most persistent facts within the sociology of education, that is, if we compare groups on the basis of father's occupation the differences in educational achievement are great and persistent. Halsey (1975) has shown that children born during the period 1910 to 1919 to fathers in professional and high managerial jobs (doctors, bank managers, judges, etc.) had five times the average chance of going to university while children of unskilled workers had less than a quarter the average chance. For children born between 1930 and 1949 the chances were three times the average for the children of professional workers and less than half of the average chance for children whose fathers were employed in an unskilled occupation, evidence which supports the conclusion reached by Little (1971) that, 'Two decades of explicit social and educational policy, not only in this country but in many industrial societies, have indicated how difficult it is to narrow social inequalities through educational policy and practice.' The social inequalities identified are apparently related to social class and before we look at the links between class and education we need to clarify the term, 'social class'.

Social class

As we have already stressed, each concept within the social sciences is dependent for its meaning upon the theoretical framework within which it is used. For Durkheim, class was not a concept which was central to his explanatory framework. He argued that as the division of labour progressed, as the initial stages of organic solidarity became more developed, then society would reach a stage where 'social inequalities exactly expresses natural inequalities' (1938, p. 377). For Durkheim it was not the inequalities as such but the regulation of those inequalities which was at issue.

Weber makes an important distinction between class and status, both aspects of the distribution of power within society. By class, Weber means one's relationship to the economy and labour market, and by status, 'every typical component of the life fate of men that is determined by a specific, positive or negative, social estimation of *honour*' (quoted in Gerth and Mills, 1946, p. 187). Unlike Marx, Weber's classes are not communities, 'they merely represent possible and frequent bases for communal action'. Thus Weber makes a distinction between social classes sharing the same *life-chances*, and status groups which are communities of people sharing the same *life-style*.

In Marx's analysis of society, class is a central concept. At the start of *The Manifesto of the Communist Party*, Marx and Engels write, 'The history of all hitherto existing society is the history of class struggles.' In essence there are two great classes, the bourgeois and the proletarians, the former owning the means of production and the latter nothing but their own labour. Though these form the two great classes of society Marx does speak of the 'lumpenproletariat', or those right at the bottom of a hierarchical society, and also at times distinguishes between the capitalist and the landowners in discussing the bourgeois. Unlike Durkheim, Marx argued that it was the class struggle which carried a society forward, though not in a deterministic way (quoted in Bottomore and Rubel, 1963, p. 196):

> The small-holding peasants form a vast mass, the members of which live in similar conditions but without entering into manifold relations

with one another. Their mode of production isolates them from one another instead of bringing them into mutual intercourse. . . . In so far as millions of families live under economic conditions of existence that separate their mode of life, their interests, and their culture from those of the other classes, and put them in hostile opposition to the latter, they form a class. In so far as there is merely a local interconnection among these small-holding peasants, and the identity of their interests begets no community, no national bond, and no political organization among them, they do not form a class.

It is only when members of a class have a consciousness of their common class position that they form a social class; history is always made by men and women and it is in coming to recognize their objective class position that people unite to bring about change.

Both Marx and Weber used social class as a unit of analysis; their concepts formed part of their theories of society. Social class is also used in a descriptive sense and in many research projects it forms the critical independent variable – people are compared on the basis of their social class. The usual method of allocating a person to a social class is on the basis of his, or his father's, occupation. Occupations which are judged to be of similar standing are grouped together to form six social classes ranging from social class one (professional and managerial) to social class five (unskilled workers). In this classification the largest social class, three, is divided into two, non-manual and manual, the former being clerks and secretaries and the latter skilled workers such as toolmakers, plumbers and electricians.

More recently there has been a move to increase the sensitivity of class as a research tool by dividing the population into socio-economic groups. The Registrar General uses seventeen such groups for the analysis of census data. The Hope-Goldthorpe scale which codes occupations on the general desirability of occupations as popularly assessed has 124 categories though these may be collapsed to a 36 category version of the scale (Goldthorpe and Hope, 1974). Both scales implicitly take a Weberian approach to stratification in recognizing the importance of status as well as the more economic concept of class.

At best social class is a crude research instrument in whatever form it is operationalized. There may be a greater variation within a category than between categories, thus the range of behaviour of bus drivers and their families may be far greater than the difference between bus drivers and for example, school teachers. In the discussion that follows it must be remembered that class is a way of grouping people together which is somewhat arbitrary, thus for every statement made about any class there will be individual members for whom the statement is completely inappropriate. Like all concepts in social science, class must be treated with caution.

Social class and equality

In placing together concepts like class and equality the question must be raised as to whether the two are linked. In an influential paper written in 1945, Davis and Moore argue that 'Social inequality is . . . an unconsciously evolved device by which societies insure that the most important positions are conscientiously filled by the most qualified persons.' Social class is necessary to all societies as it reflects the relative importance of different positions in society to its survival, the relative rank of different positions being determined by the functional importance of the position together with the scarcity of personnel able to occupy that position. Thus refuse collectors may have a high functional importance to society but they occupy a low position because there is no shortage of possible recruits. A design engineer is both important and scarce and thus society rewards him sufficiently for the individual to be attracted to the position and once there to continue to perform the duties attached.

The functionalist position adopted by Davis and Moore has not gone uncriticized. In a debate with Davis and Moore, Tumin (1953) argues that although each society must distribute power unequally it does not follow that differences in prestige and esteem should be a necessary consequence. Tumin attacks the logic of Davis and Moore. A more telling criticism is that the latter's position does not accord with historical fact. It assumes a rationality in organizing our affairs which does not accord with reality, for example, Davis and Moore stress the functional importance of religion as a legitimating force for the central value system and hence deduce that the religious official will enjoy high rewards. In England the Archbishop of Canterbury earns about the same as the head of a large comprehensive school and most of the clergy less than a basic scale schoolteacher. Their status is by no means guaranteed and even the esteem given to the Primate of all England may be quickly lost if he is seen to become too involved in matters not of his immediate responsibility. Within Davis and Moore's discussion there is no concept of struggle either between classes or between status groups.

The perspective which Davis and Moore develop is important for its links with a more influential position, that of *human capital theory*. Vestiges of this theory can be traced back in economics as far as Adam Smith in the eighteenth century. Its contemporary formulation is associated with the work of Theodore Schultz (1961) and Mark Blaug (1970). The latter opens his text on the economics of education by stating that, 'In all economies of which we have knowledge, people with more education earn on average higher incomes than people with less education.' In essence the theory states that both individuals and nations will find it profitable to invest in education as such investment will increase skills and hence productivity, which in turn will generate wealth. The assumption behind both functionalist and human capital theory is that there is a free market for labour. That is each society has a set of high-skill jobs which carry high remuneration, the supply of labour for these jobs is regulated through the education system so that those which most ability get the most demanding jobs. To reiterate Durkheim, the classes which result will be based upon natural inequalities, we will achieve what Young (1958) satirized as *The Rise of the Meritocracy*.

The influence of these views for policy in education has been immense. Third World countries were urged, and indeed given financial help, to invest in education. Only then could their economies be expected to take off into self-sustained growth, free of the bottlenecks caused by a lack of skilled manpower. For domestic policy investment in education would enhance social justice; poverty could be eliminated so long as the poor had access to schools. In the words of the Plowden Committee, 'The first step must be to raise the schools with low standards to the national average; the second, quite deliberately to make them better.' Again, however, the evidence of the past two decades suggests that the theory remains unproven. Thurow (1972) showed that education among adult white males had become more equal in the USA between 1950 and 1970. Measured as the percentage share of years of educational attainment, the lowest fifth had increased their hold on education and the highest fifth had reduced theirs. But at the same time, contrary to the predictions of human capital theory, the distribution of income had become less equal. Thurow concludes that investment in education is not sufficient to promote a more egalitarian society. The difficulty in interpreting Thurow's conclusion lies in knowing what in fact is being measured. There has been greater equality in the years of schooling which is not the same as saying there has been any equality in measured learning outcomes. All children could have the same schooling, and yet a fixed percentage of children attain educational qualifications which they can use on the market. Before turning to look more specifically at the contribution that education makes to the development of a more egalitarian society we need to extend our discussion of class to include an allied concept, that of social mobility.

159

Social mobility

Our specific interest in this chapter is the relation between education and the occupational structure. Education can be seen, amongst other things, as a preparation for the occupational structure and we may ask to what extent education promotes the individual's chances of increasing his occupational status as against, for example, that of his father. In comparing the occupational status of fathers and sons we are looking at *inter-generational* mobility and asking to what extent sons follow the occupation of their fathers. Mobility can also be examined in terms of *intra-generational* movement, or the extent to which the same individual experiences a change in status during his own lifetime. In both cases we are interested in the amount of openness in the society. At the extremes, a completely open society would be one where the relationship between the occupations of fathers and the occupations of sons, for example, was completely random. This would be a society where status was earned by *achievement*, where knowing the father's occupation would not help one to predict the occupation of his children. A completely closed society would be one where status was *ascribed* at birth, the street-cleaner produced street-cleaners, nurses produced nurses and judges produced judges. In each society, however, there is a mixture of both achievement and ascription, the inter-relationships of endeavour and birth are complex and changing.

Within a decade of the 1944 Education Act in England, Glass and his colleagues were examining some of the possible consequences of the Act for social mobility. The purpose of this study was to note the extent of movement in social status, or social position, by individuals of diverse social origins. Using a model of society divided into layers – hierarchies rather like an elaborate multi-tiered sandwich – the task was to assess the movement between the layers both upwards and downwards. Glass found, for example, that 46 per cent of those sons born between 1900 and 1909 whose fathers had been in the upper occupational categories were, by 1949, downwardly mobile and 53 per cent of those whose fathers had been semi-skilled or unskilled manual workers were upwardly mobile. Education appeared to have two effects. In the first place the type of secondary schooling influenced the association between the status of fathers and sons. The grammar school stood out as preserving the links between upper-status fathers and sons and in increasing the distance moved by sons of low occupational status fathers. In other words the age of eleven was crucial to mobility chances; selection to a grammar school was a powerful determinant of eventual status and income. The second effect noted by Glass was that further education (by which was meant any full-time education after the statutory school-leaving age) acted as a reinforcing rather than a second-chance agency underlining the critical position of the secondary school selection examination. Further education was not the avenue to mobility for the failed 11-plus student but tended to attract those who had been selected for grammar school and who had decided not to follow the conventional path into higher education.

One of the specialized studies associated with the central study of mobility was that conducted by Floud, Halsey and Martin (1956), into the relative chance of selection into grammar schools in two regions of England. The study of an affluent area of south-east England and a northern industrial city compared the numbers entering grammar schools in each area. As might be expected, for each there were more middle-class, non-manual pupils attending grammar school than re-presented in the area and fewer working-class children. In the industrial city, Middlesborough, for example, 77 per cent of the population was classified as working-class although only 55 per cent of grammar school pupils in the town were working-class. Floud, Halsey and Martin agree, 'the present differences in proportion of the contribution of the various occupational classes to the grammar school intake can be explained almost entirely in terms of the unequal distribution of measured intelligence' (1956, p. 58). That is the selection examination at eleven was efficient in picking out high-ability children for grammar school places. But, as we saw in Chapter 4, intelligence is not an objective and absolute quality. As Floud, Halsey and Martin comment, 'measured intelligence is well known to be largely an acquired characteristic' (p. 65). The test results allowed the identification of those children whose cultural background was contiguous to that of schools rejecting others, potentially just as capable, whose background does not immediately relate to the school.

Government studies and a note of scepticism

During the 1950s the pattern of mobility within English society was becoming clearer to see. Upward mobility depended largely on selection for grammar schools at eleven. The inefficiency of the education system in identifying, and having identified holding on to, the most able children, especially from working-class homes, was demonstrated both by the Crowther Report on the education of fifteen- to eighteen-year-olds, and the Robbins Report on higher education. Using as a sample men who were undertaking their national service in the late 1950s, the Crowther Committee were able to demonstrate the wastage within the system, illustrated in Table 9.1. Taking those men who were in the top ability group, 11 per cent of the total sample, 42 per cent had left

TABLE 9.1

Left school at age	15 years (%)	16 years (%)	17 years (%)	18 years (%)
All men in top 11 per cent of ability	9	33	17	41
Men in top 11 per cent of ability whose father's were manual workers	19	44	13	24

Adapted from Crowther Report, 1959, vol. 1, page 9, Table 4.

school by the age of sixteen. If we look at those men in the top 11 per cent whose fathers were manual workers we see that 63 per cent had left full time education by the age of sixteen. It was on the basis of evidence such as this that the Robbins Committee in 1963 argued for the expansion of higher education to soak up the pool of ability which was not being utilized by the existing system. The evidence seemed unequivocal, the selection examination used at age eleven was not differentiating among children as precisely as was expected and in consequence there were large numbers of able children who were not completing their education. The implications of such findings were clear, selection ought to be delayed for as long as possible and opportunities for education must be expanded.

In 1961 Anderson wrote a closely argued paper which expressed some doubt on the easy relationship between education and mobility. Using the data of Hall and Glass, together with evidence from Sweden and the USA, he concluded, 'education is but one of many factors influencing mobility, and it may be far from a dominant factor'. In other words there were people with high formal qualifications who did not gain high-status employment, just as there were those with few formal requirements who nevertheless were successful. Anderson's article was a forerunner of the work of the next two decades which explored what Bourdieu terms 'the relative autonomy' of education, of particular importance being the Oxford study into occupational mobility of men aged 20 to 64 and resident in England and Wales in 1972.

After analysing data on 10,309 men in the Oxford study, Goldthorpe and Llewellyn (1977 a and b) show that the analogy with a multi-tiered sandwich, a hierarchical pattern of stratification, is too simplistic. The top layer has been expanding throughout this century, thus recruiting new members, new in that their fathers were in occupations below this level, and the bottom layer has shown a tendency to diminish and to recruit from itself. Thus the layers of the cake are changing in size. To be more specific, Goldthorpe and Llewellyn used a seven-fold class model from the 36-category version of the Hope-Goldthorpe occupational scale, and for much of their analysis group this into three: a *Service* class of professionals, administrators and managers, an *Intermediate* class of clerical, self-employed artisans and supervisors and a *Working* class of manual workers. Table 9.2 is adapted from 1977a, p. 262.

TABLE 9.2   *Class composition by class of father when the respondent's age was 14*

Father's class	Respondent's class in 1972		
	Service	Intermediate	Working
	percentage by column		
Service	32	13	5
Intermediate	34	38	24
Working	34	49	71
	n = 2,280	n = 2,540	n = 3,755

This table shows that the Service class is more heterogeneous in its recruitment than the Working class. Reading down the columns, 32 per cent of Service class occupants originate from this class, 34 per cent from the Intermediate class and 34 per cent from the Working class. The Working class is much more homogeneous, 71 per cent of its members coming from working-class homes. Bechhofer, Elliott and McCrone (1978) support these findings, arguing that 'the middle class in Britain today is a *less established, less unified* middle class' (their stress), and is thus less likely to become a focal point for political action. Conversely the working class may be becoming more a class for itself, in the Marxist sense, but it is also becoming a smaller class, representing 73 per cent of the male workforce in 1911 and 58 per cent in 1971. The social structure of modern England and Wales is becoming more complex, and with technological advance is likely to become more so. The diminution of the working class is not in the face of an enlarging middle class but of a diversifying class structure. An important question is the contribution that education plays in this process. Was Anderson's note of scepticism as to the role of education justified?

School and life chances – England and Wales

It is widely held that as society becomes more bureaucratic the bond between education and occupational placement will get tighter. The critical period in the life of an individual is his years of formal schooling because the qualifications he gains then will have a strongly determinant influence on his life-chances. An aspect of this thesis has been labelled by Goldthorpe and Llewellyn (1977a) as a 'counter balance' thesis of mobility. The thesis has it (1977a, p. 274)

> that any increase in upward mobility achieved in recent decades via educational channels will have been offset by the decrease in chances of advancement in the course of working life. The self-sustaining properties of the class structure – as one of power and advantage – will be little altered by reforms which do not touch basic inequalities of *condition*.

The evidence they present from the Oxford study compares respondents born between 1908 and 1927 (the older group) with those born between 1928 and 1947 (the younger group) at three points in the life-cycle – the first point the social class of the respondent's father when the respondent was fourteen years old, the second the social class of the occupation the respondent first entered and the third the respondent's class position in 1972. Table 9.3 presents their results for men originating from the working class.

Looking at the amount of mobility at first entry to work, the younger group show increased mobility compared to the older group, 30 per cent upwardly mobile as against 21 per cent. But if we look at the percentage who are upwardly mobile *after* having started work, we see that the number is about the same for each group – roughly a third are upwardly mobile after starting work. The nature of social structure and the contribution of education is much more complex than many theorists acknowledge, a simple correspondence between the structure of capitalism and the occupational structure distorts the evidence which the Oxford study has presented. Goldthorpe and Llewellyn in pointing to the complexity note that much more research needs to be done into the process of reproduction, possibly starting with more biographical studies to begin to unravel the nature of social mobility.

One way of trying to assess the importance of education relative to other variables like family background in determining occupational success is to construct a path diagram. Path analysis is a technique for assessing how much of the difference in, for example, income can be attributed to antecedent variables like occupation, education and so on. The most striking features of all path diagrams are their high residual factors, or the amount of difference which cannot be explained

TABLE 9.3.

1908–27 group (older group)			1928–47 group (younger group)		
Father's class	Respondent's class on first entering work	Respondent's class 1972	Father's class	Respondent's class on first entering work	Respondent's class 1972

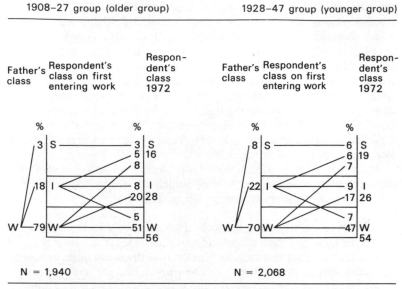

N = 1,940	N = 2,068

Adapted from Goldthorpe and Llewellyn, 1977a, p.276.

by the variables in the model. Using the Oxford data to account for the variance in individual occupational status in 1972, Halsey (1977) is able to explain 36 per cent of the variance by variables like father's education and his occupation, son's education and his first job. In other words, most of the variance, 64 per cent, is attributable to factors outside the model. Using data from the 1972 General Household Survey in the United Kingdom Psacharopoulos (1977) accounts for 31 per cent of the variance in earnings from variables of schooling, ability, occupation and family background. the high residual reflects the complexity of social life; were an individual to list the determinants of her specific income one would see the problems confronting any attempt to estimate the effects of a single variable, like education. However given these difficulties and the limitations of their method, both Halsey and Psacharopoulos see education playing an important part in the determinants of occupational status and of income. Halsey sees what has been happening over the past generations to be 'the weighting of the dice of social opportunity according to class, and "the game" is increasingly played through strategies of child rearing refereed by schools through their certifying arrangements' (1977, p. 184), a conclusion which supports Anderson's thesis that the effects of education are filtered through both status and class before directly influencing mobility.

165

School and life-chances – the USA

As part of 'the war on poverty' launched by President Johnson's administration, the US Congress passed the Civil Rights Act of 1964 which directed the Commissioner of Education 'to survey inequalities in educational opportunities for major racial, ethnic and religious groups in the United States'. The expectation was that the different school achievement between whites and negroes was a reflection of different levels of educational provision. The policy implication was clear: equalize the resources going to the two groups and the educational outcomes would be similarly equated. The report of the survey, *Equality of Educational Opportunity*, otherwise known as the Coleman Report, was published in July 1966.

Having collected information from 4,000 schools and 600,000 children, their teachers and school principals, throughout the USA, Coleman reached the conclusion (1966, p. 325) that

> Schools bring little influence to bear on a child's achievement that is independent of his background and general social context; this very lack of independent effect means that the inequalities imposed on children by their homes, neighbourhood, and peer environment are carried along to become the inequalities with which they confront adult life at the end of school.

In sum, the expected difference *between* schools in terms of buildings, library facilities, teachers' qualifications and so on was not found. For each of the six racial groups examined (negroes, Puerto Ricans, American Indians, Mexican Indians, Oriental Americans and whites) most of the differences in achievement were between groups within the same school.

Summarising the report in 1969, Coleman wrote

> The major result is that the closest portions of the child's social environment – his family and fellow students – affect his achievement most, the more distant portion of his social environment – his teachers – affect it next most, and the non-social aspects of his school environment affect it very little.

Thus although equality of access existed in the USA equality of outcomes remained very large. Predictably the Coleman Report was the subject of a very heated debate, its methodology was criticized, its data re-analysed, but the major conclusion stayed. Interestingly the Plowden Report on English primary education, published six months after Coleman, had similar results. The Plowden enquiry found that differences between schools explained little of the variance in the abilities of English children, leading the Plowden Committee to conclude that the parental attitude of the home had a greater influence.

A more optimistic assessment of the affects of education was provided by Blau and Duncan (1967). Using data collected with the monthly Current Population Survey of the US Bureau of Census they examined the relative determinants of male occupational status in the USA. They concluded that, 'Education assumes increasing significance for social status in general and for the transmission of social standing from fathers to sons in particular' (1967, p. 430). They see a trend within American society where status is conferred on the basis of achieved rather than ascribed criteria. The trend implies 'that superior status cannot any more be directly inherited but must be legitimated by actual achievements that are socially acknowledged'. Their work has been criticized by Crowder (1974) for its uncritical acceptance of the Davis and Moore model of stratification and for depending on a path model with a residual of 83 per cent, that is, the Blau and Duncan model accounts for 17 per cent of the variation in income. Crowder suggests that one of the reasons for this is that 'the total amount of income rewards from occupational pursuits is to a large extent beyond the ascriptive or achievement characteristics of any particular person or group of persons in the occupational system'. Thus a vital determinant of income left out by Blau and Duncan is the control of the occupational structure within any society.

One of the most publicized studies into the relationship between education and the opportunity structure is that of Jencks and colleagues (1973). This work indicates an awareness of a political dimension to mobility having been initiated in the belief that the liberal social reforms of the 1960s in the USA had been misdirected. The reason, according to Jencks, was the enthusiastic adoption of human capital theory which carried the prescription that the abolition of poverty was possible through investment in the skills of the poor. The political position of Jencks and colleagues is that if inequality is to be reduced, then it must be attacked at source, namely the economic system, and not through proxy variables like education.

The data base for this study was that collected by Coleman and by Blau and Duncan, as well as over a dozen other studies relating to family background, educational outcomes and 'success' as measured by income. The conclusions reached by Jencks have provoked considerable discussion. For Clark (1973) 'Jencks has closed the circle. The last possibility of hope for the under-educated and oppressed minorities has been dashed.' For Thurow (1973), 'Inequality' might be summarized as 'nothing affects anything'; for Pullman (1974), the book is 'a bench mark in the study of how I.Q., education, occupational status, and

167

income are interrelated'. Let us turn, then, to look at the conclusions that Jencks and his colleagues came to having completed their data reanalysis.

First, as a consequence of policies of compulsory schooling between the ages 6-16 years, the amount of time that people spend in school is becoming more equal. Jencks states, without comment, that 'at this level almost all inequalities are qualitative', thus it is important to note that his study does *not* include variables like teacher effectiveness, school climate, or curriculum. Beyond the statutory school year, in both pre-school and post-school education, middle-class white children make far greater use of the facilities available than other groups. Turning to quality, the data used is the amount of money spent on schools. Jencks acknowledges that there is little or no evidence to support a direct link between resources inputs and educational outputs but suggests there may be an indirect link in 'that both teachers and students *feel* there is a connection'. He estimates that in America the average white child receives something like 15-20 per cent more resources per year than the average black child, an estimate slightly larger than that made by Coleman in 1965 for an 8-10 per cent difference in favour of white children.

Turning to the distribution of cognitive skills measured by standardized tests, Jencks shows that both genetic and environmental inequality were important in determining cognitive inequality. He concludes that about 45 per cent of the variation in intelligence across a population is attributable to heredity, though this estimate could easily be off by as much as 20 per cent either way. Environment accounts for about 35 per cent of the variance, again with a similar margin of possible error, and the tendency of environmentally advantaged families to have genetically advantaged children accounts for the remaining 20 per cent.

Although occupational status of adult males is related more closely to educational attainment than to anything else which Jencks has measured, he shows that there are still large status differences among people with the same amount of education. This remains true when he compares people who have not only the same years of schooling, but the same family background and the same scores on tests of ability. At most, these characteristics explain about half of the difference, or the variance, in occupational status between individuals.

Finally, when analysing the determinants of income variation, Jencks concludes 'that there is nearly as much income variation among men who come from similar families, have similar credentials, and have similar test scores, as among men in general' (1972, p. 254). Jencks constructs a path model of the type subsequently used by both Halsey and Psacharopoulos, and which explains 22 per cent of the variance in income, in other words the residual, or unexplained variance, is 78 per cent. In comparing Jencks's results with thirty-six other attempts to explain variation in income in the USA, Psacharopoulos (1974) notes that only five studies explain a lower amount of variance than Jencks, that is less than 22% and the majority explain about 40% of the variance. Psacharopoulos concludes 'Jencks owes it to us to explain to what the differences are due'. Jencks attributes the large residual to 'luck', an unfortunate word as he admits, but which encapsulates, 'chance acquaintances who steer you to one line of work rather than another, the range of jobs that happen to be available in a particular community when you are job hunting, the amount of overtime work in your particular plant, whether bad weather destroys your strawberry crop, whether the new superhighway has an exit near your restaurant, and a hundred other unpredictable accidents' (1972, p. 227).

In short, Jencks concludes that equalizing educational opportunity would do very little to make adults more equal because, (a) children seem to be far more influenced by what happens at home than what happens at school; (b) the way teachers and students actually treat each other minute by minute seems to be the most important aspect of school and is largely out of control of educational planners; and (c) any changes which are exerted by the school are likely to diminish as the individual grows older. It may seem that the implication from Jencks's work is that we should cut expenditure on education. Jencks's counsel is against reducing the money being spent on schools on the grounds that schools are an important contributor to the quality of life as it is experienced in the present. By improving the quality of education now we are improving the quality of life of a significant proportion of the population, the children.

Jencks's own estimate of his work is both humble and realistic. He writes (1973):

> The evidence presented in *Inequality* seems to me to show that
> variations in family background, I.Q., genotype, exposure to
> schooling, and the quality of schooling cannot account for most
> of the variation in individual or family incomes. This means we
> must reject the conservative notion that income inequality is largely
> due to the fact that men are born with unequal abilities and raised
> in unequal home environments. We must also reject the liberal
> notion that equalizing educational opportunity will equalize people's
> incomes. The evidence in *Inequality* cannot carry us much further,
> even though its rhetoric sometimes tries.

The major lack of the study is a neglect of the actual process of education within the schools, a neglect of what is often referred to as the inside of the black box of education. Jencks is not unaware of this, noting, 'A high school's impact on individual students seems to depend on relatively subtle "climatic" conditions, not on the size of the budget or the presence of the resources professional educators claim are important.' There is some support here for the work of Phillipson (1971), Reynolds (1976), and Rutter *et al*. (1979), as discussed in Chapter 8. Over large samples, education may appear to have little impact on individuals' life-chances, but this is not to say that for any one individual education is not the major determinant of occupational success. Jencks does not deny this, but the importance of the intra-school factors remain to be fully developed. Jencks reinforces the points made by both Plowden and Coleman that a naive belief in the efficacy of education to bring about social equality is misplaced. However this does not imply that schools make no difference. One needs to clarify the level of the debate as well as the limitations to social policy.

The evidence from both Britain and America is that education, while a necessary factor in the promotion of mobility, is not a sufficient factor. Lipset (1972) argues that even a change from capitalism to communism would have no effect on mobility, as the critical feature is industrial society as such, not its ideological underpinning. Boudon agrees, along with Thurow (1972) that 'the social structure (i.e. the distribution of social status), is largely independent of the evolution of the educational structure' (1977, p. 187), and that 'cultural inequality probably plays a much more restricted role with respect to I.E.O. [inequality of educational opportunity] than many people believe' (1974, p. 110). In essence Boudon holds a model of social mobility which starts with the assumption that the distribution of individuals according to educational attainment varies as a function of social class background and that within each social class there are different probabilities for the decisions that are made. In other words, the upper social class are more likely to aim for elite jobs and make decisions contingent upon this while the lower class, still wishing to maximize their life chances, will nevertheless anticipate lower-level jobs. From his model, Boudon calculates the changing pattern of mobility over time, validating his results against mobility data which is available, such as Glass's work and data from OECD (Organization for Economic Co-operation and Development) studies, to conclude that there is no doubt 'in industrial societies, and in particular in liberal industrial societies, *educational inequality* shows a constant tendency to decrease' (1977, emphasis in original) while social inequality remains. Boudon agrees with Thurow, 'that our reliance on education as the ultimate public policy for curing all problems, economic and social, is unwarranted at best and in all probability ineffective.' The scepticism of Anderson in 1961 has been supported by empirical studies in both Europe and the USA.

The mode of social mobility

So far we have looked at the extent of mobility and shown, that in England and Wales at least, there is greater mobility than frequently supposed. We have also seen, in the words of Bowman (1975), 'how schooling affects the lives of individuals and how it contributes to the restructuring of society depends as much on policies for labour markets as on policies intended to redistribute schooling.' In accounting for mobility we have shown the influence of changes in the occupational structure, but as well as this dimension there is also an ideological dimension to mobility. There is within society a set of values, often conflicting, which relate to what is considered to be an appropriate mode of mobility within society. In one mode, entry to the elite status may be seen as the privilege of the few; only those with special attributes enter the governing class. In another mode, entry to the elite may be seen as a prize awarded to those who do best in open competition. Turner (1961) in making this distinction called the first type of mobility *sponsorship*, comparable to the sponsorship necessary to join an elite club, and the second *contest* mobility, or a race in which each competitor has the same chance as any other. The first which represents a pure ascriptive society could, Turner argued, be found in England in the late 1950s while the second, a pure achievement society, was closer to American social structure. In using the word 'mode', Turner is drawing on Durkheim's idea of 'collective conscience' or, 'the totality of beliefs and sentiments common to average citizens of the same society forms a determinate system which has its own life . . . it has specific characteristics which make it a distinct reality' (1933, p. 79).

Each mode of mobility has consequences for the nature of social control within society as it has for the values of education, the timing of selection and the curriculum of schools. Turner argues, 'The most conspicuous control problem is that of ensuring loyalty in the disadvantaged classes toward a system where they receive less than a proportional share of society's goods' (1961, p. 125). Under the contest mode this is managed through the creation of a universal norm of ambition through which each person is led to believe that if only he had the drive, the dedication, then the top positions would be open to him. The elite is composed of individuals who are the same as those in the mass of the population but who have worked hard to earn their prize of elite status. On the contrary the sponsorship mode holds the belief in the natural superiority of the elite, a group possessing esoteric skills which mark their difference from common man.

As the nature of social control differs, so does the form of selection which operates in each system. The prime task of the education system within sponsorship is to separate out the potential elite as soon as possible so that the novitiates may receive an education which marks their enhanced status. Contest mobility has as its major preoccupation the avoidance of any sharp separation into inferior and superior students. All are encouraged to stay within the system though this eventually creates a problem of 'inconsistency between encouragement to achieve and the realities of limited opportunity' (Clark, 1961), or as Hopper (1971) sees it, the crucial dilemma of all contest systems of 'warming-up' and 'cooling-down' at the same time, encouraging all to succeed yet limiting the areas where success can be experienced.

Finally, the content of education will differ within each mode. Education under sponsorship is for elite values; for taste, discrimination, style and distinctiveness. Eliot (1948) defined the condition for this, writing, 'For it is an essential condition of the preservation of the quality of the culture of the minority, that it continues to be a minority culture.' Knowledge transmitted in schools will tend, therefore, to be theoretical, to be 'pure' and divorced from the mundane problems of everyday life. In contrast, education under the contest mode is a preparation for open partnership in society; knowledge transmitted will tend to be practical, that which is considered of use to both the individual and society. The differing curricula reflect different values held for education. The prized value in contest mobility is 'getting ahead', thus credentials matter as a symbol of one's position within the race; they reflect a status open to all who have the will to try. The distinguishing marks of sponsorship are not available in the market place; style is not a common attribute but the product of the elite culture as embodied in the Public Schools of England or the Gymnasia of Western Germany.

Turner's article is seminal in that it has had a widespread influence on various aspects of the way in which the education–mobility inter-relationship has been conceptualized. It has led to empirical work into the nature of different kinds of mobility, Lipset (1963) and Kerckhoff (1974), and into the links between mobility and personality, Turner (1964) and Elder (1965). Turner's discussion of the relationship between the form of mobility and the form of the content and evaluation of educational practice relates to aspects of the work of both Bernstein and Bourdieu, the attempt to locate the process of education and the form of its transmission to the social structure of the age. The most direct link, however, is with the work of Hopper (1968, 1971) and Collins (1977), both of whom use Turner's discussion in their respective analyses as to why a particular form of educational system has evolved within a specific society.

Hopper (1968) attempts to broaden Turner's two-fold system into a typology which could be used for the classification of educational systems as a base from which one could begin to explain why each has taken the form it has. For Hopper the primary function of all educational systems is one of selection; by asking how, when, who and why the selection process takes place it should be possible to construct the base from which comparisons may be made. In other words if we were going to compare the system of education in France with that in Germany, or Thailand with that in Malaysia, then the management of selection would be the dimension we would use. In the end, Hopper only manages to supplant Turner's two categories with two of his own, the first is *ideology of implementation* and the second *ideology of legitimization*.

Under ideologies of implementation Hopper groups the 'how' and the 'when' questions. The 'how' question being of the order, Is selection centrally controlled and administered, as in, for example, Malaysia, or is it the responsibility of individual education authorities as in England? The 'when' question is, Is selection early, as in Germany, or late in the educational career of the individual as in the USA? In discussing ideologies of legitimization Hopper groups together the 'who' and the 'why' questions and builds onto two of Parsons's pattern variables (see Chapter 1), universalistic/particularistic and individualistic/collectivist to produce a fourfold typology for the justification of selection. Thus a country falling into the first cell, Communist, would be expected to justify selection in terms of collectivist criteria, 'society needs the skills of its people', and universalistic criteria, 'we shall select those who achieve the necessary grades in the common examination' (see Table 9.4).

TABLE 9.4

Why should they be selected?	Who should be selected?	
	Universalistic	Particularistic
Collectivist	Communistic	Paternalistic
Individualistic	Meritocratic	Aristocratic

Adapted from Hopper, 1968.

In struggling to build a typology, Hopper tends to pass over the complexity within any educational system. In each society there are different modes of mobility which co-exist, the educational system responds partially and unevenly to a number of different, and often competing, values. The search to develop a model for the whole educational system can lead one to ignore its diversity. Collins (1977), working within a Weberian perspective, tries to respond to this diversity.

He argues that any educational system is the product of economic (class) interests, but at the same time is also the product of cultural (status) and bureaucratic (party) interests. Thus in creating a theory of social reproduction where the extent of mobility is juxtaposed alongside the mode of mobility the three factors of class, status and party must be seen as interdependent dimensions of the process. The organizational form of education within any society cannot be explained as just reproducing the factors of production needed to sustain capitalism. Historically, most training for practical skills has taken place within factories through apprenticeships and on-the-job training and not through the formal educational system. Further, Collins argues, the establishment of compulsory education does not always follow industrialization and he gives Prussia and Japan as two nineteenth-century examples of countries where compulsory education has been established before industrialization.

Building on his Weberian model, Collins sees education as a *cultural market* in which social factors simultaneously attempt to attain certain goals. Within the market, different groups may be following similar purchasing patterns but for different reasons. Central government, for example, may see education as a means of underwriting its control over particular classes while at the same time members of that class see education as a means of increasing their status. The way in which the market adjusts to its different demands is through the currency of credentials, formal qualifications. The tendency within every society is towards a credential inflation, the demand for higher and higher formal certificates as licences to enter particular occupational groups. Looking at trends in America in 1964, Folger and Nam report that about 85 per cent of the rise in educational attainment may be attributed to increased educational levels within occupations, and only 15 per cent to shifts in the occupational structure from occupations requiring less to occupations requiring more education. Education is part of what Hirsch (1977) calls the 'positional economy' in that the supply of high-status jobs is much less fluid than the supply of manpower able to perform those jobs. In such market conditions the price goes up, in this case measured not in dollars or pounds but in paper qualifications. As Folger and Nam conclude, 'Increasingly the future supply of educated persons may make the gross level of educational attainment a necessary, but not a sufficient, condition for occupational entry.'

The workings of the 'cultural market' are little understood. Bourdieu and Passeron (1977) see something similar to a cultural market legitimating the existing social order, 'Blessed, then, are "modest" folk who, when all is said and done, aspire in their modesty to nothing but what they have; and praise be to "the social order" which refuses to hurt them by calling them to over-ambitious destinies, as little suited to their abilities as to their aspirations.' But we have seen from the Oxford study that the pattern of mobility in England at least is not as rigid as Bourdieu and Passeron would imply for France. 'Modest folk' are to an extent upwardly mobile as a consequence of expanding Service and Intermediate sectors. The strength of Collins's model lies in its fit to empirical data, introducing a flexibility which responds to the increasing diversity of the social structure. He points out that the inflationary process does not necessarily go on indefinitely, the currency itself can break down to give way to other selection criteria. One consequence of this would be to make the criteria implicit, that is though applicants for jobs may each have the same objective qualifications, the selection process is built on hidden attributes like style, school or university attended, way of speaking; in general the values which reflect the ethos of the paticular group which is making the selection.

Conclusion

Thus, in sum, if this analysis is correct, there are two contradictory trends at work within society. At one level society is becoming more open, mobility appears to be linked to achievement, and the seeds of a meritocracy are being sown. But at the same time credentialism has the effect of shifting the grounds of selection away from achievement back to ascription. Within openness there is closure. To assess the extent to which a society like England is one in which equality of opportunity is increasing requires that we make a distinction between absolute and relative equality. In absolute terms there is greater equality of opportunity as a consequence of an enlarging occupational structure, but relative equality of opportunity has hardly changed, to reiterate Halsey's data given at the start of this chapter, the relative chance of lower-working-class children changed from less than a quarter to less than half the average chance of university access for the cohort born in 1930–49 as compared to the older 1910–29 cohort. The part played by the education system in this process of reproduction is complex, the school neither completely reflects nor determines the society in which it is located. At best it is a crude transmitter of life-chances, a transmission which is frequently distorted by the factors of class, status and party.

Chapter 10

Education and the Third World

Our discussion of equality of opportunity and of the relationship between education and the economy was within the context of advanced industrial societies like those of Western Europe and the United States of America. In this chapter the focus shifts to an examination of the contribution which education may make to the national development of countries within the Third World. The inequalities of opportunity which appear large and intractable at the national level are gross and pervasive at the international. Weiler (1978) characterizes much of the discussion of Third World problems as belonging to an 'age of innocence' built on the assumption that education would somehow achieve greater equity in the distribution of income, goods and statuses. He argues that there is, however, an emerging 'age of scepticism', where education is viewed as being dependent on changes in the political economy of societies. In accepting his view, we shall first look at different perspectives on 'development' before turning to an evaluation of the place of education within the development process.

An appropriate metaphor?

The difficulty with terms like 'developed', 'developing' and 'underdeveloped' is their implied ethnocentricitism; that is, assuming a unilinear model of development judged from the position of a 'developed' (C. Wright Mills (1959) prefers 'overdeveloped'), country like Sweden or the USA. The metaphor frequently used is of a column of countries marching through progress: those at the front – the USA, Japan and Western Germany, for example – enjoying the advantages of progress, but with development those at the rear – Bangladesh, Upper Volta and Burundi for example – will eventually be where the leading countries are now and will also enjoy the fruits of progress. There are two major weaknesses with this metaphor; first, Hirsch (1977) has pointed out that the conditions through which the column marches change as a result of the march. The first person to cross a field enjoys the grass, the springiness of the turf, but the last person becomes stuck in the mud created by the marching column: the progress of some is bought at the expense of others. The second weakness with the metaphor is that it makes the assumption that there is only one way forward, that of the overdeveloped nations.

Let us look at these weaknesses in greater detail. British wealth, for example, is not just the product of British inventiveness, ingenuity and business acumen but also the result of a colonial past which involved the expropriation of raw materials, the destruction of indigenous economies and the exploitation of world markets. The slave trade, the awful symbol of imperialism, officially came to an end in 1834; yet, talking of the migration of Chinese into Malaysia at the end of the century, Caldwell (1977a) notes:

> Conditions on the coolie boats plying between Malaya and China were universally admitted to be appalling, but government took a laissez-faire attitude. . . . It was all part of the price the coolie had to pay for the privilege of helping to maintain tin dividends for British shareholders in Virginia Water, Surbiton and Chislehurst.

Then, the sun never set on the British Empire; the present Empire of Upper Volta reaches a hundred miles from Ouagadougou. In 1970 the gross domestic product per head (a crude indicator of a country's annual wealth) was £30 per year for Upper Volta, £50 for Bangladesh, £1,135 for the United Kingdom and £2,380 for the USA. In other words, the average British citizen was forty times, and the average American eighty times, better off than the average citizen of Upper Volta. In 1973, the USA had almost two radios for every man, woman and child in the country while in Bangladesh there was one radio for every 73 people. In Britain in 1975 there were 25 cars available for every 100 people, in Malaysia (by no means at the tail of the column) there were 4 cars per 100 people. Even a country like Malaysia will never be able to reach the car ownership levels of Britain as there is not enough of the finite world resources to provide every Malaysian family with a car. Caldwell (1977b) argues that 'from quite an early point in their evolution, the currently rich countries began systematically supplementing their own domestic real resource endowments with imports drawn from the real resource endowments of economically weaker (more backward) or politically subordinate countries'. Those countries towards the tail of the column are attempting to sustain economic growth in a world where cheap raw materials and ready markets for their manufactured goods no longer exists.

The recognition of the futility of striving after the unobtainable has led some world leaders – like President Nyerere in Tanzania, Chairman Mao Zedong in China and President Castro in Cuba – to search for an alternative model of development, a model which would result in the enhanced quality of life for all citizens and not just for those who obtain employment in the 'modern sector'. In all developing countries there is a small modern sector of the economy where people obtain a regular wage and have a secure job in government or in industry and a large traditional sector of peasants growing enough food to sustain their families and hopefully a little more to sell in order to earn a small monetary income. The great majority of children, perhaps as high as 90 per cent, will *not* obtain modern sector jobs for the foreseeable future.

The realization of the inability of the modern sector to expand fast enough to absorb excess labour prompted President Nyerere to seek an alternative path through 'self-reliance'. He writes (1971):

> This means that the educational system of Tanzania must emphasize co-operative endeavour, not individual advancement; it must stress concepts of equality and the responsibility to give service which goes with any special ability, whether it be in carpentry, in animal husbandry, or in academic pursuits. And, in particular, our education must counteract the temptation to intellectual arrogance; for this leads to the well-educated despising those whose abilities are non-academic or who have no special abilities but are just human beings. Such arrogance has no place in a society of equal citizens.

Nyerere is still attempting to build an educational system where all will benefit, even though the standard of life enjoyed by the majority of Tanzanian citizens will never reach that presently experienced by citizens born into the overdeveloped world. It is worth noting that the self-reliance of Third World countries is not without relevance to the First World where standards of living may decline as the cost of raw materials increases and available world markets diminish.

Theories of development

These then, are two major weaknesses in the metaphor of development. Before looking specifically at the part education has to play in enhancing the quality of life in Third World countries, we shall look briefly at various theories of development. The history of most Third World countries must be seen in the context of the colonial policies pursued by Europe from the sixteenth century. Today, Malaysia is struggling to unite a multi-racial society which British policy helped to create and deliberately kept divided; Indo-China is fighting to create an identity after the 'concern' first of France, then the USA and now the USSR and China (imperialism is not the prerogative of capitalism) and Zimbabwe is fighting to establish itself. Many of the sociological perpsectives on development ignore the fact of colonization and continue to work within an ethnocentric framework. Frank (1971) examines four such theories, labelled the index method, stages of growth, psychological and diffusionist approaches to development. His argument is worth summarizing as illustrative of the limits of much sociological discourse to the problems of the Third World.

The index method

The ideal-typical characteristics of industrial societies are identified and compared with those which are alleged to typify the Third World. In this model 'development' becomes simply a matter of the Third World country acquiring the characteristics of the industrial country. Frank gives as an example of this approach the work of Hoselitz (1964) who, building on Parsons's *pattern variables* (see Chapter 1) sees industrial societies exhibiting the variables of universalism, achievement orientation, and role specification and Third World countries the opposite pattern variables of particularism, ascription and role diffuseness. Frank argues that Hoselitz's division is much too simplistic and does not fit with empirical reality. In Chapter 9 we discussed the movement between achievement and ascriptive criteria for social mobility within a 'developed' society, concluding that observable trends were more complex than could be explained by either achievement or ascription. Even if there were a shift from one set of variables to the other, as Hoselitz recommends, the process is by no means uniform, but a lumpy, disjointed movement with unequal costs and benefits for different members of society. Finally, Frank argues, Hoselitz's model lacks a historical dimension and does not explain why any Third World country is currently 'underdeveloped'; it lacks, in short, for a consideration of the impact of colonialism.

Stages of growth

This approach is associated with the work of W. W. Rostow (1962), at one time President Johnson's senior adviser on the Vietnam War. Rostow argues for a unilinear path of development passing through five stages. The first stage, that of the 'traditional society', is a misnomer according to Caldwell (1977b) as 'traditional societies' were

179

moulded by the impact of imperialism into societies as historically unique in their own way as the industrial countries were in theirs. Rostow's second stage is 'pre-condition for take off' where the traditional society has come sufficiently under the influence (presumably beneficial) of the developed world and has begun to dismantle some of the structures which impede growth. It is relevant to note, for example, that Western imperialism first struck south-east Asia when the Portuguese captured Malacca (now part of Malaysia) in 1511, yet almost 470 years later Malaysia, and more especially Indonesia, remain part of the Third World. The third stage is 'take off'; powered by the thrust of investment the Third World power lifts through the fourth stage, 'drive towards maturity' to stabilize at the final stage of 'high mass consumption'. The driving force for Rostow is the beneficience of the West in pursuit of aid policies to the Third World. But, as May (1978) states,

> Despite Indonesia's revenues as the world's ninth largest oil
> producer, and thousands of millions of dollars of foreign aid, the
> World Bank said in May 1975 that increased help would be needed
> if the poverty suffered by the majority were to be alleviated
> substantially in the next decade.

Aid itself is not enough; any development policy is located within the socio-political structure of a country as well as its history, religions, customs and traditions, each of which can modify the affects of economic measures.

The psychological approach

The third approach which Frank draws to our attention stems from the work of McClelland (1961; see also Chapter 3 above), for whom the basis of the development process lies in changing the psychological attributes of the people involved. Individuals must be encouraged to enhance their 'need to achieve', to become striving and efficient so that they will move into the modern sector. The major weakness of this approach is that it ignores the structural constraints within which the 'need to achieve' is generated. There is little to be gained in urging the rubber-tree smallholder to increase his yield if all the best land is owned by international companies. There may be little point in increasing individual efficiency if the peasant has no control over the market price for his produce. Obviously hard work is a necessary condition for development; it is not, however, a sufficient condition.

The diffusionist approach

The final approach identified by Frank is associated with the work of Nash (1963) and has the most direct relevance to education. It assumes that the barrier to modernization is the lack of capital and technology, as well as the appropriate institutions and infra-structure (for example, transport and educational facilities). As a society begins to acquire these from the industrial world so its own development will be enhanced. Schultz (1961) argues that the low rate by which underdeveloped countries absorb physical capital is because human capabilities, investment in human capital, does not keep pace. Hence what is required is more education, preferably of the Western type; which takes us back to the 'age of innocence' with which we began this chapter.

Education and colonialism

Frank has criticized the prevailing trends in the theory of development from a Marxist perspective. The central point that he makes is that to understand the contemporary position of Third World countries we must first understand their history, an understanding which is predicated on an analysis of colonialism or imperialism. In his analysis, colonialism is equated with capitalism such that the relations of production generated under the latter become the relations of exploitation and expropriation which keep the Third World underdeveloped. There is no column marching through progress, but a world where the rich become more affluent on the poverty of Third World peasants. An envisaged solution is to end the domination by the capitalist order – symbolized in the work of multinational corporations for example – and promote a growth in self-reliance within Third World countries, together with co-operation on technical and social development between these countries.

The development of educational systems within Third World countries was part of the colonial process. As Altbach and Kelly (1978) have it, 'Schools which emerge in colonies reflect the power and the educational needs of the colonisers.' Their model of the prevalent type of education within the metropolitan power is close to that which Turner (Chapter 9) characterized as 'sponsorship'. Thus there would be a small elite sector (in England represented by the Public Schools) giving an education best fitting a gentleman, and for the mass of the population an elementary system giving basic instruction in the skills of literacy and numeracy. There would be a small recruitment from the elementary to the elite system of the most able pupils as a token to equality of opportunity. Translated to the colonies the model would, in essence, be the same; that is, an elite education for the sons of the colonizers, elementary education conducted in the English language for the 'bright native', who could then be recruited to help administer the colony, and for the mass a short period of education conducted in the local language, vernacular education. The State Inspector of Schools for Perak (part of the then Federated Malay States, now part of Malaysia), H. B. Collinge, wrote in his report in 1895 (quoted by Loh, 1975):

> After a boy has been a year or two at school he is found to be less lazy at home, less given to evil habits and mischievous adventures, more respectful and dutiful, much more willing to help his parents, and with sense enough not to entertain any ambition beyond following the humble home occupations he has been taught to respect.

There can be few clearer statements about the real purpose of vernacular education, the creation of a docile, acquiescent population to serve the needs of the metropolitan colonial power.

The adoption of a 'Western' educational system by Third World countries is criticized by Buchanan (1975). He sees a major problem to be one of cost, and gives figures to show that in the UK, for example, the unit cost of university education is equivalent to the gross national product per head; yet in Iran the cost of university education was eight times the gross national product per head. The point is not to compare the cost of a university education in two countries but to show the relative cost in each. Coombs (1968) argues that 'in the years ahead, unit costs and expenditure per student in developing countries are destined to rise even more quickly than in the industrialized countries'.

One of the reasons for the increase in unit costs is the result of improved health measures so that more babies are surviving to maturity. In countries like Upper Volta, Bangladesh, Malaysia and Thailand over 40 per cent of the present population is under the age of fifteen as against half that percentage in Western Europe. Even if the birth rate in those countries were to drop to net replacement level, that is each woman would have two children, the population would increase as the absolute number of possible parents increases.

As well as demographic pressures on costs there is also a social demand for education, as Orr (1977) puts it, 'It is an appetite which doth grow by what it feeds on'. And it feeds on the realization by parents, as Foster (1965), Seymour (1974) and many others have shown, that education is the key to access to modern-sector jobs and hence future prosperity for their children. The combination of demographic and social demands for education means that many Third World countries are already devoting twice the percentage of public expenditure on education than industrial countries like the UK. There is a danger of reaching what the Faure Commission (1972)

182

called the 'intolerance threshold' beyond which the burden of educational expenditure could dangerously disturb a nation's economic balance.

Education and neo-colonialism

Commenting on the First Development Decade (UNESCO has given this label to the period 1960-70), Jolly (1974) notes that educational systems have expanded quantitatively in the Third World during this period but the real problem is one of qualitative improvement. The period of quantitative expansion has ushered in what has been called a period of neo-colonialism (Altbach, 1971; Thompson, 1977; Altbach and Kelly, 1978). The latter state that 'Neo-colonialism constitutes the deliberate policies of the industrialized nations to maintain their domination'. Despite the achievement of political independence the Third World remains dependent upon the industrialized world. Textbooks, for example, are often translations of those prepared in the West with minor amendments to fit local needs; teachers, especially in higher education, are often expatriate or, if local, the products of the higher education system in the West. The examinations, even if locally controlled, are tailored to Western needs because the products of the school system may well want to enter overseas universities, or as graduates from local universities may want to undertake advanced study in the metropolitan country.

Altbach (1971) notes that the USSR has just as many imperialistic tendencies as the traditional colonial powers, sponsoring courses in Russian Studies, giving scholarships to study in the USSR and subsidizing text books and equipment which are unlikely to portray the donating country in an unfavourable light. Carnoy (1974) notes that 'the institution of schooling . . . is capable of generating awareness of the dependent relationship of one society to another and of the role of the dominant groups in maintaining that dependency', though in fact this capability is seldom realized. A failure which serves to uphold, in Freire's (1972) terms, the 'domestication' of man rather than his 'liberation'.

The western model, then, is expensive, geared to the maintenance of the status quo, and inappropriate to most requirements of Third World countries. Historically it was constructed to serve the needs of the colonial government to produce an indigenous administrative class committed to the values of the metropolitan power and to provide a basic literacy for the mass of the population, although all too often this meant only those living in urban areas. Since the political independence of Third World countries, education has increasingly been seen by parents as the way for their children, or at least for one child, to move from poverty to the supposed benefits of a 'Western-type' existence. Although some individuals do make the passage, the problem which faces educational planners in the Third World is the creation of an educational system which is responsive to local needs, cheap in its use of resources, yet which allows the best students to be selected for advanced training. This problem, not just confined to Third World countries, is usually seen as the *equity* versus *efficiency* problem, or as Anderson (Anderson and Bowman, 1965) sees it, one of eliciting the maximum aggregate of learning for the available resources while keeping faith with some expression of equality of opportunity.

Education and development – dominant perspectives

We have looked at what is meant by development and sketched in the part which education has had to play in the overall process. We turn now to more detailed discussion of the relationship between education and the developmental process, starting with the contribution by a leading aid agency, the World Bank. In the *Education* Sector Working Paper (1974), the staff of the World Bank view the dilemma facing Third World countries to be dependent upon their economic systems. The modern sector of the economy tends to be dominated by government and multinational companies, and is attractive to people in the Third World because this is the sector where wages are regular – the monthly salary.

There is a high demand for jobs within the modern sector. Consequently, in simple economic terms, if demand is high for a fixed supply of goods, prices will rise. In this case, the price is educational credentials, school-leaving certificates, diplomas and degrees which regulate the flow of manpower into the modern sector. This market force is amplified by a secular trend of increasing school enrollments; there are simply more people competing for the same jobs. As a result schools become 'factories' for credentialism, schools in the first cycle producing the certificates necessary to enter the second cycle, the latter the certificates necessary to enter the tertiary sector. What is taught in school is of secondary importance because the critical area is the *level* of qualification not the *type* of education received. The staff of the World Bank argues 'the content becomes more theoretical and abstract and less practical; experience drawn on is more universal and less local; and cognitive, or purely mental, skills are emphasized over attitudes and manual, social and leadership skills'. Finally comes the heart of the dilemma we have already commented on: no matter how rapid the process of industrialization within Third World countries, no matter how impressive their economic growth, the majority of children now at school in the Third World will *not* enter the modern sector. Thus contemporary educational systems are both organized to meet the needs of a tiny minority of the population and perpetuate the myth that through schools the individual will be able to gain access to modern sector jobs.

Basic education

The major recommendation of the World Bank working paper is for the wider adoption of *basic education*. Basic education differs from universal primary education (UPE) in three major ways. The objectives and content of basic education differ from UPE in that they are defined in terms of another central idea in the vocabulary of development specialists, that of *minimum learning needs*. These have been defined by Coombs and Prosser (1973) to include functional literacy and numeracy, knowledge and skills for productive activity, family planning and health, child care, nutrition, sanitation and knowledge required for civic participation'. Thus basic education should meet the minimum learning needs of identified groups and not be seen as just a step in the educational hierarchy. The second difference is that the target group of basic education is not necessarily the same as that for UPE and may include adults and school drop-outs as well as those conventionally seen as the recipients of formal education. Finally the form of transmission of basic education will vary according to resources. Teaching is not dependent on schools with desks and classrooms.

The analysis presented by the World Bank has evoked considerable discussion (see, for example, Williams (1976) and Colclough and Hallak (1976)). Everyone, not least the staff of the World Bank, recognizes that there is no panacea for the problems facing Third World countries. The age of innocence has been replaced by the age of scepticism. Colclough and Hallak stress the fact 'that people will only use educational institutions and undergo educational programmes when it suits their own basic objectives and purposes', thereby emphasizing that the essential viewpoint which must inform the planning process is that of the intended target group. In the same paper they quote an evaluation of the efficacy of rural education centres in the Upper Volta where 'Parents of rural youths and the youths themselves . . . clearly saw what was happening and regarded the R.E.C. [Rural Education Centre] at best, as a temporary expedient that should be replaced by the real thing, the primary school, and at worst, a symbol of discrimination against rural people.' No matter what the intrinsic quality of a basic education programme there is always the danger that it will be seen as a cheap replica of 'proper' education, an opinion which is strengthened by the extent to which its graduates do not obtain the coveted modern sector jobs.

Non-formal education

Closely allied to the provision of basic education is the growing interest in *non-formal education*. Coombs (1976) sees non-formal education as a convenient label to cover a wide assortment of organized educational activities:

> the chief distinguishing characteristic of non-formal education, viewed as a whole, is its much greater flexibility, versatility, and adaptability than formal education for meeting the diverse learning needs of virtually any kind of clientele, and for changing as the needs change.

Coombs keeps to a distinction contained in much of the literature on development by distinguishing 'schooling' from 'education' and stresses that the wider perspective needed to encompass man's *educational* activities is more appropriate to the non-formal sector. He identified two important characteristics of non-formal education. The first is that its planning 'must by its very nature be decentralized and brought as close as possible to the scene of the action'. The second is that it must be seen as a part of the total process of social and economic development and not, as is often the case with the formal sector, a separate identity. Although Coombs is optimistic for the role of non-formal education, he recognizes that a major disadvantage is that, 'even where the learning results of a non-formal program may actually exceed those of its formal education counterpart . . . it does not lead to the granting of a prestige-laden certificate or diploma having a generally recognized social and economic value.'

Within both the industrial world and the Third World the view of the contribution schooling makes to economic, social and political development is dependent upon the perspective taken. For some, schooling is a necessary means for the socialization of the young to fulfil the demands of society; for others schooling is an agency of repression which legitimates the status quo. Bock (1976) applies the same perspectives to non-formal education; for some it can facilitate meaningful development by more effectively and cheaply serving to remedy the deficits of certain disadvantaged groups; for others it is yet 'another "reformist" ploy designed either implicitly or explicitly to maintain an unjust social and economic order *within* countries [his emphasis] and to sustain the conditions of dependency of poor nations upon the industrially more advanced capitalist nations.' Bock tends towards the latter view and argues that the growth of non-formal education can be explained because it meets conflicting demands within society, 'For the State is motivated to extend its authority and legitimate its elite, and, at the same time, to avoid the creation of politically explosive competitive forces by limiting the extension of legitimate claims for still scarce resources and participatory roles.' He suggests, from evidence collected in Malaysia, that non-formal education results in its graduates internalizing the 'myth of schooling' so that they view as legitimate those who gain access to scarce jobs on the basis of educational credentials earned through the formal sector. Consequently, though the non-formal education sector plays an important part in 'cooling-out' possible contenders for high-status jobs, it is an inherently unstable sector and may, Bock suggests, fail to hold the continued support of its clients.

The point is that education is a dependent variable, not creating growth, not the engine of development, but rather the product of the political economy of which it is a part. This is not to say that education is determined by the political economy. The strictures on determinism which we raised in Chapter 1 still apply. Bourdieu's concept of 'relative autonomy' is still appropriate in alerting us to the complexity of the inter-relationships between education and the political economy. The fallacy has been to see education as a neutral, self-evident and determinate route for development, particularly in those development theorists who advocate that Third World countries adopt the infrastructure of the industrial world. The problems are clear – the rapid inflation of credentials, the danger of creating a dual system of education, the escalating cost of formal schooling and the growth of unemployment among the system's graduates.

Blaug (1973) draws our attention to the wide range of problems which hide under the label 'graduate unemployment'. He suggests that the statistic that 15 per cent of India's high school and college graduates were unemployed in 1967 might be more meaningfully expressed in terms of the average waiting time before jobs were obtained. Put this way, 'the average waiting time of high school graduates was eighteen months while the average waiting time for college graduates was six weeks.' If this is the case the prudent parent may still see it worthwhile for his child to obtain the maximum education not because there is a guaranteed place in the occupational slot but because the probabilities of obtaining such a position are increased. The recommendations contained within the World Bank Sector Working Paper that 'cohort analysis' could be a useful tool for understanding the process of educational development is supported by Blaug's discussion.

Cohort analysis is really a longitudinal study of a particular group

187

over time. Thus a population would be selected, such as those living in a particular rural area, and then followed as they passed through, or missed, the educational system and began work in either the modern or traditional sectors. The advantage of this method lies in the possibility of identifying the critical factors which influence the way in which the same individual develops over time. In this way we go beyond the identification of problem areas to begin to understand the processes at work within a specific cultural setting.

Credentialism and the curriculum

If we conducted a cohort analysis we may discover, as Dore (1976) suggests, that our obsession with credentialism is largely an exercise in self-confirmation. That is, the examination simply tells us what we already know; a student who obtains high marks in a mathematics examination, for example, is good at mathematics. Dore suggests two ways in which we could fulfil the necessary task of selecting the most able students to occupy the most responsible occupational positions within a society. The first is to replace the present examination system, essentially an achievement test, with tests which could not be crammed for and which would measure a student's aptitude. The second is to revert to the position of industrial countries fifty years ago and start careers earlier, about age sixteen, and do as much of the selection as possible within work organizations. In this way one would still be able to pick out the talented but one would also be able to liberate large amounts of schooling time for education. Thus instead of teaching science as a series of facts to be learned and regurgitated at the appropriate time one would concentrate on science as a way of understanding the world. If Blaug (1973) is correct in arguing that 'education contributes to economic growth more by transforming the values and attitudes of students than by providing them with manual skills and cognitive knowledge', then it is essential that we move away from the effects produced by credentialism and begin to explore ways of promoting education.

The dilemma between education and schooling is sharply focused in the discussion about the curriculum. Most schools in Third World countries are working within what Thurow (1972) has called a 'job-competition' model of the labour market:

> In a labour market, based on job competition, the function of education is not to confer skill and therefore increased productivity and higher wages on the worker; it is rather to certify his 'trainability' and to confer upon him a certain status by virtue of this certification.

According to this model, most actual job-skills are acquired informally through on-the-job experience after a worker has started work. The critical problem facing the modern sector of the economy is to pick and train workers who will need the minimum investment in training costs. Therefore of over-riding importance is the level of the student's educational achievements, not the contents, which will have little relevance to job requirements.

However, at the same time one recognizes the absurdity of twelve-year-old children in the Tropics being taught 'Twenty biographies or important events in English History from the landing of the Romans to Henry VII' (Chang, 1973). As Third World countries achieved their independence, great energy has been poured into re-drafting the curriculum so that it accords with the political-economic context of its transmission. The Buddhist Kingdom of Srivijaya, the rise and fall of the Majapahit Empire and the history of the Mandinga people replaced Greece, Rome and the feudal lords of medieval Europe in the emergent new syllabi. An attempt has also been made to reverse the trend which Mead (1943) identified as the 'shift from the need for an individual to learn something which everyone agrees he would wish to know, to the will of some individual to teach something which it is not agreed that anyone has any desire to know'. An attempt, that is, to bring the curriculum closer to the practical and cultural needs of indigenous people.

The difficulties facing curriculum renewal have largely remained unexplored. Any adequate discussion would need to take into account the dual pressures of neo-colonialism; the continued dependency of countries on the legitimation of their educational certificates from the industrial world; and credentialism itself, the necessity to obtain a *level* of certification with which to enter the modern sector. Though the development metaphor with which we started this chapter has been shown to be inadequate, it still supports the assumptions behind neo-colonialism and credentialism, particularly the belief in the correctness of the Western model.

Education and development – alternative perspective

Nyerere (1971) recognizes the inadequacy of the development metaphor and argues that an alternative educational system can evolve in a society committed to ending the exploitation of one person by another. He identifies four deficiencies in the Tanzanian educational system: first that it is elitist in that it is geared to serve those who are intellectually stronger than their fellows. The practice of schools induces in these more fortunate people a feeling of superiority and leaves the majority with a feeling of inferiority. The school system also succeeds in divorcing its participants from the society which it is supposed to be preparing them for, 'For the truth is that many people in Tanzania have come to regard education as meaning that a man is too precious for the rough and hard life which the masses of our people still live.' The third deficiency is that education teaches people to despise know-ledge other than that which comes from books; it does not encourage an open critical mind which can appreciate that sometimes the accepted wisdom of the tribe is correct and the wisdom of books incorrect. Finally, the education system removes from productive work some of the nation's healthiest and strongest young men and women, thus underlining their remoteness from the actual needs of the village communities.

In suggesting ways in which these deficiencies could be made good Nyerere recognizes that 'we cannot solve our present problems by any solution which costs more than is at present spent'. The implication of Tanzania's poverty is that primary education must be a complete education in itself, not a preparation for the next stage. The imple-mentation of this change would require the downgrading of the value of examinations, to 'think first about the education we want to pro-vide, and when that thinking is complete think about whether some form of examination is an appropriate way of closing an education phase'. Nyerere's view of the content of the school curriculum reflects Mead's 'need for an individual to learn something which everyone agrees he would wish to know', that is the school ought to teach those things which a child needs to know if he is to live in a predominantly rural society and contribute to the improvement of life there. Educa-tion is part of the process of the liberation of human beings, liberation from colonial dependency, from feelings of inferiority, from super-stition, from 'the kind of learning which teaches an individual to regard himself as a commodity, whose value is determined by certifi-cates, degrees, or other professional qualifications' (Nyerere, 1974). Education must be tied to the productive needs of society; schools help to pay for their own running costs and becoming an integral part of the community they serve.

The contribution by Nyerere to the discussion of education and the problems facing Third World countries has aroused widespread interest, many sharing with Foster (1969) a 'warm glow' at the rhetoric. In practice there is little new in Nyerere's proposals. The memorandum issued in 1935 by the British Advisory Committee on Education in the Colonies, for example, stated 'The basis of African life is, and is likely to remain agricultural. If this is so, one of the primary tasks of African education must be to assist in the growth of rural communi-ties securely established on the land' (p. 6). The recommendation that the curriculum should reflect topics which are clearly relevant to the needs of the population is not original to Nyerere. The implementation of the recommendation, however, still remains. Morrison (1976) sees little in Nyerere's proposals to speed its adoption: 'To be specific, the programme outlined in "Education for Self Reliance" cannot achieve the objective set for it unless the overall strategy for rural development can be implemented.'

There appear to be strong pressures towards inequality in all developing societies. For so long as this continues, individuals will want to maximize their own opportunities and will resist egalitarian measures – unless these are applied to someone else. This central dilemma of equity against efficiency is common to all countries. The education sector cannot resolve the dilemma. At best investment in schools may remove some of the bottlenecks to increased efficiency, but in doing so it adds to inequalities.

Conclusion

The necessity for an overall development strategy received further stimulus from the report of the Brandt Commission (1980). The Commission was established from the initiative of the President of the World Bank, R. S. McNamara, though independent from the Bank and all other government or international agencies. Its terms of reference were 'to study the grave global issues arising from the economic and social disparities of the world community and to suggest ways of promoting adequate solutions to the problems involved in development and in attacking absolute poverty' (1980, p. 296).

The message from the Commission is clear: the *technical* means to solve the grave global issue of absolute poverty affecting 800 million people are available. The *political* will in a world which spends over £200 *billion* a year on military equipment is still not unambiguously apparent. One of the reasons for this, as we indicated at the start of this chapter, is that the eradication of world poverty has implications for the maintenance of the existing standard of living in the over-developed world.

It is of interest to note that although the Brandt Commission makes ritualistic reference to the importance of education, the Report does not discuss in any detail the contribution which might be made by the educational sector. In short, the report is written in an 'age of scepticism' and views education to be dependent on changes in other sectors of a society's infrastructure. Thus by implication, the report reaffirms the danger noted by the Faure Commission (1972) of a country reaching an 'intolerance threshold' by spending proportionately 'too much' of its GNP on education. The two aspects of education which are stressed are the need to bring more girls into schools and the need for 'international awareness'. The Commission reports that girls 'formed less than forty per cent of primary school enrollees in 27 out of 34 African countries in 1970 . . . for which information is available' (1980, p. 57). This underrepresentation of girls in schools is linked to the underrepresentation of women in development: 'economic development is often still talked about as if it was mainly a subject for men. Plans and projects are designed by men to be implemented by men on the assumption that if men, as the heads of households, benefit from these projects, the women and the children in those households will benefit too' (1980, p. 59). Finally, every school has the responsibility of alerting its pupils to the fact of global interdependency. There is a danger, especially in times of recession, for countries in the over-developed world to erect barricades and attempt to ignore the rest of the world. 'The abolition of poverty is itself not only a moral obligation. It is against everyone's interests to allow poverty to continue, with the insecurity, suffering and destruction which it brings' (1980, p. 269).

Chapter 11

Reproduction and relative autonomy

The education system of any country is beset with paradox, dilemma and contradiction. The aspirations of teachers are not necessarily shared by parents or policy-makers. For one child, schooling may afford the opportunity to develop self and facilitate transfer into an elite status, for another the same school may be repressive, intolerant and inhibitory of personal development. While being the vehicle for mobility for some people, the school system may do little to enhance the claims of the group of which the individual is a member, be this identified by region, class, race or sex. Through the school some learn to accept the prevailing order as the 'natural' way of things, yet others to challenge the basis of that order. Schools may contribute to the reproduction of the class structure, but they also contribute to its change; schools may be substantially independent of controlling groups within a society, yet those groups will attempt to impose on schools a particular view of education.

Always, schools will serve contradictory purposes. Throughout this book I have tried to emphasize the diversity of viewpoints within the sociology of education, to underline that even the best accounts are only partially true. Recognizing this, I make a general observation about human behaviour: throughout the world, parents tend to want the 'best' for their children. Such a desire is not open to precise definition and covers a multitude of forms from 'happiness' through to a better, more financially secure life than that experienced by parents. Commonplace though this observation is, even those who advocate the abolition of social hierarchies and urge the domination of collective over individual achievement must still recognize that for the parent the first concern is to promote the interests of specific, nameable, unique children. Thus, using the language of Talcott Parsons, within universalism there is particularism, within diffuseness, specificity, and within achievement there is ascription.

193

Starting from such a paradox this chapter will pull together some of the arguments introduced earlier to assess the part education plays in society. It is partly through education that the conditions for the continued survival of society are reproduced, yet education is not the finely tooled creation of those in control. Accepting Durkheim's claim that 'educational transformations are always the result and the symptom of the social transformations in terms of which they are to be explained' (1977, p. 166), it is important to locate theories of reproduction and relative autonomy in the different social contexts from which they arise. We begin, then, by returning to the development of sociology of education, and hence views on the form of education, seen as 'the result and the symptom' of its age.

Sociology of education in context

The expansion which occurred in sociology of education in the mid-1960s took place at a time of optimism in the efficacy of educational planning. The United Kingdom, in common with most of the 'north', experienced an increased affluence which improved the material condition for the majority of citizens. Affluence bred confidence, symbolized by a faith in rationalist technico-bureaucratic models and planning instruments through which the problems afflicting human life would be solved. Management by objectives, blueprints for the implementation of curriculum reform, precise techniques for the measurement of teacher effectiveness, for example, seemed to demonstrate that human beings were in control of their collective problems. Two decades later that confidence had been tempered, pessimism abounded and a hint of cynicism was in the air.

What had happened to the buoyant hope of the 1960s? First, it is important to remember that the rate by which people became affluent had never before been so rapid; it was easy to believe in the continuance of growth and therefore in the availability of resources to meet need. A cursory glance at the published statistics of most countries in the 'north' shows that people took more holidays, larger proportions owned cars, washing machines and colour televisions. If these are indicators of the quality of life then it would appear that during the 1960s life was improving for the majority. There is a danger, however, in reading such statistics, of misunderstanding what in fact was changing. Townsend (1979) argues that 'Upon analysis social changes turn out to be technical or cultural rather than structural.' This conclusion is supported by the findings from the Oxford Mobility Study (Halsey, Heath and Ridge, 1980) that *relative* inequality was much the same for those born in the period 1943 to 1952 as those born between 1913 and

1922. The surface features of society may change without disturbing the underlying structures of inequality.

Further, the war in Vietnam influenced the confidence many had in the rational, efficient and socially just processes of governments. The killing of women and children in, for example, Son My in March 1968 coincided with increasingly vociferous protests against the involvement of the USA in Vietnam. The Son My incident became a rallying point for those who felt the 'great society' was morally wrong to be involved; this was not what had been intended in the desire to support democracy in South-East Asia. If Vietnam was the catalyst, the protest was directed against the predominant values of society, as Boyd and King (1972) interpret the widespread disaffection in the universities: 'Protest was essentially against the large-scale identification of education with technological "processing" – the parcelling, distribution, and consumption of knowledge, people and expectations on an apparently automatic and illiberal basis' (p. 497).

Finally, as we outlined in Chapter 9, the evidence presented in the Coleman and Plowden Reports suggested that schools might have less influence than had been supposed in bringing about change in the wider society. By 1970, considerable unease had been expressed at the utility with which rationalist models could be used to manage the affairs of society. It is no accident that in this social context the educational ideas of Ivan Illich received such widespread attention.

Illich's thesis is that the institutions which form such a central feature of the social structure in the 'north' distort, even destroy, the purposes for which they were established: thus the Church destroys religion; hospitals, health; and schools, education. Each is what Illich calls a manipulative institution and as such is socially and psychologically addictive. 'Social addiction . . . consists in the tendency to prescribe increased treatment if smaller quantities have not yielded the desired results' (1971, p. 55). An example of psychological addiction is the individual needing more of the processes or product of the institution – more schooling, more certificates and approval from the official teacher – rather than taking responsibility for his/her own learning.

The message from the de-schoolers is that the big, centrally planned, rational institution is creating the opposite effect to that intended. De-schooling was a reaction against the technico-bureaucratic world. So also was the 'hippie' movement, the attraction of communes and the search for an alternative, self-sufficient, life-style. In social science, this protest was reflected in a renewed concern with the individual's subjective experiences, at its most extreme in the work of ethnomethodologists like Harold Garfinkel. Occult literature, such as Castaneda's *The Teachings of Don Juan* (1968), began to appear on reading lists.

In the sociology of education the so-called 'new-directions' movement reflected this trend to individualism. As we saw in Chapter 2, this perspective presented teachers making their social world, and as this world was the construct of consciousness, so could it be changed by consciousness. What mattered was a commitment to a common humanity such that children were to be encouraged to develop their own understanding of the world, be this through the English curriculum, social studies or physics (Hoskyns, 1976). For Greene (1971) the purpose of the curriculum was that 'The individual can release himself into his own inner time and re-discover the ways in which objects arise, the ways in which experience develops' (p. 266).

Of course, Greene, Illich and Reimer (1971) were correct in their analysis. Schools are anti-educational, students find much learning boring and irrelevant to their interests. The addictive quality of schools is frequently to be seen in seminars when students listen politely to one of their peers giving a paper but only write down what the teachers says – what becomes authenticated knowledge. Much learning, even in the social sciences, seems to have no relationship to how the individual understands self or appreciates the nature of the social world. It is the case that schools concentrate on the cognitive to the expense of the emotional and spiritual. Schools may well be producing individuals who are respectful of the authority of science, yet incapable of empathy with their fellow beings, stunted in their appreciation of the consciousness of others.

This, however, is only *part* of the story; there is the other side to the paradox we have already identified. Foster (1971) comments, 'Revolutionary changes are not spearheaded by the peasantry but by the outputs of the schools. The overthrow of colonial regimes can justly be attributed to the products of western education' (p. 272). In the opinion of Gintis (1972) the neglected dimension in Illich's work is the recognition that the addictive behaviour identified 'is a reasonable accommodation to the options for meaningful social outlets *in the context* of capitalist institutions' (p. 76, emphasis Gintis). Schools are not just factories for the production of a docile work force, they are also institutions in which individuals develop critical appreciations of the nature of the world. Schooling may well be addictive. It also provides the opportunity for individuals to overcome the prejudice, bigotry and superstition which may restrict their understanding. Schooling is both oppressive and liberating, restrictive and enlarging, it can stultify and also facilitate the enrichment of our common humanity.

Individuals in every social system are constrained to some extent. As a Judge in the High Court is reputed to have said, 'My freedom to wave my fist in the air is prescribed by where you place your chin.' All forms of social life impose controls on members; to say that the school reproduces the social order is to give a truism that barely enhances our understanding of the nature of education within society. My argument, therefore, is that just as the focus on individualism was a reaction to the bureaucratic, consumer-oriented world of the 1960s, so the resurgence of interest in various macro-sociologies of education in the late 1970s was a reaction to the naivety in the micro-approaches, a naivety which ignored the structural context of identity.

Correspondence thesis

An aspect of the renewed interest in macro-issues was an enthusiastic adoption of neo-Marxist approaches. The attraction of Marx's work lay in the apparent marriage it made between the individual and the structure of society. Many postulated a *correspondence thesis* in which the hierarchies within schools were said to mirror the hierarchies necessary for the sustaining of capitalist relations of production. Admitting to an 'enormous over-simplification', Benton (1974) identified schools as the arena where, 'The necessary attitudes, skills and disciplines are being inculcated into the appropriate individuals in the appropriate proportions for the requirements of the capitalist-labour market' (p. 14). One suspects that there are many capitalists whose wish would be 'if only it were so'. It is quite possible to read Benton's article with the phrase 'advanced industrial society' replacing 'capitalism'. There is no evidence that changes in the form of ownership would of itself alter the conditions of life for the majority. Benton's critique raises pertinent issues about degrading and exploitative work relationships which persist even in a modern industrial society, but the attribution of this to capitalism as such seems to me to be an act of faith rather than reason.

The striking fact about education is not how well it serves the requirements of capitalism but how badly. Finn, Grant and Johnson (1978) write as people, who, they claim, 'work in an educational system under siege or who are blocked from entering it' (p. 144). At the time of their writing, one assumes 1977, the then British Labour Government was committed to reduce planned expenditure *growth* in education; nevertheless actual expenditure in *real terms* was to be increased from £7.6 billion in 1977-8, to £7.8 billion in 1981-2. It was a little premature to see this as a system 'under siege'. The analysis which is presented by Finn, Grant and Johnson correctly identifies failures in the predominant social democratic tradition of British educational policy, failures such as the difficulty in achieving equality of outcomes, the relative failure of women in the system and the dangers in increasing professionalism in teaching.

197

Their analysis of these problems, however, is so enveloped in a faith in Marxist discourse as to be reduced to mere slogans. Apparently, the problems of working-class educability have been divorced from 'real, ongoing class relationships' (p. 166); bad behaviour in classrooms is a 'manifestation of class struggle at the level of the classroom' (p. 173). They also assert that 'The incorporation of "progressivism" into classroom practice, as an approach and a method of control, takes place within the determinants of the class struggle in the classroom' (p. 175). Such slogans re-affirm the commitment to a form of analysis which I suspect is moribund, even tragically so, as the problems identified are real and persistent.

Probably the most influential work in this loosely neo-Marxist tradition is that of Bowles and Gintis (1976). For them 'The educational system is an integral element in the reproduction of the prevailing class structure of society' (p. 126). Crucial to the maintenance of the existing order is the reproduction of a form of consciousness through which members of society come to accept hierarchies as socially just. One of the weaknesses in the analysis which Bowles and Gintis present is that the knowledge through which consciousness is at least partially formed, the curriculum, is not part of their overall framework. The heart of the process of reproduction 'is to be found not in the content of the educational encounter' (p. 265). This raises issues about the relationship between form and content which await exploration. Does the form affect content; do the social relations which obtain in a Catholic school, for example, influence the content transmitted; are we to assume that content is of little importance? The issue is complex. Foster (1965) argues that the long-standing recommendations for the introduction of agricultural studies in schools of the 'south' would, if implemented, have little influence on economic development. He shows that in Ghana 'the strength of academic education has lain precisely in the fact that it is preeminently a *vocational* education providing access to those occupations with the most prestige and, most important, the highest pay within the Ghanaian economy' (p. 145). Foster seems to be implying that at a certain stage in development the content of education is less important than the level of attainment. At the same time, however, the curriculum renewal movement of the past two decades has argued that content is critical to the promotion of a 'relevant' education. The lack of discussion of these issues, and the dismissal of content, is a major gap in Bowles and Gintis's analysis of schools as agents of reproduction in America.

There are other problems. If schools are so pervasive, so powerful in the reproduction of the consciousness necessary to support capitalist relations of production, how did Bowles and Gintis manage to escape this insidious influence? They recognize 'that people produce themselves' (p. 278), but in their desire to indict capitalism, they seem able to slide over the implications of this observation and are pushed into a conspiracy theory where the capitalist class successfully manipulates the educational system. The model of the individual which emerges from Bowles and Gintis's work is determined by the economy, duped by the ruling class and incapable of acting in his/her perceived 'best' interests.

Education and 'cultural markets'

The substantive critique of Bowles and Gintis, that they lack a theory of content, has been extended by Collins (1976) and O'Keeffe (1978) into a lack, not only of content but also of a theory of culture. For Collins, 'Education is important for elites . . . because it gives them the solidarity of an esoteric in-group culture.' That is, part of the ownership of the means of production in society is the ownership of knowledge. In the continual struggle for domination, education has an economic payoff as it enables some groups, 'to carve out professional and technical monopolies over lucrative services and vulnerable sectors' (1976, p. 251). The rise in credentialism to which we made reference in the two previous chapters is part of this process of cultural domination. For O'Keeffe, what he labels the 'consumption aspects of education' are ignored in Bowles and Gintis's work. He argues that the growth in subjects like sociology 'reflects neither the demands of the labour market nor those of the corporate state, but is rather a manifestation of intellectual consumption' (p. 256). Both O'Keeffe and Collins are re-introducing a Weberian notion to the discussion, both recognizing that the transmission of status through cultural symbols is a necessary component to any discussion of the processes of reproduction.

The importance of status as a pattern of domination within society is recognized by Musgrove (1978), who argues that the capitalist bourgeoisie has not established a cultural hegemony over the school curriculum, but that 'The culture which is "hegemonic" is in fact the gentry culture' (p. 103), a culture built on values of honour, service and courage and which is not fixed by ideas of training for jobs, or specific preparation for later stages in life. For O'Keeffe there is a distinction between the 'bourgeois' and the 'middle-class'. The former refers to the ownership of physical capital and the latter to 'specialised human capital formation, and discursive intellectual consumerism'. It is to the middle-class-dominated occupational structure, he argues, that education most obviously articulates. 'In the massive expansion of education the contemporary middle-classes have stumbled on a marvellous device for financing their direct professional interests (medicine, law and so on) and also the "investment consumerism" which characterizes their intellectual life' (1979, p. 49). But, as we saw in Chapter 9, the contemporary British middle class is an heterogeneous group and becoming more so. One consequence may be that there is likely to be less clarity in what counts as 'investment consumerism' and greater diversity of opinion as to what ought to count as school knowledge.

In discussing education and the structure of opportunity we introduced Collins's idea of *cultural markets*. By this he means that what determines the structures and contacts of educational systems is not just the product of economic forces but an amalgam of multifaceted interests. As Weber makes the distinction between class, status and party, so Collins sees the determinants of education as a kaleidoscope of economic, cultural and organizational/political demands. 'Education has been part of struggles for practical economic skills, for cultural integration and prestige or particular associational groups, and for political control by and within formal organizations' (1977, p. 5). Without pushing the analogy too far, he argues that cultural markets, as with all markets, require a common currency and independent sources of supply and demand for their goods. The currency in this case will be the certificates approved by the dominant groups in society. This currency will also tend to have a status aspect, as in the degree market in the UK. For example, subject of degree and the institution which awarded the degree may be just as much a part of the currency as the level of the degree awarded. Further, Collins argues, as in all markets it is possible to 'buy' the same object but for different uses. He gives as an example the way in which the curriculum in Classical China both met the needs of the Emperors for control and at the same time protected the status interests of the 'gentry'.

The advantage of these Weberian approaches is that they go beyond the uni-dimensionalism which is so apparent in many neo-Marxist accounts of education and the state. Conflict within education, contradictions, are necessary to the system. It is rather like rescuers at a fire holding out a blanket into which the victims of the fire can jump. The blanket only serves its purpose if the rescuers continue to pull in opposite directions; any resolution of their conflict and they would destroy the very artefact they are trying to maintain.

As well as seeing conflict as part of education, necessary in any system dedicated to the promotion of both individual talent and the general good, Collins's idea of cultural markets also suggests that the buyers are active, conscious beings using the market mechanisms for their own purposes. It seems to me that Gleeson and Mardle (1980) in their study of a college of further education in England, are struggling after some similar concept. They are aware of the dangers in both functionalist and economistic, neo-Marxist, work of portraying individuals who are dupes of external forces. Valiant though their own attempt is to escape this 'over-determined' view, they slip back into a familiar Marxist hidden hand, or conspiracy theory, in much of their analysis. Referring to apprentice-students on day release at the college, they write, 'those who enter the production process assume that they have done so voluntarily and without any compulsion from wider structural forces' (p. 125). Again, this may be true, as far as it goes. Students do face constraints of limited opportunity structures and demands for particular attributes from employers. But all this is saying is that the market is far from perfect; the claim that students are unaware of the conditions as they affect them remains unproven, as must Gleeson and Mardle's implied conspiracy theory.

The argument in this chapter has been that the correspondence thesis can neither be substantiated from recent history, nor does it adequately describe the relationship between education and the state. In a forthcoming book, O'Keeffe goes so far as to argue that the state education system of advanced capitalist society may be thought of as 'proto-socialist'. He outlines similarities between the educational systems of capitalist societies and the form of socialist societies; for example, in the former, market forces do not operate, rather education is governed by a series of administrative principles. In advanced capitalist societies, schools neither allow most of their students to express economic preference in the choices made, nor do they permit children to leave school before a prescribed time. In short, O'Keeffe argues (forthcoming):

> education is presided over by an administrative intelligentsia; that the principles of the capitalist economy obtain in education only in reduced form; that the system is for many children more coercive than the wider society and economy; and that the educative system is a middle-class world highly insulated from bourgeois production *and* the world of the working-class.

In developing his analysis, O'Keeffe draws on Bernstein's discussion of the relation between education and production, though suggesting that the distinction is false. Education can itself be seen as production, an assessment reflected in the judgment of a Chinese official at Peking University that, 'As a miner created less value than a teacher creates, he ought, in socialist theory, to get less money' (Maclure, 1980, p. 12). In elaborating his concept of classification, Bernstein argues that in capitalist societies, education and production are strongly classified and as such are *relatively autonomous* from each other; 'the principles, contexts and possibilities of production are not directly constituted in the principles, contexts and possibilities of education' (1977, p. 189).

Having recognized some degree of separation between the two, it still remains to specify the nature of the relationship that does exist. In what is an initial analysis of this problem, Bernstein uses the term *systemic relationship* to indicate the contradictions and discrepancies between the social relations of education and the social relations of work. One of these contradictions is illustrated by the tendency for the schooling of 'less-able' pupils to be regulated by reduced classification and framing strengths but at the same time for their work experience to be regulated through strong classification and framing.

In his discussion of systemic relationships Bernstein seems to mean something similar to Collins's notion of cultural markets. That is, the relationship between education and production has an economic component, but also a status and bureaucratic components. Like Collins, Bernstein uses an example from contemporary China where there is a desire to raise the economic, material base of the society and at the same time to alter status categories like those of intellectual/worker. The problem facing the development of Chinese education is one of balancing competing needs, of controlling the cultural markets such as to reproduce the human capital necessary to economic growth without creating renewed hierarchies based on intellectual status. The claim that education is relatively autonomous allows for the persistence of conflict as different groups exert pressures to achieve their goals. It seems not unreasonable, therefore, to conclude that contradiction is a necessary feature to contemporary educational systems.

Conclusion

In a sense we end where we began. At the beginning of this book I argued that there was no absolute truth in sociology, just differing perspectives. At different times different perspectives are more 'right' than others in exploring aspects of educational processes. But this authority is never inviolate, never immutable, changing in response to changing social contexts yet never in an even, mechanistic way. The relationship between education and the economy is similarly uncertain. One could argue that education has nothing to do with the economy; it is not governed by market forces, does not respond to perceived manpower needs nor teach children to honour and respect the industrial sector. On the other hand, one might argue that education completely corresponds in both content and form to the economy; schools produce a compliant labour force and through the issue of credentials legitimate existing hierarchies. In fact education does something in between, hence the theme of paradox and contradiction which has underlain this chapter. The various metaphors in use, from schools interact to schools reproduce the conditions for the maintenance of economic forms, are each attempts to capture part of the relationship. They are each a source of understanding, and also of not understanding, that web of encounters which we call education, a web which is enlivened by the competition between perspectives, as we have attempted to show in this book.

Bibliography

Chapter 1 Changing sociologies

Bauman, Z. (1977), *Hermeneutics and Social Science*, Hutchinson's University Library, London.

Benton, T. (1978), 'How many Sociologies?' *Sociological Review*, vol. 26, no. 2, May, pp. 217–36.

Berger, P. L. and Luckmann, T. (1967), *The Social Construction of Reality*, Penguin, Harmondsworth.

Blumer, H. (1965/1966), 'Sociological Implications of the Thought of George Herbert Mead', *American Journal of Sociology*, vol. 71, pp. 535–44; also in B. R. Cosin (ed.) (1971), *School and Society*, Routledge & Kegan Paul, London.

Bourdieu, P. (1977), *Outline of a Theory of Practice*, Cambridge University Press.

Central Advisory Council for Education (1953), *Early Leaving*, HMSO, London.

Central Advisory Council for Education (1959), *15 to 18* (Crowther Report), HMSO, London.

Central Advisory Council for Education (1967), *Children and their Primary Schools* (Plowden Report), HMSO, London.

Cicourel, A. V. (1971), 'The Acquisition of Social Structure', in J. D. Douglas (ed.), *Understanding Everyday Life*, Routledge & Kegan Paul, London.

Collins, R. (1975), *Conflict Sociology: Towards an Explanatory Science*, Academic Press, New York.

Committee on Higher Education (1963), *Higher Education* (Robbins Report), HMSO, London.

Corrigan, P. (1975), 'Dichotomy is Contradiction: On "Society" as Constraint and Construction. Remarks on the Doctrine of the "Two Sociologies" ', *Sociological Review*, vol. 23, no. 2, May, pp. 211–43.

Dawe, A. (1970), 'The Two Sociologies', *British Journal of Sociology*, vol. 21, no. 2, pp. 207–18.

Durkheim, E. (1938), *The Rules of Sociological Method*, Free Press, Chicago.
Durkheim, E. (1956), *Education and Society*, Free Press, Chicago.
Durkheim, E. (1961), *Moral Education: A Study in the Theory and Application of the Sociology of Education*, Free Press, Chicago.
Durkheim, E. (1964), *Essays on Sociology and Philosophy* (ed. K. H. Wolff), Harper, New York.
Durkheim, E. (1977), *The Evolution of Educational Thought*, Routledge & Kegan Paul, London.
Fauconnet, P. (1923), 'The Pedagogical Work of E. Durkheim', *American Journal of Sociology*, vol. 28, no. 5, pp. 525–53.
Floud, J., Halsey, A. H., Martin, F. M. (1956), *Social Class and Educational Opportunity*, Heinemann, London.
Glass, D. V. (1954), *Social Mobility in Britain*, Routledge & Kegan Paul, London.
Lukes, S. (1973), *Emile Durkheim: His Life and Works*, Penguin, Harmondsworth.
McLellan, D. (1969), *The Young Hegelians and Karl Marx*, Macmillan, London.
McLellan, D. (1973), *Karl Marx: His Life and Thought*, Macmillan, London.
Marx, K. and Engels, F. (1960), 'The Manifesto of the Communist Party', in *The Essential Left*, Allen & Unwin, London.
Marx, K. and Engels, F. (1970), *The German Ideology*, Lawrence & Wishart, London.
Marx, K. and Engels, F. (1962), *Selected Works*, vol. 1, Foreign Languages Publishing House, Moscow.
Meltzer, B. N., Petras, J. W. and Reynolds, L. T. (1975), *Symbolic Interactionism*, Routledge & Kegan Paul, London.
Merton, R. K. (1957), *Social Theory and Social Structure*, Free Press, Chicago.
Miller, D. L. (1973), *George Herbert Mead: Self, Language and the World*, University of Texas Press, Austin.
Mills, C. Wright (1959), *The Sociological Imagination*, Oxford University Press, New York.
Schutz, A. (1953), 'Common-sense and Scientific Interpretation of Human Action; *Philosophy and Phenomenological Research*, September, pp. 1–37.
Schutz, A. (1972), *The Phenomenology of the Social World*, Heinemann, London.
Simon, B. (1965), 'Karl Marx and Education', *Marxism Today*, August, pp. 230–41; reprinted in B. Simon, (1971), *Intelligence, Psychology and Education. A Marxist Critique*, Lawrence & Wishart, London.
Vaughan, M. and Archer, M. S. (1971), *Social Conflict and Educational Change in England and France 1789–1848*, Cambridge University Press.

Weber, M. (1972), 'The "Rationalization" of Education and Training' in B. R. Cosin (ed.), *Education: Structure and Society*, Penguin, Harmondsworth.

Williams, R. (1973), 'Base and Superstructure in Marxist Cultural Theory', *New Left Review*, vol. 82, pp. 3–16; reprinted in R. Dale *et al.* (eds), *Schooling and Capitalism*, Routledge & Kegan Paul, London, 1976.

Chapter 2 Changing sociologies of education

Althusser, L. (1971), 'Ideology and Ideological State Apparatuses', in *Lenin and Philosophy and Other Essays*, New Left Books, London, pp. 123–73; reprinted in B. R. Cosin, (ed.), *Education: Structure and Society*, Penguin, Harmondsworth, 1972.

Banks, O. (1968), *The Sociology of Education*, Batsford, London.

Banks, O. (1974), 'The "New" Sociology of Education', *Forum for the Discussion of New Trends in Education*, vol. 17, no. 1, pp. 4–7.

Bates, T.R. (1975), 'Gramsci and the Theory of Hegemony', *Journal of History of Ideas*, vol. 36, no. 2, pp. 351–66.

Bernbaum, G. (1977), *Knowledge and Ideology in the Sociology of Education*, Macmillan, London.

Bernstein, B. (1972), *Sociology and the Sociology of Education: Some Aspects*, in Open University Course Unit E282, 15/17, pp. 99–108.

Bourdieu, P. (1966), 'The School as a Conservative Force: Scholastic and Cultural Inequalities', reprinted in J. Eggleston (ed.), *Contemporary Research in the Sociology of Education*, Methuen, London.

Bourdieu, P. and Bottanski, L. (1978), 'Changes in Social Structure and Changes in the Demand for Education', in S. Giner and M. Scotford Archer (eds), *Contemporary Europe: Social Structures and Cultural Patterns*, Routledge & Kegan Paul, London.

Bourdieu, P. and Passeron, J. C. (1977), *Reproduction in Education, Society and Culture*, Sage Publications, London.

Brown, R. (ed.) (1973), *Knowledge, Education and Cultural Change*, Tavistock Publications, London.

Collins, R. (1977), 'Some Comparative Principles of Educational Stratification', *Harvard Education Review*, vol. 47, no. 1.

Davies, B. (1976), *Social Control and Education*, Methuen, London.

Demaine, J. (1977), 'On the New Sociology of Education', *Economy and Society*, vol. 6, no. 2, pp. 111–44.

DiMaggio, P. (1979), 'Review Essay: On Pierre Bourdieu', *American Journal of Sociology*, vol. 84, no. 6, pp. 1460–74.

Erben, M. and Gleeson, D. (1975), 'Reproduction and Social Structures: Comments on Louis Althusser's Sociology of Education', *Educational Studies*, vol. 1, no. 2, June, pp. 121–7.

Flew, A. (1976), *Sociology, Equality and Education*, Macmillan, London.

Floud, J. (1978), *Functions, Purposes and Powers in Education*,

University College of Swansea Press.

Floud, J. and Halsey, A. H. (1959), 'The Sociology of Education: A Trend Report and Bibliography', *Current Sociology*, vol. 7, pp. 165–235.

Floud, J., Halsey, A. H. and Martin, F. M. (1956), *Social Class and Educational Opportunity*, Heinemann, London.

Gorbutt, D. (1972), 'The New Sociology of Education', *Education for Teaching*, Autumn, pp. 3–11.

Gramsci, A. (1971), *Selections from the Prison Notebooks of Antonio Gramsci*, (ed.) Q. Hoare and G. Nowell-Smith, Lawrence & Wishart, London.

Halsey, A. H. (1975), 'The Juxtaposition of Social and Individual Approaches in Compensatory Education Projects', *Compensatory Education*, Documentation Centre for Education in Europe, Council of Europe, Strasbourg.

Halsey, A. H., Floud, J. and Anderson, C. A. (1961), *Education, Economy and Society*, Collier-Macmillan, London.

Heath, A. (1978), 'Significant Developments in the Sociology of Education?', *Oxford Review of Education*, vol. 4, no. 1, pp. 95–110.

Jenks, C. (1977), *Rationality, Education and the Social Organisation of Knowledge*, Routledge & Kegan Paul, London.

Johnson, R. (1976), 'Notes on the Schooling of the English Working Class 1780–1850', in R. Dale *et al*, (eds), *Schooling and Capitalism*, Routledge & Kegan Paul, London.

Karabel, J. and Halsey, A. H. (1977), *Power and Ideology in Education*, Oxford University Press, London.

Kennett, J. (1973), 'The Sociology of Pierre Bourdieu', *Educational Review*, vol. 25, no. 3, June 1973, pp. 237–49.

Mannheim, K. and Stewart, W. A. C. (1962), *An Introduction to the Sociology of Education*, Routledge & Kegan Paul, London.

Mardle, G. (1977), 'Power, Tradition and Change: Educational Implications of the Thought of Antonio Gramsci', in D. Gleeson (ed.), *Identity and Structure: Issues in the Sociology of Education*, Nafferton Books, Driffield, pp. 134–52.

Mead, M. (1942), 'Our Educational Emphasis in Primitive Perspective', *American Journal of Sociology*, vol. 48, pp. 633–9; reprinted in J. Middleton (ed.), *From Child to Adult*, The Natural History Press, New York.

Musgrave, P. W. (1965), *The Sociology of Education*, Methuen, London.

Shipman, M. D. (1973), 'Bias in the Sociology of Education', *Educational Review*, vol. 25, no. 3, pp. 190–200.

Swartz, D. (1977), 'Pierre Bourdieu: The Cultural Transmission of Social Inequality', *Harvard Educational Review*, vol. 47, no. 4, pp. 545–55.

Thompson, E. P. (1978), *The Poverty of Theory*, Merlin Press, London.

Whitty, G. (1974), 'Sociology and the Problem of Radical Educational Change', in M. Flude and J. Ahier (eds), *Educability, Schools and Ideology*, Croom Helm, London.

Williams, R. (1973), 'Base and Superstructure in Marxist Cultural Theory', *New Left Review*, no. 82, reprinted in R. Dale *et al.* (1976), *Schooling and Capitalism*, Routledge & Kegan Paul, London.

Williamson, B. (1974), 'Continuities and Discontinuities in the Sociology of Education', in M. Flude and J. Ahier (eds), *Educability, Schools and Ideology*, Croom Helm, London.

Young, M. F. D. (1971), *Knowledge and Control: New Directions for the Sociology of Education*, Collier-Macmillan, London.

Young, M. F. D. (1972), 'On the Politics of Educational Knowledge', *Economy and Society*, vol. 1, no. 2, pp. 194–215.

Young, M. F. D. (1973), 'Taking Sides Against the Probable: Problems of Relativism and Commitment in Teaching and the Sociology of Knowledge', *Educational Review*, vol. 25, no. 3, pp. 210–22.

Young, M. F. D. and Whitty, G. (1977), *Society, State and Schooling*, The Falmer Press, Brighton.

Chapter 3 Socialization 1. The child and the family

Aries, P. (1973), *Centuries of Childhood*, Penguin, Harmondsworth.

Berger, P. L. and Luckmann, T. (1967), *The Social Construction of Reality*, Penguin, Harmondsworth.

Bernstein, B. (1971), *Class, Codes and Control*, vol. 1, *Theoretical Studies towards a Sociology of Language*, Routledge & Kegan Paul, London.

Bernstein, B. (1977), *Class, Codes and Control*, vol. 3, *Towards a Theory of Educational Transmissions*, 2nd edition, Routledge & Kegan Paul, London.

Blumer, H. (1965), 'Sociological Implications of the Thought of G. H. Mead', *American Journal of Sociology*, vol. 71, pp. 535–44.

Brearley, M. *et al.* (1969), *Fundamentals in the First School*, Basil Blackwell, Oxford.

Byrne, E. M. (1978), *Women and Children*, Tavistock Publications, London.

Cicourel, A. V. (1973), 'The Acquisition of Social Structure: Towards a Developmental Sociology of Language and Meaning', in A. V. Cicourel, *Cognitive Sociology*, Penguin, Harmondsworth.

Clarke, J. and Jefferson, T. (1976), 'Working Class Youth Cultures', in G. Mungham and G. Pearson (eds), *Working Class Youth Cultures*, Routledge & Kegan Paul, London.

Clarke, J., Hall, S., Jefferson, T. and Roberts, B. (1976), 'Subcultures, Cultures and Class', in S. Hall and T. Jefferson (eds), *Resistance Through Rituals*, Hutchinson, London (in association with Centre for Contemporary Cultural Studies).

Colquhoun, R. (1976), 'Values, Socialization and Achievement: Aspects of Positivism in the Sociology of Education', in J. Beck *et al.* (eds), *Worlds Apart*, Collier-Macmillan, London.

Coulson, M. A. (1972), 'Role: A Redundant Concept in Sociology?

Some Educational Considerations', in J. A. Jackson (ed.), *Role*, Cambridge University Press.

Craft, M. (1970), 'Family, Class and Education: Changing Perspectives', in M. Craft (ed.), *Family, Class and Education*, Longman, London.

Davie, R., Butler, N. R. and Goldstein, H. (1972), *From Birth to Seven*, Longman, London (in association with National Children's Bureau).

Davies, B. (1976), *Social Control and Education*, Methuen, London.

Deem, R. (1978), *Women and Schooling*, Routledge & Kegan Paul, London.

Douglas, J. W. B. (1964), *The Home and the School*, MacGibbon & Kee, London.

Douglas, J. W. B. (1976), 'The Use and Abuse of National Cohorts' in M. D. Shipman (ed.), *The Organisation and Impact of Social Research*, Routledge & Kegan Paul, London.

Douglas, J. W. B., Ross, J. M. and Simpson, H. R. (1968), *All Our Future*, Peter Davies, London.

Featherstone, J. (1979), 'Family Matters', *Harvard Educational Review*, vol. 49, pp. 20–52.

Firestone, S. (1972), *The Dialectic of Sex*, Paladin, London.

Fogelman, K. (ed.) (1976), *Britain's Sixteen-Year-Olds*, National Children's Bureau, London.

Goldthorpe, J. H. and Lockwood, D. (1969), *The Affluent Worker in the Class Structure*, Cambridge University Press.

Greer, G. (1971), *The Female Eunuch*, Paladin, London.

Hoggart, R. (1958), *The Uses of Literacy*, Penguin, Harmondsworth.

Husen, T. (1975), *Social Influences on Educational Attainment*, OECD, Paris.

Hyman, H. H. (1953), 'The Value Systems of Different Classes', in R. Bendix and S. M. Lipset (eds), *Class, Status and Power*, Routledge & Kegan Paul, London.

Kahl, J. A. (1953), 'Educational and Occupational Aspirations of "Common Man's Boys" ', *Harvard Educational Review*, vol. 23, no. 3, pp. 186–203; reprinted in A. H. Halsey, J. Floud and C. A. Anderson, *Education, Economy and Society*, Collier-Macmillan, London.

Kluckhohn, F. R. (1958), 'Variations in the Basic Values of Family Systems', *Family Diagnosis*, vol. 39, pp. 63–72; reprinted in D. F. Swift (ed.) (1970), *Basic Readings in the Sociology of Education*, Routledge & Kegan Paul, London.

McClelland, D. C. (1963), 'The Achievement Motive in Economic Growth', in B. F. Hoselitz and W. E. Moore, *Industrialisation and Society*, UNESCO, Mouton, The Hague, pp. 74–96.

McRobbie, A. and Garber, J. (1976), 'Girls and Subcultures', in S. Hall and T. Jefferson (eds), *Resistance through Rituals*, Hutchinson, London, in Association with Centre for Contemporary Cultural Studies.

Mitchell, J. (1971), *Women's Estate*, Penguin, Harmondsworth.

Morgan, D. H. J. (1975), *Social Theory and the Family*, Routledge & Kegan Paul, London.

Murdock, P. (1949), *Social Structure*, Macmillan, New York.

Musgrove, F. (1964), *Youth and the Social Order*, Routledge & Kegan Paul, London.

Newson, J. and E. (1976), 'Parental Roles and Social Contexts', in M. D. Shipman (ed.), *The Organisation and Impact of Social Research*, Routledge & Kegan Paul, London.

Newson, J. and E. (1977), *Perspectives on School at Seven Years Old* (with P. Barnes), Allen & Unwin, London.

Oakley, A. (1972), *Sex, Gender and Society*, Temple Smith, London.

Parker, H. J. (1974), *View from the Boys*, David & Charles, Newton Abbott.

Parsons, T. (1951), *The Social System*, Routledge & Kegan Paul, London.

Patrick, J. (1972), *Glasgow Gang Observed*, Eyre Methuen, London.

Platt, A. (1969), 'The Rise of the Child Savers', *Annals of the American Academy*, January; reprinted in J. Beck *et al.* (1976), *Worlds Apart*, Collier-Macmillan, London.

Rosen, B. C. (1956), 'The Achievement Syndrome: A Psycho-cultural Dimension of Social Stratification' *American Sociological Review*, vol. 21, pp. 203-11.

Rosen, D. C. and D'Andrade, R. (1959), 'The Psychological Origin of Achievement Motivation', *Sociometry*, vol. 22.

Rutter, M. and Madge, N. (1976), *Cycles of Disadvantage: A Review of Research*, Heinemann, London.

Schnell, R. L. (1979), 'Childhood as Ideology: A Reinterpretation of the Common School', *British Journal of Educational Studies*, vol. 27, no. 1, February, pp. 7-28.

Sewell, W. H. (1961), 'Social Class and Childhood Personality', *Sociometry*, vol. 24, pp. 340-56.

Seymour, J. Madison (1974), 'The Rural School as an Acculturating Institution: The Iban of Malaysia', *Human Organisation*, vol. 33, no. 3, pp. 277-90.

Sharpe, S. (1976), *Just Like a Girl*, Penguin, Harmondsworth.

Swift, D. F. (1966), 'Social Class and Achievement Motivation', *Educational Research*, vol. 7, no. 2, pp. 83-95.

Swift, D. F. (1968), 'Social Class and Educational Adaptation', in H. J. Butcher (ed.), *Educational Research in Britain*, University of London Press.

Turner, R. H. (1962), 'Role-Taking: Process versus Conformity', in A. M. Rose (ed.), *Human Behaviour and Social Provision*, Routledge & Kegan Paul, London.

Wedge, P. and Prosser, H. (1973), *Born to Fail?*, Arrow Books, London (in association with National Children's Bureau).

West, D. J. and Farrington, D. P. (1977), *The Delinquent Way of Life*, Heinemann, London.

White, G. (1977), *Socialisation*, Longman, London.

Willis, P. E. (1977), *Learning to Labour: How Working Class Kids get Working Class Jobs*, Saxon House, London.

Winterbottom, M. R. (1969), 'The Relation of Need for Achievement to Learning Experiences in Independence and Mastery', in H. Prostansky and B. Seidenberg (eds), *Basic Studies in Social Psychology*, Holt, Rinehart & Winston, London.

Wrong, D. H. (1977), 'The Oversocialized Conception of Man in Modern Sociology', in D. H. Wrong (ed.), *Skeptical Sociology*, Heinemann, London.

Young, M. and Willmott, P. (1975), *The Symmetrical Family*, Penguin, Harmondsworth.

Chapter 4   Socialization 2. Language, intelligence and ability

Bane, M. J. and Jencks, C. (1977), 'Five Myths about Your I.Q.', in N. Block and G. Dworkin, *The I.Q. Controversy*, Quartet Books, London, pp. 325-38.

Baratz, S. S. and Baratz, J. C. (1970), 'Early Childhood Interaction: the Social Science Base of Institutional Reason', *Harvard Educational Review*, vol. 40, no. 1, pp. 24-50.

Berger. P. L. and Kellner, H. (1971), 'Marriage and the Construction of Reality: an Exercise in the Micro-Sociology of Knowledge', in B. R. Cosin *et al.* (eds), *School and Society*, Routledge & Kegan Paul, London.

Bernstein, B. (1971), *Class, Codes and Control*, vol. 1, Routledge & Kegan Paul, London.

Block, N. and Dworkin, G. (1977), *The I.Q. Controversy*, Quartet Books, London.

Bodmer, W. (1973), 'By the Colour of their Genes', *Times Literary Supplement*, August 1973.

Boring, E. G. (1923), 'Intelligence as the Tests Test It', *New Republic*, vol. 34, pp. 34-7.

Bourdieu, P. and Boltanski, L. (1978), 'Changes in Social Structure and Changes in the Demand for Education', in S. Giner and M. S. Archer (eds), *Contemporary Europe: Social Structures and Cultural Patterns*, Routledge & Kegan Paul, London.

Bowles, S. and Gintis, H. (1977), 'I.Q. in the U.S. Class Structure', in D. Gleeson (ed.), *Identity and Structure: Issues in the Sociology of Education*, Nafferton Books, Driffield.

Byrne, D. S. and Williamson, W. (1972), *The Myth of the Restricted Code*, Department of Sociology and Social Administration, Durham University.

Carnoy, M. (1974), *Education as Cultural Imperialism*, Longman, New York.

Cole, M., Gray, J., Gluck, J. A. and Sharp, D. W. (1971), *The Cultural Context of Learning and Thinking*, Tavistock Publications, London.

Coulthard, M. (1969), 'A Discussion of Restricted and Elaborated Codes', *Educational Review*, vol. 22, no. 1, pp. 38-50.

Durkheim, E. (1977), *The Evolution of Educational Thought*, Routledge & Kegan Paul, London.

Durkheim, E. and Mauss, M. (1963), *Primitive Classification*, Cohen & West, London.

Edmonds, R. and Moore, E. K. (1973), 'I.Q., Social Class and Educational Policy', *Change*, vol. 5, nos 8, 12, 64, October.

Edwards, A. D. (1976), *Language in Culture and Class*, Heinemann, London.

Edwards, A. D. and Hargreaves, D. H. (1976), 'The Social Scientific Base of Academic Radicalism', *Educational Review*, vol. 28, no. 2, pp. 83–93.

Gillie, O. (1978), 'Sir Cyril Burt and the Great I.Q. Fraud', *New Statesman*, 24 November, pp. 688–94.

Gladwin, T. (1970), *East is a Big Bird*, Harvard University Press.

Gumbert, E. B. and Spring, J. H. (1974), *The Superschool and the Superstate: American Education in the Twentieth Century, 1918–1970*, Wiley, New York.

Herrnstein, R. J. (1971), 'I.Q.', *Atlantic Monthly*, September, pp. 43–64.

Hextall, Ian and Sarup, M. (1977), 'School Knowledge, Evaluation and Alienation', in M. Young and G. Whitty (eds), *Society, State and Schooling*, Falmer Press, Ringmer, pp. 151–71.

Husen, T. (1975), *Social Influences on Educational Attainment*, OECD, Paris.

Jackson, L. A. (1974), 'The Myth of Elaborated and Restricted Codes', *Higher Educational Review*, vol. 6, pp. 65–81.

Jencks, C. *et al.* (1973), *Inequality: A Reassessment of the Effect of Family on Schooling in America*, Allen Lane, London.

Jensen, A. R. (1968), 'Social Class and Verbal Learning', in M. Deutsch, I. Katz and A. R. Jensen, *Social Class, Race and Psychological Development*, Holt, Rinehart & Winston, New York.

Jensen, A. R. (1969), 'How Much Can We Boost I.Q. and Scholastic Achievement?', *Harvard Educational Review*, vol. 39, no. 1, pp. 2–123.

Kamin, L. J. (1977), *The Science and Politics of I.Q.*, Penguin, Harmondsworth.

Krech, D., Crutchfield and Livson, N. (1969), *Elements of Psychology*, Knopf, New York.

Labov, W. (1972), 'The Logic of Non-standard English', in P. P. Giglioli (ed.), *Language and Social Context*, Penguin, Harmondsworth.

Lawler, J. (1978), *I.Q., Heritability and Racism: A Marxist Critique of Jensenism*, Lawrence & Wishart, London.

Mead, G. H. (1956), *On Social Psychology*, ed. A. Strauss, University of Chicago Press.

Mehan, H. (1973), 'Assessing Children's School Performance', *Recent Sociology*, no. 5, pp. 240–64; also in J. Beck *et al.* (eds) (1976), *Worlds Apart*, Collier-Macmillan, London.

Robinson, P. (1976), *Education and Poverty*, Methuen, London.

Robinson, P. (1977), 'Poverty and Education: A Pragmatic Circle', in D. Gleeson (ed.), *Identity and the Structure: Issues in the Sociology of Education*, Nafferton Books, Driffield.

Rosen, H. (1972), *Language and Class, a Critical Look at the Theories of Basil Bernstein*, Falling Wall Press, Bristol.

Rosenthal, R. and Jacobson, L. (1968), *Pygmalion in the Classroom*, Holt, Rinehart & Winston, New York.

Scott, M. B. and Lyman, S. M. (1968), 'Accounts', *American Sociological Review*, vol. 33, pp. 46–62.

Stubbs, M. (1976), *Language, Schools and Classrooms*, Methuen, London.

Thoday, J. M. (1965), 'Geneticism and Environmentalism', in J. E. Meade and A. S. Parkes (eds), *Genetic and Environmental Factors in Human Ability*, Oliver & Boyd, Edinburgh.

Trudgill, P. (1974), *Sociolinguistics*, Penguin, Harmondsworth.

Tulkin, S. R. and Konner, M. J. (1973), 'Alternative Conceptions of Intellectual Functioning', *Human Development*, vol. 16, pp. 33–52.

Weber, M. (1948), *Essays in Sociology*, ed. H. H. Gerth and C. Wright Mills, Routledge & Kegan Paul, London.

Whitty, G. (1976), 'Teachers and Examiners', in G. Whitty and M. Young, *Explorations in the Politics of School Knowledge*, Nafferton Books, Driffield.

Wilkinson, R. (1962), 'Training the Ruler: Confucian and Victorian Schools', *Teachers' College Record*, vol. 64, no. 3, pp. 236–47.

Chapter 5 Into the classroom

Amidon, E. and Flanders, N. (1967), 'Interaction Analysis as a Feedback System', in E. J. Amidon and J. B. Hough (eds), *Interaction Analysis: Theory, Research and Application*, Addison-Wesley, Reading, Mass., pp. 121–40.

Amidon, E. J. and Hough, J. B. (1967), *Interaction Analysis: Theory, Research and Application*, Addison-Wesley, Reading, Mass.

Anderson, H. H. (1939), 'The Movement of Domination and of Socially Integrative Behaviour in Teachers' Contacts with Children', *Child Development*, vol. 10, pp. 73–89; reprinted in E. J. Amidon and J. B. Hough (eds), *Interaction Analysis: Theory, Research and Application*, Addison-Wesley, Reading, Mass., 1967.

Barnes, D. (1976), *From Communication to Curriculum*, Penguin, Harmondsworth.

Barnes, D., Brittin, J. and Rosen, H. (1969), *Language, the Learner and the School*, Penguin, Harmondsworth.

Becker, H. S. (1952), 'Social Class Variations in the Teacher-pupil Relationship', *Journal of Educational Psychology*, vol. 25, pp. 451–65; reprinted in B. R. Cosin *et al.*, *School and Society*, 2nd edn, Routledge & Kegan Paul, London, 1977.

Bellack, A. A. and Davitz, J. R. (1963), *The Language of the Classroom: Meanings Communicated in High School Teaching*, Teachers College, Columbia University, New York.

Bibliography

Bellack, A. A., Kliebard, H. M., Hyman, R. T. and Smith, F. L. (1966), *The Language of the Classroom*, Teachers College Press, New York.

Bennett, N. (1976), *Teaching Styles and Pupil Progress*, Open Books, London.

Berlak, A. C., Berlak, H., Bagenstos, N. T. and Mitel, E. R. (1975), 'Teaching and Learning in English Primary Schools', *School Review*, vol. 83, no. 2, pp. 215–43.

Berlak, H. and Berlak, A. (1975), 'An Analysis of English Informal Primary Schools', *Interchange*, vol. 6, no. 3, pp. 11–22.

Biddle, B. J. (1967), 'Methods and Concepts in Classroom Research', *Review of Educational Research*, vol. 37, no. 3, pp. 337–57.

Bloom, B. S. (1954), *The Taxonomy of Objectives*, Longman, London.

Chanan, G. and Delamont, S. (1975), *Frontiers of Classroom Research*, NFER, Slough.

Cicourel, A. V. and Kituse, J. I. (1963), *The Educational Decision Makers*, Bobbs-Merrill, Indianapolis.

Delamont, S. (1976), *Interaction in the Classroom*, Methuen, London.

Delamont, S. (1978), 'Sociology and the Classroom', in L. Barton and R. Meighan (eds), *Sociological Interpretations of Schooling and Classrooms: A Reappraisal*, Nafferton Books, Driffield.

Dumont, R. V. and Wax, M. L. (1969), 'Cherokee School Society and the Intercultural Classroom', *Human Organisation*, vol. 28, no. 3, pp. 217–26; reprinted in B. R. Cosin (ed.), *School and Society*, Routledge & Kegan Paul, London, 1977.

Durkheim. E. (1956), *Education and Sociology*, Free Press, Chicago.

Edwards, A. D. and Furlong, V. J. (1978), *The Language of Teaching*, Heinemann, London.

Flanders, N. A. (1970), *Analysing Teacher Behaviour*, Addison-Wesley. Reading, Mass.

Furlong, V. (1976), 'Interaction Sets in the Classroom: Towards a Study of Pupil Knowledge', in M. Stubbs and S. Delamont, *Explorations in Classroom Observation*, John Wiley, London.

Furlong, V. (1977), 'Anancy Goes to School. A Case Study of Pupils' Knowledge of their Teachers', in P. Woods and M. Hammersely (eds), *School Experience*, Croom Helm, London.

Gannaway, H. (1976), 'Making Sense of School', in M. Stubbs and S. Delamont (eds), *Explorations in Classroom Observation*, John Wiley, London.

Geer, B. (1971), 'Teaching', in B. R. Cosin *et al.*, *School and Society*, Routledge & Kegan Paul, London.

Halsey, A. H. (1975), 'The Juxtaposition of Social and Individual Approaches in Compensatory Education Projects', in *Compensatory Education*, Council of Europe. Documentation Centre for Education in Europe, Strasbourg.

Halsey, A. H., Floud, J. and Anderson, C. A. (1961), *Education, Economy and Society*, Collier-Macmillan, London.

Hammersley, M. (1977), 'School Learning: the Cultural Reasons Required by Pupils to Answer a Teacher's Question', in P. Woods and

M. Hammersley, *School Experience: Exploration in the Sociology of Education*, Croom Helm, London.

Hammersley, M. and Woods, P. (eds) (1976), *The Process of Schooling*, Routledge & Kegan Paul, London, in association with the Open University Press.

Hargreaves, A. (1977), 'Progressivism and Pupil Autonomy', *Sociological Review*, vol. 25, no. 3, pp. 585–621.

Hargreaves, A. (1978), 'The Significance of Classroom Coping Strategies', in L. Barton and R. Meighan (eds), *Sociological Interpretation of Schooling and Classrooms: A Reappraisal*, Nafferton Books, Driffield.

Hargreaves, A. (1979), 'Strategies, Decisions and Control: Interaction in a Middle School Classroom', in J. Eggleston (ed.), *Teacher Decision Making in the Classroom*, Routledge & Kegan Paul, London.

Hargreaves, A. and Warwick, D. (1978), 'Attitudes to Middle Schools', *Education*, vol. 3, no. 13, April, pp. 25–9.

Hargreaves, D. H. (1967), *Social Relations in a Secondary School*, Routledge & Kegan Paul, London.

Hargreaves, D. H. (1972), *Interpersonal Relations and Education*, Routledge & Kegan Paul, London.

Hargreaves, D. H. (1977), 'The Process of Typification in Classroom Interaction', *British Journal of Educational Psychology*, vol. 47, no. 3, pp. 274–84.

Hargreaves, D. H. (1978), 'Whatever Happened to Symbolic Interactionism?' in L. Barton and R. Meighan (eds), *Sociological Interpretations of Schooling and Classrooms: A Reappraisal*, Nafferton Books, Driffield.

Hargreaves, D. H., Hester, S. K. and Mellor, F. J. (1975), *Deviance in Classrooms*, Routledge & Kegan Paul, London.

Harrod, P. M. F. (1977), 'Talk in Junior and Middle School Classrooms: an Exploratory Investigation', *Educational Review*, vol. 29, no. 2, pp. 97–106.

Hoetker, J. and Ahlbrand, W. P. (1969), 'The Persistence of the Recitation', *American Educational Research Journal*, vol. 6, pp. 145–67.

Jackson, P. W. (1968), *Life in Classrooms*, Holt, Rinehart & Winston, New York.

Karabel, J. and Halsey, A. H. (1977), *Power and Ideology in Education*, Oxford University Press, London.

Keddie, N. (1971), 'Classroom Knowledge', in M. F. D. Young (ed.), *Knowledge and Control: New Directions for the Sociology of Education*, Collier-Macmillan, London.

Lacey, C. (1966), 'Differentiation and Polarisation', *British Journal of Sociology*, vol. 17, no. 3.

Lacey, C. (1970), *Hightown Grammar*, Manchester University Press.

Lacey, C. (1976), 'Problems of Sociological Fieldwork: a Review of the Methodology of "Hightown Grammar" ', in M. D. Shipman (ed.), *The Organisation and Impact of Social Research*, Routledge & Kegan Paul, London.

Lewin, K., Lippitt, R. and White, R. K. (1939), 'Patterns of Aggressive Behaviour in Experimentally Created "Social Climates" ', *Journal of Social Psychology*, vol. 10, pp. 271–99.

McAleese, R. and Hamilton, D. (1978), *Understanding Classroom Life*, NFER, Windsor.

Parsons, T. (1961), 'The School Class as a Social System: Some of its Functions in American Society', in A. H. Halsey, J. Floud and C. A. Anderson (eds). *Education, Economy and Society*, Collier-Macmillan, London.

Quine, W. G. (1974), 'Polarised Cultures in Comprehensive Schools', *Research in Education*, November, p. 9–25.

Rist, R. C. (1977), 'On Understanding the Processes of Schooling: the Contributions of the Labelling Theory', in J. Karabel and A. H. Halsey (eds), *Power and Ideology in Education*, Oxford University Press, London.

Robinson, P. E. D. (1974), 'An Ethnography of Classrooms', in J. Eggleston (ed.), *Contemporary Research in the Sociology of Education*, Methuen, London.

Schutz, A. (1970), *On Phenomenology and Social Relations*, H. R. Wagner, University of Chicago Press.

Sharp, R. and Green, A. (1975), *Education and Social Control: A Study in Progressive Primary Education*, Routledge & Kegan Paul, London.

Simon, A. and Boyer, E. G. (eds) (1970), *Mirrors for Behavior*, Research for Better Schools, Philadelphia.

Sinclair, J. McH. and Coulthard, R. M. (1974), *Towards an Analysis of Discourse: The English Used by Teachers and Pupils*, Open University Press, Milton Keynes.

Stebbins, R. A. (1971), 'The Meaning of Disorderly Behaviour: Teacher Definitions of a Classroom Situation', *Sociology of Education*, vol. 44. pp. 217–36.

Stebbins, R. A. (1977), 'The Meaning of Academic Performance: How Teachers Define a Classroom Situation', in P. Woods and M. Hammersley (eds), *School Experience: Explorations in the Sociology of Education*, Croom Helm, London.

Stubbs, M. (1976), *Language, Schools and Classrooms*, Methuen, London.

Stubbs, M. and Delamont, S. (1976), *Explorations in Classroom Observation*, Wiley, London.

Taba, H. (1962), *Curriculum Development: Theory and Practice*, Harcourt, Brace & World, New York.

Tyler, R. W. (1949), *Basic Principles of Curriculum and Instruction*, University of Chicago Press.

Walker, R. (1972), 'The Sociology of Education and Life in School Classrooms', *International Review of Education*, vol. 18, no. 1, pp. 32–41.

Waller, W. (1932), *The Sociology of Teaching*, John Wiley, New York.

Werthman, C. (1963), 'Delinquents in Schools: a Test for the Legitimacy of Authority', in *Berkeley Journal of Sociology*, vol. 8, no. 1, pp. 39–60; reprinted in B. R. Cosin *et al., School and Society*, Routledge & Kegan Paul, London.

Werthman, C. (1970), 'The Functions of Social Definitions in the Development of Delinquent Careers', in P. E. Garbedian and D. C. Gibbons (eds), *Becoming Delinquent*, Aldine, New York.

Westbury, I. (1973), 'Conventional Classrooms, "Open" Classrooms and the Technology of Teaching', *Journal of Curriculum Studies*, vol. 5, no. 2, pp. 99–121.

Westbury, I. (1978), 'Research into Classroom Processes: a Review of Ten Years' Work', *Curriculum Studies*, vol. 10, no. 4, pp. 283–308.

Whitty, G. (1974), 'Sociology and the Problem of Radical Educational Change: Notes Towards a Reconceptualisation of the "New Sociology of Education" ', in M. Flude and J. Ahier (eds), *Educability, Schools and Ideology*, Croom Helm, London, pp. 112–37.

Withall, J. (1959), 'The Development of a Technique for the Measurement of Social-emotional Climate in Classrooms', *Journal of Experimental Education*, vol. 17, pp. 347–61; reprinted in E. J. Amidon and J. B. Hough, *Interaction Analysis: Theory, Research and Application*, Addison-Wesley, Reading, Mass.

Woods, P. and Hammersley, M. (1977), *School Experience: Explorations in the Sociology of Education*, Croom Helm, London.

Chapter 6   Teachers and teaching

Anderson, H. H. (1939), 'The Measurement of Domination and Socially Integrative Behaviour in Teachers' Contact with Children', *Child Development*, vol. 10, pp. 73–89.

Apple, M. (1979), *Ideology and Curriculum*, Routledge & Kegan Paul, London.

Balloch, S. (1974), 'Towards a Policy for the Professionalisation of Teachers', in *The Teacher and Educational Change: A New Role*, OECD, Paris, vol. 1, pp. 521–61.

Baron, G. (1954), 'The Teachers' Registration Movement', *British Journal of Educational Studies*, vol. 2, pp. 133–44.

Becker, H. S. (1960), 'Notes on the Concept of Commitment', *American Journal of Sociology*, vol. 66, pp. 32–40.

Becker, H. S. (1964), 'Personal Change in Adult Life', *Sociometry*, vol. 27, no. 1, pp. 40–53; reprinted in B. R. Cosin (ed.), *School and Society*, Routledge & Kegan Paul, London, 1971.

Becker, H. S. and Geer, B. (1960), 'Latent Culture: A Note on the Theory of Latent Social Roles', *Administrative Science Quarterly*, vol. 5, pp. 304–13; reprinted in B. R. Cosin (ed.), *School and Society*, Routledge & Kegan Paul, London, 1971.

Becker, H. S., Geer, B. and Hughes, E. (1961), *Boys in White*, University of Chicago Press.

Berger, P. L. and Luckmann, T. (1967), *The Social Construction of Reality*, Penguin, Harmondsworth.

Bernbaum, G. *et al.* (1969), 'Inter-occupational Prestige: Differentiation in Teaching', *Paedagogica Europaea*, vol. 5, pp. 41–59.

Biddle, B. J. (1970), 'Role Conflicts Perceived by Teachers in Four English Speaking Countries', *Comparative Education Review*, pp. 30–44.

Blease, D. (1978), 'Teachers' Perceptions of Slow-learning Children: an Ethnographic Study', *Research Intelligence*, vol. 4, no. 1, pp. 39–42.

Bledstein, B. (1976), *The Culture of Professionalism*, W. W. Norton, New York.

Bucher, R. and Sterling, J. G. (1977), *Becoming Professional*, Sage Publications, London.

Carr-Saunders, A. M. (1925/1966), 'Professions: Their Organisation and Place in Society', in H. M. Vollmer and D. L. Mills, *Professionalization*, Prentice Hall, Englewood Cliffs, New Jersey.

Carr-Saunders, A. M. and Wilson, P. A. (1933), *The Professions*, Oxford University Press, London (reprinted 1964, Frank Cass, London).

Claiborn, W. L. (1969), 'Expectancy Effects in the Classroom: A Failure to Replicate', *Journal of Educational Psychology*, vol. 60, no. 5, pp. 377–83.

Coard, B. (1971), *How the West Indian Child is made Educationally Sub-Normal in the British School System*, New Beacon Books, London.

Cogan, M. L. (1953), 'Towards a Definition of Profession', *Harvard Educational Review*, vol. 23, no. 1, pp. 33–50.

Cope, E. (1969), 'Students and School Practice', *Education of Teaching*, no. 80, pp. 25–35.

Deem, R. (1976), 'Professionalism, Unity and Militant Action; The Case of Teachers', *Sociological Review*, vol. 24, no. 1, February, pp. 43–61.

Deem, R. (1978), *Women and Schooling*, Routledge & Kegan Paul, London.

Dingwall, R. (1976), 'Accomplishing Profession', *Sociological Review*, vol. 24, no. 2, pp. 331–49.

Duggan, E. P. and Stewart, W. A. C. (1970), 'The Choice of Work Area of Teachers', *Sociological Review Monograph*, no. 15, February.

Etzioni, A. (ed.) (1969), *The Semi-Professions and their Organisation: Teachers, Nurses, and Social Workers*, Free Press, New York.

Fine, B. (1977), 'Labelling Theory: an Investigation into the Sociological Critique of Deviance', *Economy and Society*, vol. 6, no. 2, pp. 166–93.

Finn, J. D. (1972), 'Expectations and the Educational Environment', *Review of Educational Research*, vol. 41, no. 3, pp. 387–410.

Floud, J. (1973), 'Teaching in the Affluent Society', in G. Z. F. Beredoy and J. A. Lauwerys (eds), *The Education and Training of Teachers*, Year Book of Education, pp. 382–89.

Floud, J. and Scott, W. (1961), 'Recruitment to Teaching in England and Wales', in A. H. Halsey, J. Floud and C. A. Anderson (eds), *Education, Economy and Society*, Collier-Macmillan, London.

Fuchs, E. (1968), 'How Teachers Learn to Help Children Fail', *Transactions: Social Science and Modern Society*, vol. 5, no. 9, pp. 44–8; also in E. Fuchs (ed.), *Teacher Talk: Views Inside City Schools*, Doubleday-Archer, New York, 1978.

Geer, B. (1966), 'Occupational Commitment and the Teaching Profession', *School Review*, vol. 74, no. 1, pp. 31–47; reprinted in H. S. Becker *et al.*, *Institutions and the Person*, Aldine Publishing, Chicago, 1968.

Goble, N. M. and Porter, I. F. (1977), *The Changing Role of the Teacher*, UNESCO, Paris.

Gouldner, A. W. (1957), 'Cosmopolitans and locals: Towards an Analysis of Latent Social Roles – I', *Administrative Science Quarterly*, vol. 2, pp. 281–316.

Grace, G. R. (1972), *Role Conflict and the Teacher*, Routledge & Kegan Paul, London.

Grace, G. R. (1978), *Teachers, Ideology and Control: A Study in Urban Education*, Routledge & Kegan Paul, London.

Greenwood, E. (1957), 'Attributes of a Profession', *Social Work*, vol. 2, no. 3, pp. 44–55; reprinted in H. M. Vollmer and D. L. Mills, *Professionalization*, Prentice Hall, Englewood Cliffs, New Jersey, 1966.

Halmos, P. (1970), *The Personal Service Society*, Constable, London.

Hargreaves, D. H., Hester, S. K. and Mellor, F. J. (1975), *Deviance in Classrooms*, Routledge & Kegan Paul, London.

Hilsum, S. and Strong, C. (1978), *The Secondary Teacher's Day*, NFER, Windsor.

Houghton Report (1974), *Report of the Committee of Inquiry into the Pay of Non-University Teachers*, Cmnd 5848, HMSO, London.

Hoyle, E. (1969), *The Role of the Teacher*, Routledge & Kegan Paul, London.

Johnson, T. J. (1972), *Professions and Power*, Macmillan, London.

Kanter, R. M. (1974), 'Commitment and Social Organisation', in D. Field (ed.), *Social Psychology for Sociologists*, Nelson, London.

King, E. J. (1979), *Other Schools and Ours: Comparative Studies for Today*, Holt, Rinehart & Winston, London.

Lacey, C. (1977), *The Socialization of Teachers*, Methuen, London.

Leggatt, T. (1970), 'Teaching as a Profession', in J. A. Jackson (ed.), *Professions and Professionalization*, Cambridge University Press.

Leigh, P. M. (1977), 'Great Expectations: A Consideration of the Self-fulfilling Prophecy in the Context of Educability', *Educational Review*, vol. 29, no. 4, November, pp. 317–24.

Lortie, D. C. (1975), *School-Teacher: A Sociological Study*, University of Chicago Press.

Mardle, G. D. and Walker, M. (1979), 'Some Critical Aspects of Teacher Socialisation', in P. Woods (ed.), *Teacher Strategies*, Croom Helm, London.

Merton, R. K. (1949), *Social Theory and Social Structure*, Free Press, Chicago; 2nd edn 1957.

Millerson, G. (1964), *The Qualifying Associations: A Study in Professionalization*, Routledge & Kegan Paul, London.

Mills, C. Wright (1940), 'Situated Actions and Vocabularies of Motive', *American Sociological Review*, vol. 5, no. 7, pp. 904–13; also in I. L. Horowitz (ed.), *Power, Politics and People*, Oxford University Press, London, 1967.

Mills, C. Wright (1959), *The Sociological Imagination*, Oxford University Press, New York.

Murphy, J. (1974), 'Teacher Expectations and Working-class Underachievement', *British Journal of Sociology*, vol. 25, no. 3, pp. 326–44.

Nash, R. (1973), *Classrooms Observed*, Routledge & Kegan Paul, London.

Parry, N. and J. (1974), 'The Teachers and Professionalism' The Failure of an Occupational Strategy', in M. Flude and J. Ahier (eds), *Educability, Schools and Ideology*, Croom Helm, London.

Rist, R. C. (1970), 'Student Social Class and Teacher Expectation', *Harvard Educational Review*, vol. 40, no. 3, pp. 411–51.

Rosenthal, R. and Jacobson, L. (1968), *Pygmalion in the Classroom: Teacher Expectation and Pupils' Intellectual Development*, Holt, Rinehart & Winston, New York.

Sharp, R. and Green, A. (1975), *Education and Social Control: A Study in Progressive Primary Education*, Routledge & Kegan Paul, London.

Snow, R. E. (1969), 'Unfinished Pygmalion', *Contemporary Psychology*, vol. 14, no. 4, pp. 197–9.

Taylor, J. K. and Dale, I. R. (1971), *A Survey of Teachers in their First Year of Service*, University Publications, Bristol.

Thorndike, R. L. (1968), 'Review of "Pygmalion in the Classroom" ', *American Educational Research Association Journal*, vol. 5, no. 4, p. 708.

Tropp, A. (1957), *The School Teachers*, William Heinemann, London.

Vollmer, H. M. and Mills, D. L. (1966), *Professionalization*, Prentice Hall, Englewood Cliffs, New Jersey.

Waller, W. (1932), *The Sociology of Teaching*, John Wiley, New York.

Webb, J. (1962), 'The Sociology of a School', *British Journal of Sociology*, vol. 13, no. 3, pp. 264–72.

Westwood, L. J. (1967), 'The Role of the Teacher', *Educational Research*, vol. 9, no. 2, pp. 122–34; vol. 10, no. 1, pp. 21–37.

Wilensky, H. L. (1964), 'The Professionalization of Everyone?' *American Journal of Sociology*, vol. 70, no. 2, pp. 137–58.

Wilson, B. R. (1962), 'The Teacher's Role – A Sociological Analysis', *British Journal of Sociology*, vol. 13, no. 1, pp. 15–32.

Woods, P. (1979), *The Divided School*, Routledge & Kegan Paul, London.

Chapter 7 Social organization of knowledge

Apple, M. W. (1979), *Ideology and Curriculum*, Routledge & Kegan Paul, London.

Apple, M. W. and Wexler, P. (1978), 'Cultural Capital and Educational Transmissions: An Essay on Basil Bernstein, *Class, Codes and Control:* vol. 3', *Educational theory*, vol. 28, no. 1, pp. 34–43.

Berger, P. L. and Luckman, T. (1967), *The Social Construction of Reality*, Penguin, Harmondsworth.

Bernstein, B. (1971), 'On the Classification and framing of Educational Knowledge', in B. Bernstein, *Class, Codes and Control*, vol. 1, *Theoretical Studies Towards a Sociology of Language*, Routledge & Kegan Paul, London, pp. 202-30.

Bernstein, B. (1975), 'Class and Pedagogies: Visible and Invisible', in B. Bernstein, *Class, Codes and Control*, vol. 3, *Towards a Theory of Educational Transmissions*, Routledge & Kegan Paul, London.

Bloom, B. S. *et al.* (1956), *Taxonomy of Educational Objectives: 1 Cognitive Domain*, Longmans, London.

Callahan, R. E. (1962), *Education and the Cult of Efficiency*, University of Chicago Press.

Central Advisory Council for Education (1963), *Half Our Future* (Newsom Report), HMSO, London.

Cooper, C. L. (1971), *The Lost Crusade*, MacGibbon & Kee, London.

Crowther Report (1959), *15 to 18: Report of the Central Advisory Council* (England), HMSO, London.

Dale, R. (1977), 'Implications of the Rediscovery of the Hidden Curriculum for the Sociology of Teaching', in D. Gleeson (ed.), *Identity and Structure: Issues in the Sociology of Education*, Nafferton Books, Driffield, pp. 44-54.

Davie, G. E. (1961), *The Democratic Intellect*, Edinburgh University Press.

Durkheim, E. (1977), *The Evolution of Educational Thought*, Routledge & Kegan Paul, London.

Eggleston, J. (1977), *The Sociology of the School Curriculum*, Routledge & Kegan Paul, London.

Eggleston, J. and Gleeson, D. (1977), 'Curriculum Innovation and the Context of the School', in D. Gleeson (ed.), *Identity and Structure: Issues in the Sociology of Education*, Nafferton Books, Driffield, pp. 15-27.

Eisner, E. W. (1967), 'Franklin Bobbitt and the "Science" of Curriculum Making', *School Review*, vol. 75, no. 1, Spring, pp. 29–47.

Fatimah, Hamid Don (1977), 'Curriculum Issues', in F. H. C. Wong (ed.), *Readings in Malaysian Education*, Penerbit Universiti Malaya, Kuala Lumpur.

Franklin, B. M. (1976a), 'Technological Models and the Curriculum Field', *Educational Forum*, vol. 40, no. 3, pp. 303-12.

Franklin, B. M. (1976b), 'Curriculum Thought and Social Meaning: Edward L. Thorndike and the Curriculum Field', *Educational Theory*, vol. 26, no. 3, pp. 298-309.

Gleeson, D. (1979), 'Curriculum Development and Social Change: Towards a Reappraisal of Teacher Action', in J. Eggleston (ed.), *Teacher Decision-Making in the Classroom*, Routledge & Kegan Paul, London, pp. 193-203.

Hamilton, D. (1973), 'The Integration of Knowledge: Practice and Problems', *Journal of Curriculum Studies*, vol. 5, pp. 146-55.

Hamilton, D. (1975), 'Handling Innovation in the Classroom: Two Scottish Examples', in W. A. Reid and D. F. Walker (eds), *Case Studies in Curriculum Change: Great Britain and the United States*, Routledge & Kegan Paul, London, pp. 179-207.

Hamilton, D. (1977), 'The Advent of Curriculum Integration: Paradigm Lost or Paradigm Regained', in M. Stubbs and S. Delamont (eds), *Explorations in Classroom Observation*, John Wiley, London, pp. 196-212.

Hirst, P. H. (1974), *Knowledge and the Curriculum*, Routledge & Kegan Paul, London.

Inglis, F. (1974), 'Ideology and the Curriculum: The Value Assumptions of Systems Builders', *Journal of Curriculum Studies*, vol. 6, no. 1, pp. 2-14.

Jackson, P. W. (1968), *Life in Classrooms*, Holt, Rinehart & Winston, New York.

Johnson, R. (1976), 'Notes on the Schooling of the English Working Class 1780-1850', in R. Dale *et al.* (eds), *Schooling and Capitalism*, Routledge & Kegan Paul, London, (in association with the Open University).

Kirst, M. W. and Walker, D. F. (1971), 'An Analysis of Curriculum Policy-making', *Review of Educational Research*, vol. 41, no. 5, pp. 479-509.

Kliebard, H. M. (1971), 'Bureaucracy and Curriculum Theory', in V. F. Haubrich (ed.), *Freedom, Bureaucracy and Schooling*, Association for Supervision and Curriculum Development, Washington D.C.

Lacey, C. (1977), *The Socialization of Teachers*, Methuen, London.

Layton, D. (1973), *Science for the People: The Origins of the School Science Curriculum in England*, Allen & Unwin, London.

McCann, P. (ed.), (1977), *Popular Education and Socialization in the Nineteenth Century*, Methuen, London.

Mannheim, K. (1936), *Ideology and Utopia; An Introduction to the Sociology of Knowledge*, Routledge & Kegan Paul, London.

Marx, K. and Engels, F. (1970 edn), *The German Ideology*, ed. and intro. C. J. Arthur, Lawrence & Wishart, London.

Musgrove, F. (1968a), 'The Contribution of Sociology to the Study of the Curriculum', in J. F. Kerr (ed.), *Changing the Curriculum*, University of London Press.

Musgrove, F. (1968b), 'Curriculum Objectives', *Journal of Curriculum Studies*, vol. 1, no. 1, pp. 5-18.

O'Keeffe, D. J. (1977), 'Towards a Socio-economy of the Curriculum', *Journal of Curriculum Studies*, vol. 9, no. 2, pp. 101-9.

Parsons, T. (1961), 'The School Class as a Social System: Some

Functions in American Society', in A. H. Halsey, J. Floud and C. A. Anderson (eds), *Education, Economy and Society*, Collier-Macmillan, London.

Reid, W. A. (1978), *Thinking about the Curriculum*, Routledge & Kegan Paul, London.

Saad, I. (1976), 'Knowledge, Control and Curriculum Change in Developing Countries', *Journal Pendidikan (Malaysia)*, no. 4, pp. 9-17.

Shaw, B. (1973), 'The Sociology of Knowledge and the Curriculum', *British Journal of Educational Studies*, vol. 21, pp. 277-89.

Shipman, M. D. (1974), *Inside a Curriculum Project*, Methuen, London.

Shroyer, T. (1970), 'Towards a Critical Theory for Advanced Industrial Society', in H. P. Dreitzel (ed.), *Recent Sociology No. 2*, Collier-Macmillan, London.

Tyler, R. W. (1949), *Basic Principles of Curriculum and Instruction*, University of Chicago Press, London.

Vulliamy, G. (1978), 'Culture Clash and School Music: a Sociological Analysis', in L. Barton and R. Meighan (eds), *Sociological Interpretations of Schooling and Classrooms: A Reappraisal*, Nafferton Books, Driffield.

Wexler, P. (1976), *The Sociology of Education: Beyond Equality*, Bobbs-Merrill Studies in Sociology, Indianapolis.

Whitty, G. (1977), 'Sociology and the Problem of Radical Educational Change', in M. Young and G. Whitty (eds), *Society, State and Schooling*, Falmer Press, Ringmer.

Wylie, L. (1973), *Village in the Vaucluse*, Harvard University Press, New York.

Young, M. F. D. (1971), 'An Approach to the Study of Curricula as Socially Organised Knowledge', in M. F. D. Young (ed.), *Knowledge and Control: New Directions for the Sociology of Education*, Collier-Macmillan, London.

Young, M. F. D. (1977), 'Curriculum Change: Limits and Possibilities', in M. Young and G. Whitty (eds), *Society, State and Schooling*, Falmer Press, Ringmer.

Chapter 8 Schools as organizations

Argyris, C. (1973), 'The Individual and the Organization: Some Problems of Mutual Adjustment', in M. M. Milstein and J. A. Belasco (eds), *Educational Administration and the Behavioural Sciences: A Systems Perspective*, Allyn & Bacon, London.

Barr Greenfield, T. (1975), 'Theory about Organization: a New Perspective and its Implications for Schools', in V. Houghton *et al*, (eds), *The Management of Organizations and Individuals*, Ward Lock Educational, London.

Bernstein, B. (1975), 'On the Classification and Framing of Educational Knowledge', in B. Bernstein (ed.), *Class, Codes and Control*, vol. 3,

Towards a Theory of Educational Transmissions, Routledge & Kegan Paul, London.

Bidwell, C. E. (1965), 'The School as a Formal Organization', in J. G. March (ed.), *Handbook of Organizations*, Rand McNally, Chicago.

Bone, T. R. (1976), 'Comment on Barr Greenfield', *Educational Administration*, vol. 5, no. 1, pp. 12–13.

Brake, M. (1973), 'Cultural Revolution or Alternative Delinquency', in R. Bailey and J. Young (eds), *Contemporary Social Problems in Britain*, Saxon House, London.

Breton, R. (1970), 'Academic Stratification in Secondary Schools', *Canadian Review of Sociology and Social Anthropology*, vol. 7, no. 1.

Callahan, R. E. (1962), *Education and the Cult of Efficiency*, University of Chicago Press.

Cherry, N. (1974), 'Components of Occupational Interest', *British Journal of Educational Psychology*, vol. 44, pp. 22–30.

Cohen, P. (1976), 'Subcultural Conflict and the Working-class Community', in M. Hammersley and P. Woods (eds), *The Process of Schooling*, Routledge & Kegan Paul, London.

Corbishley, P. J. and Hurn, C. (1979), 'Do Schools make a Difference?', review article of *Fifteen Thousand Hours*, *British Journal of In-Service Education*, vol. 6, no. 1, pp. 48–52.

Corrigan, P. (1979), *Schooling the Smash Street Kids*, Macmillan, London.

Davies, B. (1973), 'On the Contribution of Organizational Analysis to the Study of Educational Institutions', in R. Brown (ed.), *Knowledge, Education and Cultural Change*, Tavistock, London, pp. 249–95.

Etzioni, A. (1964), *Modern Organizations*, Prentice-Hall, Englewood Cliffs, N.J.

Gray, H. L. (1979), *The School as an Organization*, Nafferton Books, Driffield.

Himmelweit, H. T. and Swift, B. (1969), 'A Model of Understanding of the School as a Socializing Agency', in P. H. Mussen, J. Lanzer and M. Covington (eds), *Trends and Issues in Developmental Psychology*, Holt, Rinehart & Winston, New York.

Hoyle, E. (1973), 'The Study of Schools as Organizations', in H. J. Butcher and H. B. Pont (eds), *Educational Research in Britain*, vol. 3, University of London Press.

Hutchinson, D., Prosser, H. and Wedge, P. (1979), 'The Prediction of Educational Failure', *Educational Studies*, vol. 5, no. 1, March, pp. 73–82.

Johnson, R. (1976), 'Notes on the Schooling of the English Working Class 1780-1850', in R. Dale *et al.* (eds), *Schooling and Capitalism*, Routledge & Kegan Paul, London.

Kahl, J. A. (1953), 'Educational and Occupational Aspirations of "Common Man's Boys" ', *Harvard Educational Review*, vol. 23, no. 3; also in A. H. Halsey, J. Floud and C. A. Anderson, *Education,*

Economy and Society, Collier-Macmillan, London, 1961.

Kanter, R. M. (1972), 'The Organization Child: Experience Management in a Nursery School', *Sociology of Education*, vol. 45, no. 2, Spring, pp. 186-211.

Karabel, J. (1972), 'Community Colleges and Social Stratification: Submerged Class Conflict in American Higher Education', *Harvard Educational Review*, vol. 42, pp. 521-62.

King, R. (1973), *School Organisation and Pupil Involvement*, Routledge & Kegan Paul, London.

King, R. (1976), 'Bernstein's Sociology of the School – some Propositions Tested', *British Journal of Sociology*, vol. 27, no. 4, pp. 430-43.

Lacey, C. (1974), 'Destreaming in a "Pressured" Academic Environment', in J. Eggleston (ed.), *Contemporary Research in the Sociology of Education*, Methuen, London.

Miller, E. J. and Rice, A. K. (1967), *Systems of Organization: The Control of Task and Sentient Boundaries*, Tavistock, London.

Miller, P. J. (1973), 'Factories, Monitorial Schools and Jeremy Bentham: The Origins of the "Management Syndrome" in Popular Education', *Journal of Educational Administration and History*, vol. 5, no. 2, pp. 10-20.

Musgrove, F. (1964), *Youth and the Social Order*, Routledge & Kegan Paul, London.

Parsons, T. (1958), 'Some Ingredients to a General Theory of Formal Organisation', in A. W. Halpin (ed.), *Administrative Theory in Education*, Collier-Macmillan, London.

Perrow, C. (1970), *Organizational Analysis: A Sociological View*, Tavistock, London.

Phillipson, C. M. (1971), 'Juvenile Delinquency and the School', in W. G. Carson and P. Wiles (eds), *Crime and Delinquency in Britain*, Martin Robertson, London.

Power, M. J. *et al.*, (1967), 'Delinquent Schools?', *New Society*, 19 October, p. 542.

Reynolds, D. (1976a), 'When Pupils and Teachers Refuse a Truce', in G. Mungham and G. Pearson (eds), *Working Class Youth Cultures*, Routledge & Kegan Paul, London.

Reynolds, D. and Sullican, M. (1979), 'Bringing Schools Back In', in P. Woods (eds), *The Process of Schooling*, Routledge & Kegan Paul, London (in association with the Open University).

Reynolds, D. and Sullivan, M. (1979), 'Bringing Schools Back In', in L. Barton and R. Meighan (eds), *Schools, Pupils and Deviance*, Nafferton Books, Driffield.

Richardson, E. (1973), *The Teacher, the School and the Task of Management*, Heinemann, London.

Richardson, E. (1975), *Authority and Organization in the Secondary School*, Macmillan, London.

Rutter, M. (*et al.*) (1979), *Fifteen Thousand Hours: Secondary Schools and their Effects on Children*, Open Books, London.

225

Silverman, D. (1970), *The Theory of Organisations*, Heinemann, London.

Smith, D. (1977), 'Codes, Paradigms and Folk Norms: An Approach to Educational Change with Particular Reference to the Work of Basil Bernstein', *Sociology*, vol. 11, pp. 1–19.

White, P. and J. (1976), 'Comment on Barr Greenfield', *Educational Administration*, vol. 5, no. 1, pp. 6–10.

Woods, P. (1979), *The Divided School*, Routledge & Kegan Paul, London.

Yee, A. H. (1972), 'The Limits of Scientific-economic-technological Approaches and the Search for Perspective in Education: The Case of Performance Contracting', *Journal of Educational Research*, vol. 66, no. 1, pp. 19–29.

Chapter 9 Education and the structure of opportunity

Anderson, C. A., (1961), 'A Sceptical Note on Education and Mobility', in A. H. Halsey, J. Floud and C. A. Anderson (eds), *Education, Economy and Society*, Collier-Macmillan, London.

Bechhofer, F. Elliott, B. and McCrone, D. (1978), 'Structure, Consensus and Action: a Sociological Profile of the British Middle Class', *British Journal of Sociology*, no. 4, December, pp. 410–36.

Bellaby, P. (1977), *The Sociology of Comprehensive Schooling*, Methuen, London.

Blau, P. M. and Duncan, O. D. (1967), *The American Occupational Structure*, Wiley, New York.

Blaug, M. (1970), *Economics of Education*, Penguin, Harmondsworth.

Bottomore, T. B. and Rubel, M. (1963), *Karl Marx: Selected Writings in Sociology and Social Philosophy*, Penguin, Harmondsworth.

Boudon, R. (1974), *Education, Opportunity and Social Inequality*, Wiley, New York.

Boudon, R. (1977), 'Education and Social Mobility: A Structural Model', in J. Karabel and A. H. Halsey (eds), *Power and Ideology in Education*, Open University Press, London.

Bourdieu, P. (1974), 'The School as a Conservative Force: Scholastic and Cultural Inequalities', in J. Eggleston (ed.), *Contemporary Research in the Sociology of Education*, Methuen, London.

Bourdieu, P. and Passeron, J. C. (1977), *Reproduction in Education, Society and Culture*, Sage Publications, London.

Bowles, S. and Gintis, H. (1976), *Schooling in Capitalist America*, Routledge & Kegan Paul, London.

Bowman, M. J. (1975), 'Education and Opportunity: Some Economic Perspectives', *Oxford Review of Education*, vol. 1, no. 1, pp. 73–84.

Clark, B. R. (1961), 'The "Cooling-Out" Function in Higher Education', in A. H. Halsey, J. Floud and C. A. Anderson (eds), *Education, Economy and Society*, Collier-Macmillan, London.

Clark, K. B. (1973), 'Social Policy, Power and Social Science Research',

Harvard Educational Review, vol. 43, no. 1, pp. 113–21.

Coleman, J. S. (1966), *Report on Equality of Educational Opportunity*, US Government Printing Office, Washington, for Department of Health, Education and Welfare.

Coleman, J. S. (1975), 'What is Meant by "an Equal Educational Opportunity"?', *Oxford Review of Education*, vol. 1, no. 1, pp. 27–9.

Collins, R. (1971), 'Functional and Conflict Theories of Educational Stratification', *American Sociological Review*, vol. 36, pp. 1002–19.

Collins, R. (1974), 'Where are Educational Requirements for Employment Highest?', *Sociology of Education*, vol. 47 (Fall), pp. 419–42.

Collins, R. (1977), 'Some Comparative Principles of Educational Stratification', *Higher Educational Research*, vol. 47, no. 1, pp. 1–27.

Crowder, N.D. (1974), 'A Critique of Duncan's Stratification Research', *Sociology*, vol. 8, no. 1, pp. 19–45.

Crowther Report (1959), *15 to 18: Report of the Central Advisory Council* (England), HMSO, London.

Davie, R., Butler, M. and Goldstein, H. (1972), *From Birth to Seven*, Longman, London.

Davis, K. and Moore, W. E. (1945), 'Some Principles of Stratification', *A.S.R.*, vol. 10, no. 2, pp. 242–9; reprinted in R. Bendix and S. M. Lipset (eds), *Class, Status and Power*, Routledge & Kegan Paul, London, 1967.

Douglas, J. W. B. (1964), *The Home and the School*, MacGibbon & Kee, London.

Douglas, J. W. B. *et al.* (1968), *All Our Future*, Peter Davies, London.

Durkheim, E. (1933), *The Division of Labour in Society*, Free Press, Chicago.

Elder, G. (1965), 'Life Opportunity and Personality. Some Consequences of Stratified Secondary Education in Great Britain', *Sociology of Education*, vol. 38, no. 3, pp. 173–202.

Eliot, T. S. (1948), *Notes Towards a Definition of Culture*, Faber & Faber, London.

Floud, J., Halsey, A. H. and Martin, F. M. (1956), *Social Class and Educational Opportunity*, Heinemann, London.

Fogelman, K. (1976), *Britain's Sixteen Year Olds*, National Children's Bureau, London.

Folger, J. K. and Nam, C. B. (1964), 'Trends in Education in Relation to the Occupational Structure', *Sociology of Education*, vol. 38, no. 1, pp. 19–33.

Frankel, C. (1973), 'The New Egalitarianism and the Old', *Commentary*, vol. 56, no. 3, pp. 54–66, September.

Gerth, H. H. and Mills, C. W. (1946), *From Max Weber: Essays in Sociology*, Routledge & Kegan Paul, London.

Glass, D. V. (1954), *Social Mobility in Britain*, Routledge & Kegan Paul, London.

Goldthorpe, J. H. and Hope, K. (1974), *The Social Grading of Occupations*, Clarendon Press, Oxford.

Bibliography

Goldthorpe, J. H. and Llewellyn, C. (1977a), 'Class Mobility in Modern Britain: Three Theses Examined', *Sociology*, vol. 11, no. 2, pp. 257–87.

Goldthorpe, J. H. and Llewellyn, C. (1977b), 'Class Mobility: Integrational and Worklife Patterns', *British Journal of Sociology*, vol. 28, no. 3, September, pp. 269–302.

Halsey, A. H. (1975a), 'Sociology and the Equality Debate', *Oxford Review of Education*, vol. 1, no. 1, pp. 9–23.

Halsey, A. H. (1975b), 'Education and Social Mobility in Britain Since World War II', in OECD, *Education, Inequality and Life Chances*, vol. 1, OECD, Paris.

Halsey, A. H. (1977), 'Towards Meritocracy? The Case of Britain', in J. Karabel and A. H. Halsey, *Power and Ideology in Education*, Oxford University Press, London.

Hirsch, F. (1977), *Social Limits to Growth*, Routledge & Kegan Paul, London.

Hopper, E. I. (1968), 'A Typology for the Classification of Educational Systems', *Sociology*, vol. 2, pp. 241–6; reprinted in J. Karabel and A. H. Halsey, *Power and Ideology in Education*, Oxford University Press, London, 1977, pp. 153–66.

Hopper, E. I. (1971), *Readings in the Theory of Educational Systems*, Hutchinson, London.

Husen, T. (1975), 'Strategies for Educational Equality', in OECD, *Education, Inequality and Life Chances*, vol. 1, Paris, OECD.

Jencks, C. *et al.* (1973), *Inequality: A Reassessment of the Effect of Family and Schooling in America*, Allen Lane, London.

Johnson, R. (1976), 'Notes on the Schooling of the English Working Class 1780–1850', in R. Dale *et al.* (eds) *Schooling and Capitalism*, Routledge & Kegan Paul, London.

Kerckhoff, A. C. (1974), 'Stratification Processes and Outcomes in England and the U.S.', *American Sociological Review*, no. 39, pp. 789–801.

Lipset, S. M. (1963), 'The Value Patterns of Democracy: A Case Study in Comparative Analysis', *American Sociological Review*, vol. 28, pp. 515–31.

Lipset, S. M. (1972), 'Social Mobility and Equal Opportunity', *Public Interest*, Summer, pp. 90–108.

Little, A. (1971), 'How Does Your Education Affect You?', *New Society*, 23 December, pp. 1245–8.

Phillipson, C. M. (1971), 'Juvenile Delinquency and the School', in W. G. Carson and P. Wiles (eds), *Crime and Delinquency in Britain*, Martin Robertson, London.

Psacharopoulos, G. (1974), 'Review of Jenck's "Inequality" ', *Comparative Educational Review*, vol. 18, no. 3, October, pp. 446–9.

Psacharopoulos, G. (1977), 'Family Background, Education and Achievement: a Path Model of Earnings Determinants in the U.K. and some Alternatives', *British Journal of Sociology*, vol. 28, pp. 321–35.

Pullman, T. W. (1974), 'Review Symposium', *American Journal of*

Sociology, vol. 78, no. 6, pp. 540–4.

Reid, I. (1977), *Social Class Differences in Britain: A Sourcebook*, Open Books, London.

Reynolds, D. *et al*, (1976), 'Schools do make a Difference', *New Society*, 24 July, p. 321.

Rutter, M. *et al.* (1979), *Fifteen Thousand Hours: Secondary Schools and their Effect on Children*, Open Books, London.

Schultz, T. W. (1961), 'Investment in Human Capital', *American Economic Review*, vol. 51, March, pp. 1–17; reprinted in J. Karabel and A. H. Halsey (eds), *Power and Ideology in Education*, Oxford University Press, London, 1977.

Thurow, L. C. (1972), 'Education and Economic Equality', *Public Interest*, vol. 28, pp. 66–81, reprinted in J. Karabel and A. H. Halsey, (eds), *Power and Ideology in Education*, Oxford University Press, London.

Thurow, L. C. (1973), 'Proving the Absence of Positive Association', *Harvard Educational Review*, vol. 43, no. 1, pp. 106–12.

Tumin, M. M. (1953), 'Some Principles of Stratification: A Critical Analysis', *American Sociological Review*, vol. 18, pp. 387–93; reprinted in R. Bendix and S. M. Lipset (eds), *Class, Status and Power*, Routledge & Kegan Paul, London, 1967.

Turner, R. H. (1961), 'Modes of Social Ascent through Education: Sponsored and Contest Mobility'; reprinted in A. H. Halsey, J. Floud and C. A. Anderson, *Education, Economy and Society*, Collier-Macmillan, London, 1961.

Turner, R. H. (1964), *The Social Context of Ambition*, Chandler Press, San Francisco.

Wedge, P. and Prosser, H. (1973), *Born to Fail?*, Arrow Books, London.

Westergaard, J. and Little, A. (1970), 'Educational Opportunity and Social Selection in England and Wales', in M. Craft (ed.), *Family, Class and Education*, Longman, London.

Young, M. (1958), *The Rise of the Meritocracy*, Thames & Hudson, London.

Chapter 10 Education and the Third World

Altbach, P. G. (1971), 'Education and Neocolonialism', *Teachers College Record*, vol. 72, no. 4, pp. 543–58.

Altbach, P. G. and Kelly, G. P. (1978), *Education and Colonialism*, Longman, New York.

Anderson, C. A. and Bowman, M. J. (1965), *Education and Economic Development*, Cass, London.

Blaug, M. (1973), *Education and the Employment Problem in Developing Countries*, International Labour Office, Geneva.

Bock, J. C. (1976), 'The Institutionalization of Nonformal Education:A A Response to Conflicting Needs', *Comparative Education Review*, vol. 20, no. 3, pp. 346–67.

Brandt Commission (1980), *North-South: A Programme for Survival*, Pan, London.
Buchanan, K. (1975), *Reflections on Education in the Third World*, Spokesman Books, Nottingham.
Caldwell, M. (1977a), 'War, Boom and Depression', in M. Amin and M. Caldwell (eds), *Malaya: The Making of a Neo-Colony*, Spokesman Books, Nottingham.
Caldwell, M. (1977b), *The Wealth of Some Nations*, Zed Press, London.
Carnoy, M. (1974), *Education as Cultural Imperialism*, David McKay, New York.
Chang, P. (1973), *Educational Development in a Plural Society*, Academia Publications, Singapore.
Colclough, C. and Hallak, J. (1976), 'Some Issues in Rural Education', *Prospects*, vol. VI, no. 4, pp. 501-25.
Coombs, P. H. (1968), *The World Educational Crisis: A Systems Analysis*, Oxford University Press, London.
Coombs, P. H. (1976), 'Nonformal Education: Myths, Realities and Opportunities', *Comparative Education Review*, vol. 20, no. 3, pp. 281-93.
Coombs, P. H. with Prosser, R. C. and Ahmed, M. (1973), *New Paths to Learning for Rural Children and Youth*, International Council for Educational Development, New York.
Dore, R. (1976), *The Diploma Disease*, Allen & Unwin, London.
Faure, E. (1972), *Learning to Be: The World of Education Today and Tomorrow*, UNESCO, Paris.
Foster, P. (1965), *Education and Social Change in Ghana*, Routledge & Kegan Paul, London.
Foster, P. (1969), 'Education for Self-Reliance: a Critical Evaluation', in R. Jolly (ed.), *Education in Africa: Research and Action*, Heinemann Educational Books, London.
Frank, A. G. (1971), *Sociology of Development and Underdevelopment of Sociology*, Pluto Press, London.
Freire, P. (1972), 'Education: Domestication or Liberation', *Prospects*, vol. 2, no. 2, pp. 173-81.
Hirsch, F. (1977), *Social Limits to Growth*, Routledge & Kegan Paul, London.
Hoselitz, B. F. (1964), 'Social Stratification and Economic Development', *International Social Science Journal*, vol. 16, no. 2, pp. 237-51.
Jolly, R. (1974), 'The Judo Trick', in F. C. Ward (ed.), *Education and Development Reconsidered: The Bellago Conference Papers*, Praeger Publications, New York.
Loh, P. (1975), *Seeds of Separatism: Educational Policy in Malaya 1874-1940*, Oxford University Press, Kuala Lumpur.
McClelland, D. (1961), *The Achieving Society*, Van Nostrand, Princeton.
May, B. (1978), *The Indonesian Tragedy*, Routledge & Kegan Paul, London.

Mead, M. (1943), 'Our Educational Emphasis on Primitive Perspective', *American Journal of Sociology*, vol. 48, pp. 633–9.

Mills, C. Wright (1959), *The Sociological Imagination*, Oxford University Press, London.

Morrison, D. R. (1976), *Education and Politics in Africa: The Tanzanian Case*, C. Hurst, London.

Nash, M. (1963), 'Introduction: Approaches to the Study of Economic Growth', *Journal of Social Issues*, vol. 19, no. 1, January, pp. 1–5.

Nyerere, J. K. (1971), 'Education for Self-Reliance', in J. K. Nyerere, *UJAAMA: Essays on Socialism*, Oxford University Press, London.

Nyerere, J. K. (1974), *Daily News*, 21 May, reprinted in R. McCormick (ed.) (1976), *Nyerere on Education and Society*, Open University Press, Milton Keynes, Course E203.

Orr, K. (ed), (1977), *Appetite for Education in Contemporary Asia*, The Australian National University, Canberra.

Rostow, W. W. (1962), *The Stages of Economic Growth. A Non-Communist Manifesto*, Cambridge University Press.

Schultz, T. W. (1961), 'Investment in Human Capital', *American Economic Review*, vol. 51, March, pp. 77; reprinted in J. Karabel and A. H. Halsey (eds), *Power and Ideology in Education*, Oxford University Press, London, 1977.

Seymour, J. Madison (1974), 'The Rural Schools as an Acculturating Institution: The Iban of Malaysia', *Human Organization*, vol. 33, no. 3, Fall, pp. 186–203.

Thompson, A. R. (1977), 'How Far Free? International Networks of Constraint upon National Educational Policy in the Third World', *Comparative Education*, vol. 13, no. 3, pp. 155–68.

Weiler, H. N. (1978), 'Education and Development: from the Age of Innocence to the Age of Scepticism', *Comparative Education*, vol. 14, no. 3, October, pp. 179–98.

Williams, P. (ed.) (1976), *Prescription for Progress? A Commentary on the Education Policy of the World Bank*, University of London Institute of Education, London.

Williamson, B. (1979), *Education, Social Structure and Development: A Comparative Analysis*, Macmillan, London.

World Bank (1974), *Education* (Sector Working Paper), World Bank, Washington.

Chapter 11 Reproduction and relative autonomy

Benton, T. (1974), 'Education and Politics', in D. Holly (ed.) *Education or Domination?*, Arrow Books, London.

Bernstein, B. (1977), 'Aspects of the Relation between Education and Production', in B. Bernstein (ed.), *Class, Codes and Control*, vol. 3, *Towards a Theory of Educational Transmissions*, 2nd edn, Routledge & Kegan Paul, London.

Bibliography

Bowles, S. and Gintis, H. (1976), *Schooling in Capitalist America*, Routledge & Kegan Paul, London.

Boyd, W. and King, E. J. (1972), *History of Western Education*, 10th edn, A. & C. Black, London.

Castaneda, C., (1968), *The Teachings of Don Juan: A Yaqui Way of Knowledge*, University of California Press; Penguin, Harmondsworth, 1970.

Collins, R. (1976), Review of *Schooling in Capitalist America, Harvard Educational Review*, vol. 46, no. 2, pp. 246–51.

Collins, R. (1977), 'Some Comparative Principles of Educational Stratification', *Higher Educational Research*,vol. 47, no. 1, February.

Durkheim, E. (1977), *The Evolution of Educational Thought*, Routledge & Kegan Paul, London.

Finn, D., Grant, N. and Johnson, R. (1978), 'Social Democracy, Education and the Crisis', in *On Ideology*, Centre for Contemporary Cultural Studies, Hutchinson, London.

Foster, P. J. (1965), 'The Vocational School Fallacy in Development Planning', in C. A. Anderson and M. J. Bowman (eds), *Education and Economic Development*, Cass, London, pp. 142–66.

Foster, P. J. (1971), 'The Revolt against the Schools', *Comparative Education Review*, vol. 15, no. 3, October, pp. 267–75.

Gleeson, D. and Mardle, G. (1980), *Further Education or Training?*, Routledge & Kegan Paul, London.

Gintis, H. (1972), 'Towards a Political Economy of Education: a Radical Critique of Ivan Illich's "Deschooling Society" ', *Harvard Educational Review*, vol. 42, no. 1, pp. 70–96.

Greene, M. (1971), 'Curriculum and Consciousness', *Teacher's College Record*, vol. 73, no. 2, pp. 253–69; reprinted in J. Beck *et al.* (eds), *Worlds Apart*, Collier-Macmillan, London, 1976.

Halsey, A. H., Heath, A. F. and Ridge, J. M. (1980), *Origins and Destinations: Family, Class and Education in Modern Britain*, Clarendon Press, Oxford.

Hoskyns, A. (1976), 'An Experiment in the Teaching of Physics', in G. Whitty and M. Young (eds), *Explorations in the Politics of School Knowledge*, Nafferton Books, Driffield.

Illich, I. D. (1971), *Deschooling Society*, Calder & Boyars, London.

Maclure, S. (1980), 'After the Revolution', *Times Educational Supplement*, 21 March, p. 12.

Musgrove, F. (1978), 'Curriculum, Culture and Ideology', *Journal of Curriculum Studies*, vol. 10, no. 2, pp. 99–111.

O'Keeffe, D. J. (1978), 'Profit and Control: The Bowles and Gintis Thesis', *Curriculum Studies*, vol. 10, no. 3, pp. 251–61.

O'Keeffe, D. J. (1979), 'Capitalism and Correspondence: A Critique of Marxist Analyses of Education', *Higher Educational Review*, Autumn, pp. 40–54.

O'Keeffe, D. J. (forthcoming), *The Sociology of Human Capital*, Routledge & Kegan Paul, London.

Reimer, E. (1971), *School is Dead: An Essay on Alternatives in Education*, Penguin Books, Harmondsworth.
Townsend, P. (1979), *Poverty in the United Kingdom*, Penguin Books, Harmondsworth.

Name index

Name index

Wexler, P., 128
White, G., 42
White, P. and J., 142–3
White, R.K., 73
Whitty, G., 26, 69, 81, 127
Wilensky, H.L., 94
Wilkinson, E., 154
Wilkinson, R., 68
Williams, P., 185
Williams, R., 28
Williamson, W., 58
Willis, P., 43
Willmott, P., 49–50
Wilson, B.R., 107, 108

Wilson, P.A., 99
Winterbottom, M.R., 36
Withall, J., 73
Wittgenstein, L., 88
Woods, P., 104–5, 106, 146, 148–9, 153
Wylie, L., 121

Yee, A.H., 139
Yerkes, R., 63
Young, M., 49–50, 159
Young, M.F.D., 24, 25, 26, 32, 118, 126, 127

Subject index